The Black Queer Work of Ratchet

Nikki Lane

The Black Queer Work of Ratchet

Race, Gender, Sexuality, and the (Anti)Politics of Respectability

Nikki Lane
Washington, DC, USA

ISBN 978-3-030-23321-1   ISBN 978-3-030-23319-8 (eBook)
https://doi.org/10.1007/978-3-030-23319-8

© The Editor(s) (if applicable) and The Author(s) 2019
This work is subject to copyright. All rights are solely and exclusively licensed by the Publisher, whether the whole or part of the material is concerned, specifically the rights of translation, reprinting, reuse of illustrations, recitation, broadcasting, reproduction on microfilms or in any other physical way, and transmission or information storage and retrieval, electronic adaptation, computer software, or by similar or dissimilar methodology now known or hereafter developed.
The use of general descriptive names, registered names, trademarks, service marks, etc. in this publication does not imply, even in the absence of a specific statement, that such names are exempt from the relevant protective laws and regulations and therefore free for general use.
The publisher, the authors and the editors are safe to assume that the advice and information in this book are believed to be true and accurate at the date of publication. Neither the publisher nor the authors or the editors give a warranty, express or implied, with respect to the material contained herein or for any errors or omissions that may have been made. The publisher remains neutral with regard to jurisdictional claims in published maps and institutional affiliations.

Cover illustration: Delmaine Donson/Getty Images

This Palgrave Macmillan imprint is published by the registered company Springer Nature Switzerland AG.
The registered company address is: Gewerbestrasse 11, 6330 Cham, Switzerland

For Leo. My wish is for you to be a little bit ratchet, a little bit boojie, and completely yourself.
For Billye. Thank you for always watching over me, Grandma.

Acknowledgements

"First of all, giving honor to God who is the head of my life…"

I have always wanted to write about the women I hold dearest—Black women who love women—and the worlds that they create in the midst of overlapping systems of oppression that try to erase them. This book is a dream come true. Not just because I have always wanted to write *this* book, but because I grew up with a love for words, writing and reading everything I could get my hands on, using those words as balm for the daily cuts that come from living poor, Black, woman, and queer in the world. Doing things with words, whether reading books, writing in my journal, or running my mouth, has made life bearable during some particularly rough times. And then I became an anthropologist who studies what people do with words. I would have never been able to make this dream a reality without the support, generosity, and love from some very important folks some of whom I name below.

Thank you to the informants who shared their stories with me, for being candid and honest, open, and available. This would not have been possible without the 40 women and trans men whose beautifully complicated lives were the source for this intellectual engagement with Black queer lives in DC.

To my Momma, Cheryle Lane, for teaching me to "drive a bus," because we're Lanes, and we can do anything. And my Auntee, Rebecca Footman, who is the very definition of loyalty, service, and vitality.

To my sister-friends Carletta Girma, Shannon Vassel, Brittney Thomas, Ashley Williams, Rahema Mooltrey, Kelly Leon, and Fade Adetesoye Olatoye, thank you all for being on call when I needed some love.

To an accompaniment of advisors who have advocated for me and lent their ears throughout my career. William Leap, Jennifer C. Nash, Sabiyha Prince, Rachel Watkins, Katharina Vester, Sue Taylor, Ami Lynch, and Nemata Blyden. Thank you for encouraging and advising me in the ways of scholarship, teaching, and life in general. To colleagues who were generous in their encouragement, in their readings, and commentary including Laura Jung, Matthew Thomman, Lauren Boussard, Bill Harder, and Ashante Reese.

To my dear Ruth Ost, excuse me, Dr. Ost, thank you for being the brilliant example of what it means to live a meaningful, rich intellectual life. To Lorraine Savage of Temple University's Writing Center for making space for me to get the work done.

Funding for the research conducted to write this book came from American University's Office of the Vice-Provost of Graduate Studies and the Dean of the College of Arts and Sciences. My hope is that more institutions will invest in research about queer life, especially in projects that capture the vitality and unique contributions of Black queer people to American culture.

I also have to say that there have been a whole host of people throughout my movement within higher-ed who have helped me along the way, including the lunch ladies whose names I don't know who always made sure I ate through college and grad school, the cleaning ladies who always looked out for me, and the staff of various offices who made sure my forms got to the right places. And the countless people who have helped me along the way, but whose names I failed to remember, but whose contributions I have not. Thank you.

And to my wife, Julie Lane. Thank you for holding me down. You share my love and adoration for Black women, you have invested time, energy, and money into me writing this book, and I cannot thank you enough for being the solid rock I have needed throughout this journey. And thank you pushing our baby, aka "lion emoji," into my heart. The kid's presence was just what I needed to push me past the finish line.

Contents

1 **The Ethnography of Ratchet: Studying Language Practices of the Black (Queer) Middle-Class**   1
   "I Don't Like Ratchet Music, But I Like This Song"   1
   The Ethnography of Ratchet   7
   Why Black Queer Women?   12
   The Black Middle-Class and Respectability   15
   Homo- and Heteronormativity   22
   Putting Ratchet to Work   29
   References   31

2 **Defining Ratchet: Ratchet and Boojie Politics in Black Queer Space**   35
   Definitions   35
   Ratchet/Boojie Politics in the BQW Scene   42
   On That Act Right   44
      Jay, "Everyone Didn't Get a Flyer"   44
      Sade, "I Learned Quickly"   48
      Timi, "Southeast Tracy"   51
      Renee, "Not the Best DC Had to Offer"   53
   Working with Ratchet   55
      Anna, "Sometimes You Need Ratchet"   55
   Continuum   60
   References   64

3	**Being Ratchet: Undoing the Politics of Respectability in Black Queer Space**	67
	Un/LadyLike	67
	Amber, "The Divide"	71
	"I'm 'Bout to Hit the Club and Dance Like a Stippa"	76
	Ratchet Music	76
	Ladies Day Party	79
	Conclusion	85
	References	89
4	**Representing Ratchet: Screening Black Lesbian Sex and Ratchet Cultural Politics**	91
	Screening Ratchet/Boojie Politics	91
	Black Lesbians on TV	92
	Black Lesbians on YouTube	94
	Black Lesbian Gender Politics and Ratchet/Boojie Politics	95
	District Heat	99
	Representing Sex in District Heat	100
	Black Lesbian Hypermasculinity	102
	Quare Work of District Heat	108
	References	110
5	**Coming Out Ratchet and Whole: Black Women and the Struggle to Just Be**	111
	Selling BQW's Sexual Stories	111
	#LHHAtl and the Commodification of Ratchet	114
	#LHHAtl's BQW's Coming Out	117
	Ariane Comes Out for K. Michelle	118
	Joseline Comes Out for No One	122
	Mimi Comes Out for Herself	129
	"Tightrope"	136
	"They Probably Know"	139
	References	144

6	**"I Said What I Said": Final Notes on Ratchet/Boojie Politics**	**147**
	Bad and Boojie	147
	"Am I Freak for Getting Down?"	152
	"We All Need to Get a Little Ratchet"	155
	Lingering Questions	158
	Class	158
	The South	159
	Final Remarks	160
	Ratchet *and the "Nigga"*	160
	References	163
Index		**165**

CHAPTER 1

The Ethnography of Ratchet: Studying Language Practices of the Black (Queer) Middle-Class

"I Don't Like Ratchet Music, But I Like This Song"

I conducted ethnographic fieldwork between 2012 and 2016 for my research about what is colloquially referred to as the *Scene* in DC among Black Queer Women (BQW). The BQW's Scene is an amorphous, loosely connected set of social networks comprised of BQW and their allies, as well as the spaces those social networks create in order to socialize (Lane 2015). I refer to these spaces, where the Scene was most often instantiated, as scene spaces. Scene spaces included sites such as house parties, book club meetings, social support groups, professional women's sporting events, semi-private parties at restaurants, lounges, and bars. Additionally, musical performances by queer artists, burlesque shows, one-off Black queer-themed events, and Meetups organized by Black queer people were also scene spaces. During my fieldwork, I made it a point to go to *all* of the scene spaces that were available to me. And so when I was invited to Timi's[1] birthday celebration at a "Women's Happy Hour" at a new gay bar just off U Street, I happily accepted. There were five of us, including the "birthday girl," standing together amongst the crowd. We stood nursing our drinks and, as is customary at happy hours with casual acquaintances, we engaged in small talk and someone asked me, "Oh, so what do you do?"

Scene spaces were often *classed* in particular ways. The location of the party, the price of admission, or, as was of particular importance to me and

---

[1] Pseudonym.

© The Author(s) 2019
N. Lane, *The Black Queer Work of Ratchet*,
https://doi.org/10.1007/978-3-030-23319-8_1

my work, language practices within, often served as important indicators of the *kind* of class performances that were to be expected. On the BQW's Scene in DC during my research, happy hours were often spaces where upwardly mobile, middle-class women met. Happy hours were typically spaces where the music was at a volume low enough to have a conversation. Asking and answering "what do you do?" was one way of demonstrating one's cultural and economic capital. Issues of class performance were often of supreme importance in scene spaces, and language practices such as these indicated the way that issues of race, sexuality, and class were inextricably linked within this particular social formation. Music could also serve as an indication of how a space was classed, and discussions about music revealed particular ideological investments in certain kinds of class performances. The DJ at the Women's Happy Hour played hip-hop from the Top 40 with songs like Kanye West's "Mercy" that included rapper Big Sean's lyrical gem, which I mouthed along to the music:

> *Drop it to the floor, make that ass shake (whoa)*
> *Make the ground move, that's an ass-quake*
> *Built a house up on that ass, that's an ass-state*
> *Roll my weed on it, that's an ass-tray*

The DJ also played one of my favorites from that year "No Lie" (2012) by 2 Chainz featuring Drake who says eloquently:

> *She came through, she brought food*
> *She got fucked, she knew wassup*
> *She think I'm the realest out*
> *And I say "damn, that makes two of us"*

Then the DJ played Tyga's "Rack City" (2011) whose most memorable lines were its hook:

> *Rack city, bitch*
> *Rack rack city, bitch*
> *Ten ten ten twenties and them fifties bitch*

As the song began, Timi turned to the group of us and said, "I don't like ratchet music, but I like this song." We all laughed, backed it up,[2] and

---

[2] Cash Money Records took over the '99 and the 2000 with rapper Juvenile's hit "Back that azz up." The phrase, "back that ass up," was not necessarily new, but entered into

dropped it like it was hot[3] to the next few songs. We took a break from dancing and refreshed our drinks, and ended up in a conversation about the kind of hip-hop that had come to be referred to as *ratchet music*. Curious, I asked everyone "What do you mean when you say 'ratchet music'?" Everyone, including myself, tried their hand at a definition of *ratchet music*.

By 2012, *ratchet music*, generally, had become associated with any contemporary hip-hop song that featured sexually explicit and suggestive themes. Timi and her friends said as much by naming rappers and songs they thought were ratchet. It was not necessarily "new" music. It was simply a subgenre of primarily Southern hip-hop that often referenced drug dealing (oftentimes referred to as its own genre, Trap[4] Music) stripping, explicit sexual acts, public drunkenness, and other behavior deemed outside of the notions of respectability. It was the kind of music that revolved around being inappropriate—drunk, angry, loud, and horny. It also revolved around being Black and bad, on purpose. It associated Blackness with badness and the South. It was "non-conformist, daring, [broke] social conventions, [went] against the established (read: White) norms for Black folk," (Smitherman 2006) and it was as Geneva Smitherman might argue "Bad Nigger[5]" music. It was the kind of music that Black middle-class people standing around sipping on $12 drinks *should not* enjoy because it associated Blackness with poor (read: lower-class) behavior.

The word *ratchet* itself wasn't a new "made up word," but a part of the legacy of African American English (AAE) which often stretched and bent the meanings of English words (Alim 2006; Smitherman 2000). In fact, I

---

broader use and when said within the context of African American English users, often evokes the song itself. If you find yourself at a club where the majority of the people there are Black, if the DJ plays this song from the very beginning, you will witness people "backing that ass up." The movement involves shaking one's buttocks, or ass, while simultaneously thrusting out and backward rhythmically.

[3] "Drop it like its hot" is a 2004 song by Snoop Dogg featuring super producer and performer, Pharell. The actual act of "dropping it like it's hot," refers to dipping one's ass down as low as possible.

[4] The Trap refers to the world of dealing illicit substances. Dealing illicit substances is inherently dangerous and will, most often, result in death and/or prison. Entering into that line of work is an acknowledgment that one has signed up for being "trapped" within one of those two possibilities. "Trap music," therefore, discusses the realities (and perhaps fantasy) of dealing illicit drugs and the dangers associated with it.

[5] I strongly encourage white people reading this to use "n-word" when reading this out loud, and to themselves.

was certain I heard a mother in my church[6] refer to people who were standing around on a street corner drinking out of brown paper bags as ratchet one Sunday evening[7] while my family was dropping her off to her retirement home after services. I remember knowing exactly what she meant. They were raggedy, disheveled, and inappropriate. They were the "Bad Nigger." I had grown up learning, and it was consistently reinforced, that when you behaved as a "nigger" in public, whatever happened to you, you deserved. "Niggers" I learned, growing up as a Black girl in the American South, were not worthy of respect, let alone sympathy. I didn't learn until I was a young adult that this idea was rooted in an investment in assimilationist racial politics. Black folks who enjoyed leisure time on the street corner, especially on a Sunday, were no less im/moral than church folk who were in the church treating one another with contempt. What was different though was that those on the corner made other Black folk *look bad* in the eyes of white people. And that seemed to be what Black middle-class folks feared the most.

Iton describes "the nigger" as a kind of non-citizen, haunting America's promise of democracy. "The nigger" haunts Blackness for "the nigger, the other, must be identified, isolated, and deployed in such a manner as to sustain a viable, marketable, assimilable, and respectable Blackness" (Iton 2008, 181). If the nigger is the specter that haunts Blackness, he does so by disrupting the fiction that Black people could ever have full access to American citizenship. He must be rooted out because he threatens every other Black person in America who is trying to "act right" and prove they're worthiness. I would argue that ratchet describes the *sensibility* and, perhaps, the imagination of "the nigger."

Claiming, acting, and being ratchet, involves an indirect (or direct) political orientation. To be Black and to be ratchet, on purpose, means that you ascribe no value to assimilation into the American "way of life." It is neither a possibility, nor a goal. Being ratchet makes you an outsider within American cultural politics and being a "nigger" makes you one

---

[6] Title of an elder woman in a Black church.

[7] Black churches notoriously keep their "flock" in church for several hours. The church of my childhood was one such church. My church also required elaborate set-up and break down as it often took place in either the home of the pastor or a hotel meeting room. Following Sunday school which began around 10 am and ended around 11:30 am, there were several church announcements. Then, praise and worship service, which, depending on the move of the spirit, could last anywhere between an hour or two. If the pastor was feeling particularly boisterous that afternoon, services could last until 2 pm–3 pm.

within assimilationist, Black middle-class politics, but in either case, you're still Black. That outsider-within positionality, we learn from Collins (1986), produces a great number of possibilities. One such possibility is a *new* word. According to Smitherman, the *nigga* (where the -er is replaced by the -a) is an example of African American counter-language where Black folks upend the "White man's language ... transforming *bad* into *good*" (Smitherman 2006, 51). Similarly, Southern hip-hop artists upended the potentially invective intent of ratchet—particularly its concern over what is "bad" behavior according to some Black folks—in the process, reanimating debates over respectability (Stallings 2013; Lewis 2013), racialized class politics (Pickens 2014; Brown and Young 2015), and, as I'll argue, the intersection of each of these within the politics of normative sexuality. As our conversation about ratchet and ratchet music unfolded at happy hour, I immediately recognized that each of us had a different investment in how *ratchet* was defined.

Consider the words *twerk*, *bling*, and *swag*. African American English words frequently end up in the American lexicon without much attention to what they *do* when they get there. That is, while many people use these terms, not enough attention is paid to how they operate in the everyday lives of people. But here was Timi, using the word in a discussion about how she understood herself in the world. Timi wanted us to know that, even though she knew some of the songs, it wasn't the type of music that she listened to at home, nor was it the kind of music that she preferred listening to. During my research, I found that *ratchet* was sometimes discussed as something that could "rub off" on you. If you spent too much time doing ratchet things, such as listening to ratchet music, then someone might think you were actually ratchet. The fear of being mistaken for ratchet reminded me of the fear of being seen as a lower-class Black person sometimes experienced by Black middle-class folks. Vershawn Young (2011) analyzes Chris Rock's joke in his comedy special *Bigger and Blacker* which highlights the anxiety that Black people, particularly Black middle-class people, have about being mistaken for "niggas" who behave in ways that are outside of the boundaries of respectability. Geneva Smitherman, concerned with the broad language practice of Black folks using the n-word, argues that one of the ways Black folks use the word is to describe a "vulgar, disrespectful, anti-social" Black person who "conforms to negative stereotypes of African Americans" (Smitherman 2006, 52). Black women who engaged in ratchet behavior, are seen as suspicious; self-serving and "playing into stereotypes" of Black women as uncouth, unsophisticated, and unjustifiably short-tempered (Pickens 2014). Being associated, therefore, with a ratchet person, could cause others to question whether you had "class," here referring to a sensibility that can be possessed. And one's ability to be "classy" can be especially important to those who already live on the edge of Black respectability politics such as Black lesbian, gay, bisexual, and transgender people.

Timi wanted us to know that she was *not* ratchet. She'd rather hear house music or Afrobeats, and for happy hours, she wished people played more Erykah Badu-like songs. One of Timi's friends agreed with her, but departed in that she occasionally enjoyed indulging in ratchet things such as music or television shows like *Love & Hip-Hop,* but only as "guilty pleasures." I was alone in enjoying ratchet music not simply as a "guilty pleasure," but because it was fun, light, and a part of the legacy of Southern hip-hop music[8] I came of age to. And yet, in the spirit of celebration, we all agreed that whether or not it was the primary music we listened to, or if it was "good" music, or whether the topics lacked "taste" or "class," we knew the words and could recognize the infectious beats of popular ratchet music, including the one that was playing, Louisiana rapper Hurricane Chris' "Halle Berry" (2009) and so we two-stepped, shook our hips as "classy" as we could, and sang along:

> *Halle Berry, Halle Berry*
> *Halle Berry, Halle Berry*
> *Well let's get ratchet*
> *Let's get ratchet*

This conversation about *ratchet* inspired me to seriously consider the connection between class politics and racialized sexuality and gender within the context of BQW's Scene in DC. I had similar conversations with BQW during my time in the field. I conducted formal interviews with 40 BQW in DC. In those interviews, seven of which were oral history interviews, informants talked about the places where they spent their leisure time, and how they made choices about where they spent their time. What I quickly learned was that class politics saturated the social and cultural landscape of BQW's lives in DC, and that only by closely examining what work class politics was doing within BQW's Scene would I understand how a word like *ratchet* mattered.

---

[8] Songs such as Juvenile's "Back that Azz Up" would always bring people out to the dance floor in Atlanta.

The Ethnography of Ratchet

This book is about the word *ratchet*.[9] Whenever I talk about having written a book about *ratchet*, people either want me to tell them what it means, or they want to know what I think about _____ (insert the name of a ratchet person, place, or thing). They are often disappointed about my resistance to offer a neat definition or when I don't confirm their suspicion about a person, place, or thing they have evaluated as being ratchet. They are disappointed still when I refuse offer what they (sometimes) feel should be my admonishment of the existence of ratchet representations of Black people. My lukewarm responses are not a matter of indifference, or coyness, but one of a very strong anti-racist, anti-sexist, and anti-capitalist politic rooted in the very same resistance to respectability politics as other Black women intellectuals[10] that have come before me. In this book, you will learn what I have come to find out about *ratchet* and the work that it does to animate particular kinds of conversations about race, gender, sexuality, and class. And while I will offer a definition of the word in Chap. 2, I only do so as a means of turning a slippery referent into a tangible object of study rather than as a way of fixing a definitive set of means to it.

Like the words *funk* and *bad*, *ratchet* is an African American English (AAE) word with multiple definitions, any and all of which may operate in a single utterance. For this reason, it can be hard to pin down definitions of AAE words. Sociolinguist Marcyliena H. Morgan explains that AAE is rooted in set of language practices borne out of necessity to resist subjugation. As Morgan explains, "until the 1960s, Southern segregationist could, without consequences, control and regulate the verbal interactions of Blacks, and especially interactions between blacks and whites" (Morgan 2002, 23). AAE developed under racism, a system of inequity which maintained "unwritten—but enforced—policy […] which functioned to mark a presumed belief in the superiority of a white audience/hearer" (Morgan 2002, 23). Under such conditions, Black folks have developed counter-language with different language ideologies or norms and beliefs about the use of language (Alim 2004; Morgan 2002; Smitherman 2000). This new counter-language included the use of words and phrases with multiple meanings, sometimes meanings that were the opposite from Standard

---

[9] When I refer to the word in the form of a noun, it is italicized. When using the word with its specified connotation it is in regular type.

[10] See Brittney C. Cooper's *Beyond Respectability: The Intellectual Thought of Race Women* (2017).

American English. This is in part because Black people may need or want to talk in the presence of a white audience without said audience fully understanding their true meaning. This is a simple way of explaining a language practice referred to as "indirectness." Therefore, AAE may be difficult to understand for the non-native AAE speaker but makes perfectly good sense to those who have grown up using a language that frequently operates within varying forms of indirectness, a linguistic resource that helps to mask the intent of the speaker. Indirectness involves a recognition of the power of words and an ability to bend the symbolic nature of words in order to undermine dominant society and their beliefs about their superiority (Morgan 2002, 24). Simply put, you could be talking to a white audience/hearer and they hear one thing—your acquiescence, but a Black audience might hear something else—your agency and true intent, camouflaged (Morgan 2002, 24). For example, in AAE you can be "bad," but with the right intonation, that may actually mean you're good at something.

I often describe *ratchet* as a word that points out bad Black behavior. *Bad* here meaning that it falls outside of standards set forth as acceptable within Black middle-class ideologies, but also that one might be good at calling out particular kinds of assumptions about how Black people are supposed to behave. *Ratchet* typically indexes, or calls attention to, aspects of behavior most often associated with the Black working-class including non-normative sexual configurations (Brown and Young 2015). Interestingly enough, *ratchet* also refers to the purposeful lack of pretense for what has been defined as socially acceptable by Black or white middle-class, heteronormative logics. As a sensibility that skirts the need to perform *respectability*, it points out the limits of assimilationist racial politics. Therefore, it functions both as a tool for pointing out and critiquing bad Black behavior, and as a tool for resisting the notion that there are such things as "good" and "bad" behavior in the first place. "Good" for whom? *ratchet* asks. "Bad" for whom? *ratchet* asks.

Ratchet has entered into a wider[11] American discourse the same way that many words in AAE have—through hip-hop and other forms of social exchange, especially public profiles of individuals on social networking sites such as YouTube, Twitter, and Instagram. Through this expansion, often the actual definition of the word becomes lost on those who use it indiscriminately (Brown and Young 2015). I have found that the word has

---

[11] Read: *whiter*. More white people have been using the word, giving the impression that it is "new," however, it is not.

come to take the place in many people's vocabulary that had previously been reserved for *ghetto*.¹² And yet, despite its strikingly similarity to *ghetto*, I would argue that in this moment, *ratchet* does a unique kind of work. In the Age of Obama, which overlaps with the Ages of Twitter, YouTube, the Rise of Trump, memes, hashtags, viral images of police violence against Black bodies, #BlackLivesMatter, the repeal of the Defense of Marriage Act and "Don't Ask, Don't Tell," *ratchet* shows us the contours of an emerging set of socio-political, economic, and cultural anxieties taking shape within African American communities of practice.

In *The Black Queer Work of Ratchet*, I am interested in the work *ratchet* does among Black queer women (BQW) in Washington, DC. During my fieldwork, I often heard BQW, the majority of whom were middle-class and upwardly mobile,¹³ using the word *ratchet*. These were women who, arguably, fell outside of the Black middle-class framework because they were not heterosexual. Their refusal to reproduce a heteronormative Black family and the Black patriarchy meant that they were not following the rules of proper Black middle-class womanhood. If anyone was ratchet, certainly it was them. And yet, it was the parties and events considered ratchet on the Scene which drew the largest audiences; BQW were often the objects of Black men's sexual fantasies in hip-hop that was considered ratchet, and they were often featured on Black reality television shows, arguably to demonstrate just how ratchet (and thus, for some, low-brow) the shows were. So, what was the work that *ratchet* did for these women?

I like to think of this book as an ethnography of a word. Ethnography is a social science methodology whereby a researcher studies the contemporary, lived experiences of the individuals within a specific place and time. Linguistic anthropologists frequently use ethnography in concert with the sustained study of specific ways of speaking, speech acts, or groups of speakers. We look for patterns in the way language is used, that is, how language practices are enacted by groups of people. Since language is in constant flux, there is value in studying a language practice *in context*, or as a function of a specific place and time. In this book, I explore the way *ratchet*, a word loaded with interracial and intraracial

---

[12] Being "ghetto," was to act as if one was from a lower-class, or "underclass" and without the dignities required for "civilized," "respectable" living.

[13] Meaning that their immediate families may have been working-class, but they experienced a "bump" in material resources often as a result of attainment of undergraduate or graduate education that allows them to experience middle-class lifestyles.

class politics, circulated within a very narrow and specific context—within the BQW's Scene in DC. This, I decided, was the best strategy for managing the inherent instability and unruliness of the subject. Rather than consider how everyone in America uses *ratchet*, I consider how the word traveled among a specific group of people whose voices we rarely hear, especially in the broad set of conversations which revolve around *ratchet* including the politics of respectability, homonormativity, and representations of the Black middle-class and Black working-class.

I use an analytical approach I call a Quare Linguistic Anthropological approach which borrows from E. Patrick Johnson's notion of quare (Johnson 2001) and William Leap's Queer Linguistic anthropological approach to Critical Discourse Analysis (CDA) (Leap 2008, 2015). E. Patrick Johnson offered "quare" as a critique of queer studies for its failure to render legible the experiences of queer bodies of color. Quare is as an AAE term meaning "odd and slightly off kilter" and is characterized by an "excess incapable of being contained within conventional categories of being" (Johnson 2001, 2). Johnson wishes to "'quare' 'queer' such that ways of knowing are viewed both as discursively mediated and as historically situated and materially conditioned" (Johnson 2001, 3). Such interventions are critical in order to make Black same-sex desiring subjects legible, because of the way Whiteness tends to stand in as the dominant and normative subject position from which queerness is theorized. Similarly, Black cultural theory has tended to elide the sexual differences between Black subjects and thus has participated in the "straight washing" of Blackness. In other words, while queers of colors have always been there, the theoretical tools for analyzing the specificity of their experiences have emerged primarily from challenging their absence. I wish to extend a quare approach in my application of linguistic anthropology primarily as a means of calling attention to the ways that topics of language and sexuality are by their very nature about the topics of race, gender, and class because these discourses always travel together, fixing certain kinds of differences on bodies in particular ways. Approaches to gender and sexuality in language, what Leap (2015) has referred to as "queer linguistic analysis," are closely tied to Critical Discourse Analysis (CDA) and are concerned with analyzing the power-laden practices of discursive formations of sexuality broadly, and queer subjects specifically. Leap champions a broad set of analytical techniques such as analyzing systems of appraisal, the examination of the use of metaphors, and narrative analysis all of which bring to the researcher closer to understanding "the role of discourse in the (re)production and challenge of dominance" (van Dijk 1993, 249). Leap's approach to discourse analysis holds that the goal of our research is to "[locate] connections between gender and other forms of social location that are being addressed within the social moment. This requires a close reading of text, and careful consideration of speaker biography and speaker intention, but it also requires social and historical perspectives that extend far beyond the textual boundary" (Leap 2008, 295). By quaring CDA, I want to think about the ways that the "different 'standpoints' found among lesbian, bisexual, gay, and transgendered people of color—differences that are also conditioned by class and gender" (Johnson 2001, 3) are embedded within social spaces and linguistic practices in any given moment. Leap (2015) argues that queer linguistics "engages the linguistic dimensions of affective and intersectional alignments, thereby exploring the many ways in which desire itself becomes expressed—or materialized—in everyday experience." Not only must one be concerned with analyzing the textual data, but one must also understand the social contexts in which the textual data emerges. This moves us closer to understanding how sexuality becomes material in people's everyday lives, particularly in the way that they express themselves through language. This is the crucial difference between a project that is only concerned with the theoretical uses of language and one which is interested in, as E. Patrick Johnson has points out, the very real conditions of subjects "on the street" (Johnson 2001).

Therefore, I utilize a *Quare* Linguistic Anthropological approach in this examination of *ratchet* because it compels me to pay strict attention to the ways that discussions of sexuality are already about race, gender, and class as the discourses tend to travel together. It also helps me to stay attuned to the ways that Black heterosexuality can be and should be analyzed for its queerness (Bailey and Shabazz 2013), and its continued use of queer configurations to make particular kinds of claims about authenticity and social value (Lane 2011; Ferguson 2000). Further, "quare studies acknowledges the different 'standpoints' found among lesbian, bisexual, gay, and transgendered people of color—differences that are also conditioned by class and gender" (Johnson 2001, 3). Anthropology, ethnography, in particular, allows us to bring into focus how difference is navigated at those various standpoints. When we focus on individual, local experiences of larger macro-processes, we begin to acknowledge the various ways individuals and groups have defined their subjectivity, with and against, seemingly all-encompassing cultural, political, and social forces. By focusing on individual, local uses of a specific word—*ratchet*—I will demonstrate how projects of neoliberalism and homonormativity come to structure the sensibilities, tastes, everyday life, and ordinary experiences of Black queer women in DC.

Why Black Queer Women?

Black women within the American mainstream are, at best, "trendy," and at worst, abnormal (Harris-Perry 2011; Collins 2000). Given the growing interest in dynamic Black women intellectuals and entertainers such as Roxane Gay, Brittney Cooper, and Patrisse Khan-Cullors as well as the meteoric rise of pop star Lizzo, the pop dominance of Beyoncé, and the quiet takeover of Rihanna, who is engaged in fashion and beauty, Black women would seem to be enjoying the moment. As Black women who skirt the Black heteropatriarchal politics of respectability, BQW fall outside of the of racialized gender script of proper Black womanhood and are often marginalized within Black cultural and sexual politics as well (Fogg-Davis 2006; Richardson 2003; Isoke 2014; Khan-Cullors and asha bandele 2018). Though, it is important to keep in mind that within the American mainstream as Cathy Cohen (2005) argues, both homosexual and heterosexual Black women occupy a similar denigrated position within the American mainstream since both are unable to enact American middle-class (read: proper) modes of (white) womanhood. In referring to my informants as *Black Queer* women, I follow E. Patrick Johnson and Mae Henderson and evoke the heterogeneity implicit in the terms *Black* and *queer*.

> [J]ust as "queer" challenges notions of heteronormativity and heterosexism, "Black" resists notions of assimilation and absorption. And so we endorse the double cross of affirming the inclusivity mobilized under the sign of "queer" while claiming the racial, historical, and cultural specificity attached to the marker "Black." (Johnson and Henderson 2005, 7)

Johnson and Henderson (2005) do not use either *Black* or *queer* to simply modify the other but to disturb the boundaries of both. BQW have different ethnicities, (non-normative) sexualities, and have different relationships to class and Black cultural politics. Part of what I intend my analysis to demonstrate is just how much those differences affect their experiences. BQW differ greatly along important axes in this project including age, ethnicity, class, and gender presentation and yet I contend that all of them face choices about how to define themselves, how to be, and how to represent themselves in a mainstream American cultural imagination where they are rarely seen or heard from. There are very few examples of BQW or the spaces that they create for socializing with one another in the mainstream, though, for most people, it is the exceptions to this rule that are more easily called up.

For example, Queen Latifah has portrayed two same-sex desiring characters on screen (in addition to being rumored to be a lesbian herself). She played the title role of HBO biopic of the blues songstress Bessie Smith titled *Bessie* (2015). And most famously, in 1995, she played the lesbian character Cleo in the film *Set it Off* which placed her female masculinity within the context of an ensemble cast of Black female bank robbers. As Kara Keeling argues, Cleo serves as "a receptacle for the embattled, outlawed, and virulently 'heterosexual' articulations of 'Black masculinity'" further carrying "the burden of 'Black masculinity' so that the film's other perceptibly 'female' characters [...] can be recognized as simply 'Black women' (a category that carries an assumed orientation towards heterosexuality)" (Keeling 2003). Sonya Sohn played police detective Kima on HBO's hit drama *The Wire*. Similarly, her female masculinity was positioned in relation to white masculinity such that they produced similar screened effects. In Starz's *Survivor's Remorse*, M-Chuck, played by Erica Ash, is the older sister of the main character, a budding basketball star. More often than not, however, Black lesbians, when they are portrayed, are token—ancillary—characters who operate to make the main characters (or the shows themselves) seem more progressive. In all most of these cases (Kima and M-Chuck, especially), the characters are what I would call "heterowashed." They spend all their time with their heterosexual counterparts in heterosexual spaces. They seemingly have no Black queer friends and are rarely, if ever, depicted as being in Black queer space. The seemingly "progressive" nature of inclusion of BQW in mainstream ends up reiterating the fact that BQW are spaceless, and exist "comfortably" in normative spaces as long as they act like heterosexual people expect them to. This does not reflect the lived experiences of the majority of BQW I encountered during my fieldwork. Their lives were more like to be characterized as a constant movement between white and Black heterosexual spaces, and Black queer spaces. My informants spoke of the importance of being connected to other Black queer people, or broadly queer people of color. I would argue that BQW and the spaces that they create, tend to occupy a position within the American mainstream as illegible (Hancock 2004), ungrieveable (Fogg-Davis 2006; Isoke 2014), and invisible (Moore 2011).

BQW are situated within dominant ideologies of racism, sexism, heteronormativity, and homonormativity such that they are typically invisible in many analyses. This is in many ways surprising given that BQW and their experiences offer compelling insights into the interconnectedness of race, gender, sexuality, and class. Class analyses, especially, tend to disregard the experiences of BQW. Rarely are BQW in any context the subjects of class analysis. Black lesbians, for example, are impossible to see if looking only at statistical analyses of class in America where women or Black people are typically aggregated from large samples. On rare occasions are Black women aggregated usually to compare their income to Black men, which still yields no information about BQW. There remain few sources to draw from which address the specific ways that non-heterosexuality structures Black women's access to social, economic, cultural, and symbolic capital (Bourdieu 1984). Further, there is little information about the way that social and cultural capital structures their experiences, their talk, or their relationships to social space. I would argue that the dearth of information pertaining to BQW and class is what Evelynn Hammonds might refer to as one of the many (w)holes that exists where it pertains to Black women's sexuality (Hammonds 1994). This gap in our understanding may in part be related to the fact that BQW are generally invisible and illegible in the American mainstream.[14]

The widened use of *ratchet* in American popular media over the past several years as well as the engagement with the concept in academe mark it as a topic for which many are beginning to take seriously (Brown and Young 2015). What seems to be missing, however, are the actual voices and experiences of the individuals of those whom have so much at stake in how the word gets deployed; those who have always existed on the margins of the politics of respectability and Black Sexual Politics—BQW. In particular, by exploring how BQW's bodies are often positioned against many notions of propriety, this book uses as a case study the various ways BQW in DC situate themselves against such renderings of their lives as antithetical to Black middle-class respectability.

---

[14] It should be noted that two films, the successful independent film *Pariah* and HBO's biographic film *Bessie* staring Queen Latifah, both directed by Dee Rees, a self-identified Black lesbian, have gained notable mainstream attention. However, these representations of Black queer women are "atypical."

The Black Middle-Class and Respectability

In May 2012, then President Barack Obama publicly declared his shifting stance on Marriage Equality. In an interview with Robin Roberts of Good Morning America, who had recently "come out," Obama said, "I've been going through an evolution on this issue."[15] Obama wasn't the only Black person having personal evolutions on LGBT issues, but his public support of lesbian, gay, and bisexual people's right to marry certainly opened the door for other middle-class Black people who were invested in heteronormativity to begin to openly show their support. But questions remain about what that "support" looks like and to whom that support is extended. What kind of Black lesbian, gay, bisexual, or trans person was acceptable now? Which one's would be seen as worthy of support? Which one's would be respectable? How should Black queer people act now that middle-class Black people would now allow *some* of us to come to "the table"? My research took place within the context of the repeal of the Defense of Marriage Act, the (Black) President of the United States gravitating toward support for LGBT communities, and the increased self-representations of Black same-sex desiring subjects in American visual media, offering a unique opportunity to ask how Black queer subjects would be engaged in redefining the borders of acceptable Black behavior in public. Borrowing from Johnson (2011) who argues that Black middle-classness is performative, I consider how deployments of *ratchet* as well as its attendant discourses, allowed some of my informants to engage in performances of Black middle-classness to demonstrate their worthiness of having a set at the proverbial "table."

It is important to understand that white supremacist logic and policies in the United States created a link between Blackness and lower-classness (Young and Tsemo 2011, 17). Further, it has been argued that African American existence was purposefully rendered "non-heteronormative" in the United States to justify ongoing social, cultural, and economic exclusion (Ferguson 2000). In attempting to enter into the folds of "the Black middle-class" some BQW put into practice some of the very discourses that maintain their exclusion. This behavior is situated within intersecting sets of concerns for Black women some of whom, at the turn of the twentieth century, reacted to being excluded from the "cult of true womanhood" by doubling down on a version of immaculate womanhood. At the

---

[15] Transcript: Robin Roberts ABC News Interview With President Obama.

same time, the Era of Segregation had the long-lasting effect of making it appear as if one's race determined one's class, because Black people were relegated to poor amenities and impoverished neighborhoods leading to the formation of "ghettos" whether they had access to capital or not (Johnson 2011, 15). In other words, middle-class Black people could still be treated as if they were lower-class (Johnson 2011, 15), a point that even Barack Obama makes clear in his autobiography.

> Only white culture had individuals. And we, the half-breeds and the college-degreed, take a survey of the situation and think to ourselves, "Why should we get lumped in with the losers if we don't have to?" [...] and we're never so outraged as when a cabbie drives past us or the woman in the elevator clutches her purse, not so much because we're bothered by the fact that such indignities are what less fortune coloreds have to put up with every single day of their lives [...] but because we're wearing a Brooks Brothers suit and speak impeccable English and yet have somehow been mistaken for an ordinary nigger. (Obama 2007, 100)

Like Chris Rock, Obama explains the outrage some middle-class and upwardly mobile Black people experience at being mistaken for a "nigger." Here the issue is related to being unable to reap the public benefits of not being one: common decency, a cab ride, people not automatically associating you with anti-social behavior. E. Patrick Johnson argues that "the social inequality that some middle-class Blacks still protest always has been and already is about class" (Johnson 2011, 12). Working-class Blackness has always been situated as the true, "authentic" representation of Black behavior. This allowed for whatever "benign behaviors" associated with Blackness to be "deemed problematic only because they are associated with being Black and thus lower class" (Johnson 2011, 16). Thus being "mistaken for an ordinary nigger" often fueled the Black middle-class's need to "perform themselves" (perform their class) in situations where they should have be able to "be themselves'" (Johnson 2011, 20). During the Era of Jim Crow, they were forced to sit at the back of a train in their tailored suits and pockets full of money with the rest of "the niggas." Both *de jure* and *de facto* redlining kept Black middle-class people out of white middle-class neighborhoods meaning that Black middle-class people are more likely to live in mixed class neighbors closer to working-class Black people, the niggas. Since the introduction of Affirmative Action policies, Black middle-class people have had to defend their fitness for jobs or seats in undergraduate and graduate programs due to some people's hatred of race-conscious policies that attempt to (marginally) address racial inequality. And so, regardless of how close to achieving individuality those in the Black middle-class have tried to come, they're never allowed to truly sit at tables with white people as individuals, but as "credits" to their race, "exceptional Negros" (Kendi 2016) or worse yet, a "well-trained, well-paid nigger" (Obama 2007, 97). Simultaneously, from within Black communities, Black middle-class protest at not wanting to be thought of as belonging to the same group of Black people who were consistently mistreated, would be used as evidence for the charge that those Black middle-class folks were being *boojie*, or "acting white." Here, we see the real cost of racial segregation. Whiteness comes to function as a form of property that Black folks are kept from (Harris 1995), and their attempts to get even a piece of what it confers to the owner: decency, respect, individuality, access to better resources, is viewed suspiciously from both white and Black folks alike.

Cheryl Harris (1995) looks at the intersection of white racial privilege in the law and economic domination. She uses the concept of fair-skinned Blacks being able to "pass" (for white) as a way of examining the ability to own white identity. She says "passing" can only occur "when oppression makes self-denial and the obliteration of identity rational and, in significant measure, beneficial" (Harris 1995, 285). In describing the persistence of Whiteness as a form of property she argues Whiteness does not automatically mean wealth and power; on the contrary, those have been retained for a rather small group of white (male) ruling elite. Whiteness does, however, remain significant because while "it does not mean that all whites will win" it does mean "they will not lose, if losing is defined as being on the bottom of the social and economic hierarchy—the position to which Blacks have been consigned" (Harris 1995, 286). We should understand that the work middle-class Black people do when attempting to not be mistaken for "niggers" is a performance designed to recalibrate the boundaries of the bottom of the hierarchy. Some middle-class Black people were adamant about proving their *worth* even under such conditions as these which were designed to ensure that regardless of how Black people behave we all ultimately lose within a white supremacist structure.

The Black church as an institution has considerable influence on Black values (Douglas 2011, 235), and has been concerned with the shaping with the moral character of the Black community in the United States since its introduction on the outskirts of slave plantations. However, it is not the only place where Black folks have talked about morality and how to behave properly. Booker T. Washington and W.E.B. Du Bois published "conduct books" in the late nineteenth century. Nazera Sadiq Wright argues that they "elevated the Black elite's role as instructors to the Black reading public and were designed to contribute to the moral good of Black people and the nation at large" (Wright 2011, 95). What constituted "moral," however, seemed to be more about acting in line with how white people had constructed virtuous characteristics of masculinity and femininity. Thus, these books demonstrate evidence of a long-standing tradition in the politics of Black racial progress: a strong assimilationist logic. The logic goes that if individual Black people act like morally, upright American citizens (and the only such people are white), then Black people as a group will be treated like true Americans (white people). In and of itself, it wasn't a bad idea, but we now know that these ideas were misguided and didn't include in their calculation the lengths to which white people would go to protect their place at the top of America's racial hierarchy including violence. Thus the books reveal a set of "self-imposed restrictions Black people were under to avoid violence ... [a] strict etiquette least the community be condemned by the behaviors of one or a few" (Wright 2011, 103). Examining Silas X. Floyd's book *Floyd's Flowers* (1905) in more detail, Wright (2011) considers how the rules of proper (or assimilationist) behavior were carefully gendered. For example, little Black girls who were "loud," were cast as "hardly human" by Floyd (Wright 2011, 101). And if they wore unfeminine attire, were loud, or aggressive they were deemed "unladylike" (Wright 2011, 102). Unfortunately, authors of the conduct books seemed to have bought into racist ideas about Black people. Ibram X. Kendi defines a racist idea as any idea that holds that a racial group, in this case Black people, are inferior, for any reason. When being "unladylike" as a little Black girl means that you "hardly human," the same language used to describe Black people of the same era, then we should know that we're likely dealing with a racist idea. We can also speak this racist idea being laced with heterosexism, since all girls are expected to want to be "ladylike" and, implicitly, desirable to men. The oral tradition of many Black families and the persistence of respectability politics, particularly the insistence on telling Black women to "behave" to avoid mistreatment in a racist white America (that would go on to mistreat them anyway), mean that these ideas have not gone anywhere. They remain the lessons that many young Black women learn early in childhood. Downplay any behavior that might be seen as "unladylike," (or too Black) in order to mitigate how you're treated in the world. What is most striking given my interest in BQW is that the very things that could make a woman "hardly human" and "unladylike," are the very things that could make her seem, in the terms of the early twentieth century, a "bulldagger."[16]

Evelyn Brooks Higginbotham classically lays out the origins the politics of respectability which she describes as a discursive effort of self-representation that Black Baptist women undertook in the late nineteenth and early twentieth century meant to contest the racist and sexist representations of themselves (Higginbotham 1993, 185). Higginbotham argues that respectability, or the condition of being worthy of respect, became a matter of political importance for Black women who spread the notion that Black people needed to begin to act like those who are worthy of being respected so that the white majority would begin to see them as such. The "politics of respectability" would get dispersed within various kinds of Black publics and discursive arenas, and would get transfigured and refracted through other Black cultural theorists, artists, and philosophers of the time (Andrews 2003; Beauboeuf-Lafontant 2008; Bergner 1995; Higginbotham 1993). While it contested the racist assumptions that Blacks were lazy, unkempt, and immoral, the politics of respectability "led to their insistence upon Blacks' conformity to the dominant society's norms of manners and morals" (Higginbotham 1993). Emphasizing manners and morals as a strategy for combatting racism and white supremacy, the politics of respectability "reflected and reinforced the hegemonic values of white America, as it simultaneously subverted and transformed the logic of race and gender subordination" (Higginbotham 1993, 187). Arguably, the politics of respectability was rooted in the desire to assimilate to normative white middle-class ways of being and was problematically aligned with the racist rhetoric of the time. However, for Higginbotham, by simply calling attention to the fact that there were, in fact, Black women with "class" and who were worthy of respect, the politics of respectability also called out the inherent problem with racial and gendered subordination.

The politics of respectability was, at least in part, shaped by Black middle-class women in response to white supremacist notions about the morality and worth of Black women specifically, and Black people more broadly. It could also be said that the politics of respectability instigates a

---

[16] An early twentieth century epithet for lesbian; often used to refer to Black lesbians.

particular kind of anxiety among Black people who wanted to "prove" their worth in the wake of their newfound freedoms in America. As members of an emerging Black middle-class at the turn of the twentieth century struggled to change white people's minds about Black people, they became concerned with policing the behaviors of "poorly behaved," working-class, Southern, uneducated, dark-skinned Black people for fear of being mistaken for them. As the politic of respectability took a firm hold within progressive racial politics, it would position the Black middle-class and elite as the moral arbiters of the Black community, policing the borders of Black respectability. For example, Alain Locke, a gay man and one of the most important Black intellectuals of the early twentieth century and known as the "Architect of the Harlem Renaissance," argued in a 1925 essay titled "Enter the New Negro" that due to rapid class differentiation taking place at the turn of the century "if it ever was warrantable to regard and treat the Negro *en masse*, it is becoming with every day less possible, more unjust and more ridiculous" (Locke 1925, 631). He continued that "social gain" for all Black people would happen with "the releasing of our talented group from the arid fields of controversy and debate to the productive fields of creative expression" (Locke 1925, 634). Here Locke recognizes that all of the racist ideas that Americans had formed about Black people were based on the Southern, agrarian, working-class Black folks many of whom were poor and lacked formal education. The New Negro was urban, talented, and educated, and thus had access to class mobility which made him more different from the Old Negro, than he was from the learned, white middle-class and elite. However, to demonstrate their value on the American cultural stage, the New Negro had to struggle to escape the "controversies and debates" generated by the Old Negro. The problem with race in America, as Locke describes in this essay, was not simply America's *de jure* and *de facto* white supremacist laws, or the state-sanctioned white supremacist violence against Black bodies, but "race relations" including how white people thought of Black people's contributions to American culture. Good Negro art produced by the New Negro in Harlem could repair that relationship. Locke believed that "the cultural recognition they win should in turn prove the key to that revaluation of the Negro which must precede or accompany any considerable further betterment of race relationships" (Locke 1925, 634). Locke's logic is rooted in an assimilationist politic and suggests that Black people simply need to be reevaluated by white people based on a small group of smart, articulate, and artistic Black men geographically located outside of the South, and then white people would see that not all Black people were bad. This logic of assimilation would set up a small group of highly educated, middle-class and elite Black men, for the New Negro was always male in the imagination of Locke (Stewart 2018, 512), to represent all Black people in all race-related matters, even if their experiences did not reflect the majority. Further, it would set these men as the idealized version of Blackness, producing a conundrum for Black women trying to understand what it meant to be Black within the context of American cultural life. How these questions play out within the politics of representation of Black women is of particular importance here.

Those engaging in the study of images of Black women, almost always encounter Patricia Hill Collins on the path to understanding how Black women's bodies are treated within the American visual emporium. Her seminal essay on the subject "Mammies, Matriarchs, and Welfare Queens" offered us the concept of the "controlling image," a neologism, a new, explanatory word for a previously unnamed phenomenon. The American visual emporium is saturated with images of Black women as maids, sex workers with hearts of gold, and dotting best friends of white women. According to Collins, controlling images are not simply stereotypes—short-hand ways of thinking about Black women—they are technologies of oppression, as they justify the mistreatment of Black women at the hands of the State. For example, the figure of the welfare queen justifies the policies enacted to reduce state and federal spending on the social safety net, placing poor women and children in an even more precarious position within a racist, capitalist society (Collins 2008). One of the effects of this new language to talk about the representations of Black women according to Jennifer Nash was that it provided a way of understanding what clearly appeared to be "an ideologically consistent set of visual practices which insist on Black women's sexual deviance and train viewers to interpret Black women's alterity" (Nash 2014, 33). Nash clues us in to how many people use the concept to simply place any representation of Black women that they see within an already predetermined box such that a character like Olivia Pope in Shonda Rhimes *Scandal* is read by some as simply another iteration of the mammy. Nash also suggests why it is important to utilize different reading practices as well, for if any image a Black woman is somehow, always already an example of how Black women are injured in the American visual emporium, then how do we explain the pleasure that some Black women experience when seeing these images? Further, what do we do with self-authored images of Black womanhood that might be attempting to work outside of those narrow boxes. What is needed is a decidedly anti-racist reading practice that does what the politics of respectability cannot—allow Black women to *live*. Joan Morgan in her essay "Why We Get Off: Moving Toward a Black Feminist Politics of Pleasure" describes the challenges in theorizing around pleasure within Black Feminist Theory. In placing "Black women's damaged sexuality" and "reoccurring trauma" at the center of all analyses concerning Black women's sexuality means that we miss out on exploring "the complex, messy, sticky, and even joyous negotiations of agency and desire that are irrevocably twinned with our pain" (Morgan 2015a,b, 36).

Nicole Fleetwood's work on racial iconicity offers another strategy for reading the images of Black women (Fleetwood 2011). A much-needed departure from a reading strategy that always assumes that images of Black women fit into one or more of the molds of the controlling image, Fleetwood suggests that it is within the field of the visual that Black women also do reclamatory work (Fleetwood 2011). Rather than reduce all images of Black women to moments of injury, she attempts to account for the work that Black women do to engage audiences via the assumptions about Black women's bodily "excess." In other words, even while engaging in visual practices that may imply particular controlling images, Black women can also make alternative claims about the form and structure of their difference or sameness (Fleetwood 2011; Nash 2014). Such reading strategies will be of particular importance when examining the self-authored representations of BQW as I intend to do here, for it becomes nearly difficult, if not impossible, to place them within the existing framework of controlling images, in part because all of the controlling images are presumably heterosexual—the Welfare Queen, the Baby Mama, the Sapphire, the Hoochie Mama—or, in the case of the Mammy, asexual.

Homo- and Heteronormativity

When sexuality is discussed in studies of the Black middle-class, heterosexuality typically stands as the unquestioned vantage point from which any issues related to gender and sexuality are discussed or analyzed. For example, Mary Pattillo's *Black Picket Fences: Privilege and Peril among the Black Middle-Class* (2013) is a rich and thorough examination of the Black middle-class in a neighborhood of Chicago. In it, she examines the role of gender and sexuality in the lives of youth growing up in the neighborhood. Pattillo contends that both boys and girls have equal access to the benefits of their middle-class parents, however, the kinds of "temptations" they might experience outside of the home that might prevent them from maintaining and reproducing their middle-class lifestyle in adulthood were gendered (Pattillo 2013, 111). Discussing some of these potential "temptations," Pattillo suggests that "boys and young men join gangs and sell drugs … and girls and young women get pregnant before they are married" (Pattillo 2013, 111). While this might be true of her sample, I would contend that gendering these temptations, or more importantly adult anxieties, in this way gives the impression that all the girls and young women are heterosexual. During my research, I spoke to BQW women who had come from Black middle-class families (in and around DC), and several spoke about the disappointment their families—their mother's especially—experienced when they told them about their sexual identity. A child or loved one being gay is, in many contexts, an *unspeakable* "temptation" that some Black middle-class and working-class families living in Black neighborhoods fear. In William Leap's (2009) ethnographic research in Washington, DC in the late 1990s and early 2000s, one his informants, a Black gay man named Bolton, explained,

> To me … it seems that with a lot of black gay residents, they tend to be just kind of mixed in with other working-class families in uh row houses in certain parts of the city. Their identities are kept kind of concealed. [...] And people tend to respect them for not revealing "quote unquote" their business. (Leap 2009, 203)

According to Bolton, one way of earning "respect" as a Black gay person in a Black neighborhood was to "not reveal" one's homosexuality. Mignon Moore's findings in her study of Black lesbian mothers in New York suggest that Black lesbian, gay, or bisexual women in seemingly homonormative partnerships—two parents and children—often make use of strategic "covering" (Goffman 1967) to navigate their relationships within Black communities. They downplayed the benign, outward signs of their sexuality such as masculine attire, opting for gender-neutral attire when in social spaces and situations where the majority of people were Black heterosexual, middle-class people. Some BQW are accepted by the Black middle-class, but their acceptance is often conditioned on their ability to practice temperament, restraint, and other forms of self-management as to not shake the foundations of heteronormativity. Therefore, as long as they do not represent a kind of Black homosexuality that is *too* sexual, *too* queer, they are fine.

In the United States, the majority of Black LGBTQ people live in predominantly Black neighborhoods (Kastanis and Gates 2013), many of which are likely mixed-income (Pattillo 2013). According to a 2013 statistical study conducted by the University of California Los Angeles' Williams Institute, DC has the highest percentage of African American LGBT identified individuals among its population than anywhere else in the United States with 9.7% of the African American population being LGBT identified (Kastanis and Gates 2013). One of the key findings of the report was that African American LGBT people tended to "flock" in cities where there was a high density of African Americans (Kastanis and Gates 2013). This is significant for DC because while African Americans make up roughly 14% of the country's total population, according to the 2010 U.S. Census, DC had a Black population of just over 50% (U.S. Census 2010). While this percentage is steadily decreasing,[17] DC and its surrounding suburbs are still have some of the highest percentages of Black people relative to other similar sized cities in the country, and evidence would suggest that these suburbs, like the city, are, relatively speaking, very gay. Therefore, the absence of these subjects in discussions of the Black middle-class in the region is odd.

Karyn Lacy's book *Blue-Chip Black: Race, Class, and Status in the New Black Middle-Class* about the new Black middle-class in and around Washington, DC offers little indication of how sexuality might structure the experiences of the Black middle-class. The word "sexuality" appears in the book only once, and "lesbian," "gay," and "homosexuality" are nowhere in the book. Yet evidence suggests that the regulation of sexuality is foundational to the State's regulation of both the Black middle-class and the Black working-class. Consider what Roderick Ferguson calls the State's "taxonomy of Black nonheteronormativity" which included "common law marriages, out-of-wedlock births, lodgers, single-headed families, nonmonogamous sexual relationships, unmarried persons, and homosexual persons and relationships" (Ferguson 2000, 423). Apart of the maintenance and reproduction of the Black middle-class, as both Pattillo and Lacy describe, there is a concern with the reproduction of the *ideals* about what it means to be middle-class. Therefore, those things

---

[17] Current U.S. Census Bureau estimates have 47.1% of the population to be Black or African American, and 45.1% as white, and 11% Hispanic. United States Census Bureau, "Quick Facts: District of Columbia" Last accessed July 22, 2018. https://www.census.gov/quickfacts/fact/table/dc/PST045217.

which mark Black people as non-heteronormative are to be avoided. For a young, Black middle-class girl in a predominantly Black neighborhood, depending on the normative investments of her family, being gay might be as "bad" as, or worse than, getting pregnant "out of wedlock." That neighborhood-level research about the Black middle-class rarely treats conceptions about non-heteronormativity is unfortunate given how connected sexuality is to the reproduction of class ideologies. The absence of a discussion of sexuality is not a "fault" per se of either study, and certainly doesn't take away from their broader analyses, but it raises important questions about why sexuality (even normative modes of heterosexuality) has not be regarded as a relevant lens. The result is that there are few sources from which to draw that address the specific ways that being (or not) heterosexual might structure a Black woman's experiences of her class status.

During my time in my field site in Washington, DC, a metropolitan area with one of the highest proportions of Black middle-class people, I found that the majority of the BQW that I engaged with held on to Black middle-class ideologies despite the fact that by simply *being* gay, or partnering with women, they were often positioned outside of Black middle-class notions of propriety. I would speak to women who would talk about their mother's difficulty with them being gay—their mothers often being embarrassed or disappointed by their daughter's unwillingness to conform to a certain vision of Black middle-class womanhood and heterosexual coupling, and then she would go say that she didn't like going to *ratchet* clubs because the women were "unladylike," or didn't conform to Black middle-class versions of propriety. There was clearly tension in the way that these women understood themselves and their own class positions. That Black lesbian, bisexual, and queer women, who are already outside of the framework of a "proper" Black femininity, would be engaged in a struggle *within* their own communities of practice around the politics of respectability points to the nature of a politics of respectability to structure the way people understand their place in the world.

The politics of respectability demonstrates one of the many ways that African Americans have been engaged in symbolic and cultural struggle to prove that they too can be "normal" (Ferguson 2000). If the politics of respectability would seek to rectify the "problems" of African American families starting with Black women, then what L. H. Stallings has referred to as the "Black Ratchet Imaginary" would seem to work against this logic. For Pickens (2014) ratchet performances have an oppositional relationship to progressive racial politics.

> The ratchet imaginary has no desire to participate in narratives of racial progression or social uplift; instead, it articulates a desire for individuality regardless of the ideas and wants of a putative collective. It functions as a tertiary space in which one can perform a racialized and gendered identity without adhering to the prescriptive demands of either. (Pickens 2014, 4)

For the ratchet woman then, her presence and her success call into question the very tenants of the politics of respectability which are based on the assumption that if a Black female subject *acts right*, then and only then, can she expect to be treated with respect, and thus be successful. Pickens (2014) also argues the continued propagation of images of Black female subjects who are ratchet, Karrine Steffans, self-described hip-hop "video vixen," Tamar Braxton, reality television star and sister of R&B legend Toni Braxton, and the girlfriends and mistresses on the reality television show *Love and Hip-Hop* "reinforce dominant and racist views of Black female sexuality" (Pickens 2014, 7). However, following Ibram X. Kendi who argues that racist ideas are the "children" of racist policies, I depart from Pickens (2014) on this point and would argue that it is not ratchet people or representations of ratchet people that reinforce racist and sexist ideas, instead it is the continued investment in racist and sexist policies. According to a report by the Institute for Women's Policy Research, 60% of Black women in the United States participate in the formal economy and 80% are breadwinners in their home, but their earnings lag behind most men and women of any race.[18] Black women are some of the hardest working women in the country, and yet, they experience poverty at a rate higher rate than Black men and women of any other race.[19] The continued need to justify racist and sexist policies which maintain Black women's place within the current patriarchal and racial hegemonic structures are what reproduce racist and sexist ideas. In other words, absent racist and sexist structures including policies, we might be able to read these women who behave in ratchet ways as individuals who represent only themselves. Ratchet women on television don't make policy, and

---

[18] DuMonthier, Asha, Chandra Childers, and Jessica Milli. "The Status of Black Women in the United States." Washington, DC: Institute for Women's Policy Research, 2017.
[19] Ibid.

more importantly, they are attempting to wrestle from the grips of these racist and sexist structures a sense of individuality; they are individuals who do not—despite assimilationist anxieties and racist people's assumptions which often preceded those representations—represent all Black women.

Black women's desire for individuality and self-determination *outside* of structures which silence us is a matter of collective and political importance. In expounding upon ratchet's lack of respectability, L. H. Stallings leans on the work of Jack Halberstam's *The Queer Art of Failure* where Halberstam argues that "under certain circumstances failing, losing, forgetting, unmaking, undoing, unbecoming, not knowing may in fact offer more creative, more cooperative, more surprising ways of being in the world" (Halberstam 2011, 2). Through "the performance of the failure to be respectable, uplifting, and a credit to the race," the Black Ratchet Imagination *undoes* discourses of Black sexual politics that posit ratchet individuals and ratchet ways of being as "the promotion of failure" based on fixed notions of what it means to do the right kind of Blackness (Stallings 2013, 136).

Often depicted as falling outside scripts of both heterosexuality and patriarchal ideals, African Americans are at once figured as aberrantly heterosexual and persistently non-heteronormative (Ferguson 2000, 420). Matriarchal family structures, fictive kin networks, high rates "out of wedlock" births, low rates of Black women getting married all have been pointed to as "problems" plaguing the "Black Community." Women heading households supposedly meant that Black women emasculated Black men. Out of wedlock births meant that Black men would not be raising their kids, and therefore, those kids, without a Black man in the house, would turn into "monsters." Black women putting their careers before finding a man means that they were more likely to be emasculating breadwinners and heads of households. Black women have consistently been viewed as the source of the problems Black people have with being viewed as respectable (Smith 1991, 91). But what is most illuminating about these constructions of Black gender relations within the context of normative constructions of sexuality is that the comparisons are both ahistorical and rooted in a presumption that Black people should want to mimic the problematic patriarchal family structure of white people. Further, comparing Black families to the "average," or white American family, despite our cultural differences and the persistent effects of white supremacy, is effectively comparing those things they call peaches in cans at the grocery store to actual, fresh Georgia peaches. Nonetheless, Black middle-class ideologies rooted in the politics of respectability frequently point to the very same differences between Black and white gender relations and family structures as evidence of the numerous "crises" within the "Black Community." The politics of respectability demonstrates one of the many ways that the Black middle-class have been engaged in symbolic and cultural struggle to prove that they too can be "normal," which often translates into *heteronormative* (Ferguson 2000). Similarly, throughout this book, I will argue that the politics of respectability as it plays out within Black queer women's cultural spaces, suggests a *homonormative* striving of the Black queer middle-class subject. If, the politics of respectability is one way that Black bodies become invested in the very systems that are implicated in the construction of racist and sexist assumptions of Black women's sexuality, therefore it is not at all a surprise that BQW would also be interested in participating in the conversations animated by it.

Following Lisa Duggan (2004), homonormativity as a politic, not unlike the politics of respectability, "does not contest dominant heteronormative assumptions and institutions but upholds and sustains them while promising the possibility of a demobilized gay constituency and a privatized, depoliticized gay culture anchored in domesticity and consumption" (Duggan 2004, 50). To those who participate in the twin discourses of the politics of respectability and homonormativity, ratchet operates as tool of disciplining and regulating Black women's behavior (Pickens 2014, 15). In BQW scene space, the question of who is and what constitutes ratchet is a struggle over which configurations of race, class, gender, and sexuality are most legitimate. It places BQW in the center of ongoing debates and concerns over who gets to determine what are and what are not legitimate forms of Black female sexuality.

There are two different, but interrelated discursive frames in which the politics of respectability appear and they often overlap. They are both about an internal management of behavior for African Americans living within the context of hostile American public, however, each is interested in the internal mechanization of "acting right" for different ends.

The first is based on the notion that if Black people act right, then we'll be seen as proper American subjects and citizens (e.g. if we win Gold medals at the Olympics, then we can just be "American"). The second is based on the notion that it is Black people's personal responsibility for escaping and overcoming any and all State-sanctioned obstacles or barriers to their success. It is common for both to be referenced at the same time. For example, one might argue that once you remove any and all "African" or

Black cultural sensibility, assimilate, or at least appear to, then you can be considered a proper subject/citizen, and then you will have "taken responsibility" for your own success and pulled yourself up by your bootstraps to become the "first" or the "only" Black person to ever do the thing that you've always wanted to do. This argument presupposes that people will treat you differently (because you're not acting like a "nigger") and that this differential treatment is what will allow you to be successful. Or, following the second approach, one might argue that if you only take responsibility for your own actions rather than "blaming the system," then you'd be "respectable" and therefore able to overcome any institutional and structural barriers to your success. This, of course, presupposes that anyone claiming injury due to institutional barriers simply have not taken personal responsibility for their own lack of success. Once they do this, the argument goes, they'll be able to be successful. Because, presumably, all it takes is a change of clothes and a change of attitude to overcome racism, sexism, and homophobia.

To those who participate in the twin discourses of the politics of respectability and homonormativity, it is easy to see how *ratchet* ends up operating as tool of disciplining and regulating Black women's behavior (Pickens 2014, 15). On the BQW Scene in DC, the question of who is and what constitutes ratchet is a struggle over which configurations of race, class, gender, and sexuality are most legitimate, and worthy of respect. So that by considering how *ratchet* works within Black queer women's linguistic practices, I aim to understand how and why *homonormativity* and the politics of respectability work in and on the bodies of queer Black middle-class subjects. These questions place BQW in the center of ongoing debates and concerns over who gets to determine the legitimate forms of *any* and *all* expressions Black female sexuality in the American public.

Putting Ratchet to Work

I will argue throughout this book that the word *ratchet* does things. I ask about the way issues of class, respectability, and representation mark the experiences of BQW. I interrogate how my informants made use of the word and its attendant discourses to make sense of their "place" within broader context of African American public life. When we address what *ratchet* does discursively, we begin to see the boundary work that it does, specifically around notions of respectability and authenticity. Therefore, this book is about how BQW defined, experienced, and represented *ratchet*.

It is also about a group of people whose experiences are often ignored when considering the lived experiences at the border of respectability—Black lesbian, gay, bisexual, and otherwise queer women. In Chap. 2, we listen to how BQW define and use *ratchet*. I draw your attention to examples of the ways that *ratchet* effected the BQW's Scene in Washington, DC. This chapter is most concerned with the ways that Black middle-class ideologies circulate among BQW through their deployment of *ratchet*, and what was, in this particular site, its inverse: "professional." Using *ratchet*, I will argue, had consequences for how people used space—decidedly marking certain bodies as in-place, or out-of-place, based on their ability to be demonstrate middle-class notions of propriety. Popular depictions, uses, and anxieties over who and what is *ratchet* animate the interrelated dimensions of the politics of race, gender, sexuality, and class.

In Chap. 3, I take you to a BQW party at a strip club, a commonly understood site for ratchet people, music, and behavior. I analyze an ethnographic moment I encountered during my fieldwork at a BQW's party at a strip club. I'll discuss the way that ratchet music uses Black same-sex desiring women's bodies to make certain claims about hip-hop authenticity and its relationship to notions of propriety. I also demonstrate how BQW use ratchet music to create the conditions for their voices to be heard and their spatial practices to be recognized within Black cultural politics. In Chap. 4, we'll binge watch *District Heat*, a web series that centers on the love lives of Black lesbians in DC. The show is created, directed, and produced by Shanovia McKenzie, a BQW in DC. In this chapter, I consider what kinds of readings of Black female sexuality are possible when we pay close attention to the screening of explicit sex between Black women, paying close to how *ratchet* points out the continuing role of heteronormativity and homonormativity in shaping the representations and lived experiences of Black lesbian, gay, bisexual, and queer people. Chap. 5 analyzes "coming out" narratives of Black women on Ratchet TV shows. I analyze the "coming out" storylines of 3 Ratchet TV stars alongside the *Rolling Stone* cover article that featured Janelle Monáe's disclosure (some would say confirmation) of her non-heterosexuality and an informant who purposefully decided to let her colleagues "figure out" whether or not she was a lesbian.

The book does not include arguments about why you should or should not like ratchet music, people, places, or television. Instead, this book aims to illuminate the "slight werk" that *ratchet* does to animate issues of race, gender, sexuality, and class in and on a very specific set of bodies—Black women who identify as lesbian, gay, bisexual, and/or queer. When I say I wish to illuminate the "slight werk" *ratchet* as a concept does in/on the bodies of BQW, I want to explore the ways that it produce a set of effects in/on actual, real-life people. In short, this book enters as a corrective to a tendency to misuse, trivialize, and (mis)appropriate African American English words. *Ratchet* is not an innocent word; it is not a vacuous term, absent intention, and power. It can be used as a tool for disciplining and coercing Black queer, working-class, and poor people to perform their race, gender, and sexuality in a way that conforms to conservative, heteronormative, and homonormative Black middle-class ideologies of appropriate behavior. This is not to say that all Black middle-class people hold on to the same kind of ideas about what "appropriate" means, but that those who fall neatly within the category of the Black middle-class and those who conform to Black middle-class standards of appropriateness, exert a great amount of control over whom and what gets to count as the "best" versions of Black in the American mainstream. I want to show you how people define ratchet, what being ratchet feels like, what being inside a ratchet space feels like, and I want you to show you what deep engagement with ratchet images of Black lesbian sexuality can do if we refuse to look away or judge those images as unworthy of our deep consideration. I'll take you close enough to touch *ratchet*, maybe even her hair; and, by the end of this book, you'll know—if you didn't already—why it would be unwise to do so.

References

Alim, H. Samy. 2004. Hip Hop Nation Language. In *Language in the USA: Themes for the Twenty-First Century*, edited by Charles Albert Ferguson and Shirley Brice Heath. Cambridge University Press, 387–406.

———. 2006. *Roc the Mic Right: The Language of Hip Hop Culture*. London and New York: Routledge.

Andrews, William L. 2003. *Classic African American Women's Narratives*. New York: Oxford University Press.

Bailey, Marlon M., and Rashad Shabazz. 2013. Gender and Sexual Geographies of Blackness: New Black Cartographies of Resistance and Survival (Part 2). *Gender, Place & Culture* 21 (4): 449–452.

Beauboeuf-Lafontant, Tamara. 2008. Listening Past the Lies that Make Us Sick: A Voice-Centered Analysis of Strength and Depression Among Black Women. *Qualitative Sociology* 31 (4): 391–406.

Bergner, Gwen. 1995. Who Is that Masked Woman? Or, the Role of Gender in Fanon's Black Skin, White Masks. *PMLA* 110 (1): 75–88.

Bourdieu, Pierre. 1984. *Distinction: A Social Critique of the Judgement of Taste.* Cambridge, MA: Harvard University Press. Reprint, 2000.

Brown, Nadia E., and Lisa Young. 2015. Ratchet Politics: Moving Beyond Black Women's Bodies to Indict Institutions and Structures. In *Broadening the Contours in the Study of Black Politics: Political Development and Black Women,* ed. Michael Mitchell and David Covin. New Brunswick, NJ: Transaction Publishers.

Cohen, Cathy J. 2005. Punks, Bulldaggers, and Welfare Queens: The Radical Potential of Queer Politics. In *Black Queer Studies: A Critical Anthology,* ed. E. Patrick Johnson and Mae Henderson, 21–51. Durham: Duke University Press.

Collins, Patricia Hill. 1986. Learning from the Outsider Within: The Sociological Significance of Black Feminist Thought. *Social Problems* 33 (6): S14–S32.

———. 2000. Gender, Black Feminism, and Black Political Economy. *Annals of the American Academy of Political and Social Science* 568 (The Study of African American Problems: W. E. B. Du Bois's Agenda, Then and Now): 41–53.

———. 2008. *Black Feminist Thought: Knowledge, Consciousness, and the Politics of Empowerment.* New York and London: Routledge.

van Dijk, Teun A. 1993. Principles of Critical Discourse Analysis. *Discourse & Society* 4 (2): 249–283.

Douglas, Kelly Brown. 2011. The Black Church and the Blues Body. In *From Bourgeois to Boojie: Black Middle-Class Performances,* ed. Vershawn Ashanti Young and Bridget Harris Tsemo. Detroit: Wayne State University Press.

Duggan, L. 2004. *The Twilight of Equality: Neoliberalism, Cultural Politics, and the Attack on Democracy.* Boston: Beacon Press.

Ferguson, Roderick A. 2000. The Nightmares of the Heteronormative. *Journal for Cultural Research* 4 (4): 419–444.

Fleetwood, Nicole R. 2011. *Troubling Vision: Performance, Visuality, and Blackness.* Chicago: University of Chicago Press.

Fogg-Davis, H.G. 2006. Theorizing Black Lesbians Within Black Feminism: A Critique of Same-Race Street Harassment. *Politics & Gender* 2 (01): 57–76.

Goffman, Erving. 1967. *Interaction Ritual: Essays in Face-to-Face Behavior.* Chicago: Aldine Publishing Company.

Halberstam, J. Jack. 2011. *The Queer Art of Failure.* Durham, NC: Duke University Press.

Hammonds, Evelynn. 1994. Black (W)holes and the Geometry of Black Female Sexuality. *Differences: A Journal of Feminist Cultural Studies* 6 (2/3): 126–145.

Hancock, Ange-Marie. 2004. *The Politics of Disgust: The Public Identity of the Welfare Queen.* New York: NYU Press.

Harris, Cheryl. 1995. Whiteness as Property. In *Critical Race Theory: The Key Writings that Formed the Movement,* ed. Kimberlé Crenshaw, N. Gotanda, and K. Thomas, 276–291. New York: The New Press.

Harris-Perry, Melissa V. 2011. *Sister Citizen: Shame, Stereotypes, and Black Women in America.* New Haven, CT: Yale University Press.

Higginbotham, Evelyn Brooks. 1993. *Righteous Discontent: The Women's Movement in the Black Baptist Church, 1880–1920.* Cambridge, MA: Harvard University Press.

hooks, bell. 1990. *Yearning: Race, Gender, and Cultural Politics.* Boston, MA: South End Press.

Isoke, Zenzele. 2014. Can't I Be Seen? Can't I Be Heard? Black Women Queering Politics in Newark. *Gender, Place & Culture* 21 (3): 353–369.

Iton, Richard. 2008. *Search of the Black Fantastic: Politics and Popular Culture in the Post-Civil Rights Era.* New York: Oxford University Press.

Johnson, E. Patrick. 2001. "Quare" Studies, or (Almost) Everything I Know About Queer Studies I Learned from My Grandmother. *Text and Performance Quarterly* 21 (1): 1–25.

———. 2011. *Sweet Tea: Black Gay Men of the South.* Chapel Hill: The University of North Carolina Press.

Johnson, E. Patrick, and Mae Henderson. 2005. *Black Queer Studies: A Critical Anthology.* Durham, NC: Duke University Press.

Kastanis, Angeliki, and Gary J. Gates. 2013. *LGBT African-American Individuals and African-American Same-Sex Couples.* Los Angeles: The Williams Institute, UCLA School of Law.

Keeling, Kara. 2003. "Ghetto Heaven": Set It Off and the Valorization of Black Lesbian Butch-Femme Sociality. *The Black Scholar* 33 (1): 33–46.

Kendi, Ibram X. 2016. *Stamped from the Beginning: The Definitive History of Racist Ideas in America.* New York: Nation Books.

Khan-Cullors, Patrisse, and asha bandele. 2018. *When They Call You a Terrorist: A Black Lives Matter Memoir.* New York: St. Martin's Press.

Lane, Nikki. 2011. Black Women Queering the Mic: Missy Elliot Disturbing the Boundaries of Racialized Sexuality and Gender. *Journal of Homosexuality* 58 (6–7): 775–792.

Lane, Charneka. 2015. *In the Life, On the Scene: The Spatial and Discursive Production of Black Queer Women's Scene Space in Washington, D.C.* PhD Dissertation, Department of Anthropology, American University.

Leap, William. 2008. Queering Gay Men's English. In *Gender and Language Research Methodologies,* ed. K. Harrington, L. Litosseliti, J. Sunderland, and H. Sauntson. New York: Palgrave Macmillan.

———. 2009. Professional Baseball, Urban Restructuring, and (Changing) Gay Geographies in Washington, D.C. In *Out in Public: Reinventing Lesbian/Gay Anthropology in a Globalizing World,* ed. Ellen Lewin and William Leap, xii, 365. Chichester and Malden, MA: Wiley-Blackwell.

———. 2015. Lavender Language. In *The International Encyclopedia of Human Sexuality,* ed. Patricia Whelehan and Anne Bolin. Malden, MA: Blackwell.

Lewis, Heidi R. 2013. Exhuming the Ratchet Before It's Buried. *The Feminist Wire,* January 7. https://thefeministwire.com/2013/01/exhuming-the-ratchet-before-its-buried/. Accessed 15 Sept 2019.

Locke, Alain. 1925. Enter the New Negro. In *Harlem: Mecca of the New Negro,* ed. Alain Locke. Special edition. Survey Graphic, 631–634.

Moore, Mignon R. 2011. *Invisible Families: Gay Identities, Relationships, and Motherhood Among Black Women*. Berkeley, CA: University of California Press.

Morgan, Joan. 2015a. Why We Get Off: Moving Towards a Black Feminist Politics of Pleasure. *The Black Scholar* 45 (4): 36–46.

Morgan, Marcyliena. 2002. *Language, Discourse and Power in African American Culture*. Vol. 20. Studies in the Social and Cultural Foundations of Language. Cambridge: Cambridge University Press.

———. 2015b. African American Women's Language: Mother Tongues Untied. In *The Oxford Handbook of African American Language*, ed. Sonja Lanehart, 817–833. Oxford: Oxford University Press.

Nash, Jennifer Christine. 2014. *The Black Body in Ecstasy: Reading Race, Reading Pornography*. Durham, NC: Duke University Press.

Obama, Barack. 2007. *Dreams from My Father: A Story of Race and Inheritance*. New York: Crown Publishers.

Pattillo, Mary. 2013. *Black Picket Fences: Privilege and Peril Among the Black Middle Class*. Chicago: University of Chicago Press. Original edition, 1999. Reprint, Second Edition.

Pickens, Therí A. 2014. Shoving Aside the Politics of Respectability: Black Women, Reality TV, and the Ratchet Performance. *Women & Performance: A Journal of Feminist Theory* 25 (1): 1–18.

Richardson, Mattie Udora. 2003. No More Secrets, No More Lies: African American History and Compulsory Heterosexuality. *Journal of Women's History* 15 (3): 63–76.

Smith, Barbara. 1991. Ain't Gonna Let Nobody Turn Me Around. *The Black Scholar* 22 (1/2): 90–93.

Smitherman, Geneva. 2000. *Black Talk: Words and Phrases from the Hood to the Amen Corner*. Rev. ed. Boston: Houghton Mifflin.

———. 2006. *Word from the Mother: Language and African Americans*. New York and London: Routledge.

Stallings, LaMonda Horton. 2013. Hip Hop and the Black Ratchet Imagination. *Palimpsest: A Journal on Women, Gender, and the Black International* 2 (2): 135–139.

Stewart, Jeffrey C. 2018. *The New Negro: The Life of Alain Locke*. New York City: Oxford University Press.

Wright, Nazera Sadiq. 2011. Black Girls and Representative Citizenship. In *From Bourgeois to Boojie: Black Middle-Class Performances*, ed. Vershawn Ashanti Young and Bridget Harris Tsemo, 91–110. Detroit: Wayne State University Press.

Young, Vershawn Ashanti. 2011. Introduction: Performing Citizenship. In *From Bourgeois to Boojie: Black Middle-Class Performances*, ed. Vershawn Ashanti Young and Bridget Harris Tsemo, 1–38. Detroit: Wayne State University Press.

Young, Vershawn, and Bridget Harris Tsemo, eds. 2011. *African American Life Series: From Bourgeois to Boojie: Black Middle-Class Performances*. Detroit: Wayne State University Press.

CHAPTER 2

Defining Ratchet: Ratchet and Boojie Politics in Black Queer Space

"Ratchet" Etymology
(with apologies to E. Patrick Johnson [2001] and Alice Walker [1983])

Ratchet (ra-CHit), adj. 1. meaning wretched, raunchy, and/or raggedy; also, opp. of highbrow; having low taste, or tacky; from the African American Southern vernacular for wretched; sometimes negative in connotation; denotes a purposeful or careless excess of funk, attitude, filth, and/or grime. Antonyms, classy, professional, and boojie.

—adj. 2. socially unacceptable, and/or outside of norms within Black sexual and cultural politics and community; often used to describe a person who acts out and "acts up" intentionally, or not, with excess.

—adv. 3. lack of pretense, or care for socially acceptable standards; often used to describe an action performed with total disregard for propriety.

4. *ratchet* is to wretched as *quare* is to queer.

Definitions

In the essay "'Quare' Studies, or (Almost) Everything I Know about Queer Studies I Learned from My Grandmother" E. Patrick Johnson provides an etymology and definition of the word *quare*, wherein, following Alice Walker's definition of *womanism* (Walker 1983), Johnson lays out his understanding of what *quare* means and its relationship to *queer*. *Queer*, though perhaps radical in its original intent, has tended to leave

Black non-heteronormative bodies out of its theorizing, activism, and thus, its politics (Cohen 2005). *Quare*, according to Johnson is a Southern African American English variant of the word *queer* and it does a particular kind of work to animate the specificity of (Southern) Black queer experience within what had begun to emerge within academia as "queer studies" (Johnson 2001). In this spirit, I am following Johnson (2001) "out on a limb,"[1] and though it might break under the strain, I wish to ask what it might mean for us to bring along with our attention to Southern Black queer experience, an attention to situated language use. I offer here what I consider to be a preliminary etymology and definition of *ratchet*. It is culled together from the way interlocutors in both formal and informal interviews used the word during my time in the field, but in no way is it meant to stand in for or be treated as the actual definition which is in constant flux. Instead, I am interested in its function and use value to those who put the word into operation. Employing a Quare Linguistic Approach in this chapter, I examine how uses of *ratchet* are situated within a network of overlapping ideological commitments.

Ratchet is a Southern African American English (AAE) variant of the English verb *to ratchet* that is thought to have originated among Southern AAE users in Louisiana (Brown and Young 2015). *Ratchet*, as it functions in Southern AAE, carries with it some of the connotation found in the "standard" English definition, defined in the Oxford English Dictionary as "[to] cause something to rise (or fall) as a step in what is perceived as a steady and irreversible process" (Stevenson and Lindberg 2018). In Southern AAE it does not typically function as a verb, however, it can be paired with a verb to make it actionable. For example, one can "get ratchet" or "be ratchet." It can also be turned into a noun with a drastically different meaning than the "standard" definition of the word. One might have "a bit of ratchet inside them." Typically, however, it is used as a modifier, describing actions, persons, places, and things. One can watch "ratchet television," listen to "ratchet music," or "drop that ass to ground like them ratchet girls" do, for example. What is most important to understand about *ratchet* is that it is a word that demonstrates the persistence of AAE speakers to bend and twist "standard" English to their whim

---

[1] In the first sentence of the essay Johnson writes, "I am going out on a limb." He is remarking on the high stakes of attempting to re-conceptualize what was still forming as "queer studies." He goes on to say, "This is a precarious position, but the stakes are high enough to warrant risky business" (Johnson 2001, 2).

(Smitherman 1994, 2000). Where some of the standard definition of *ratchet* is implied, people tend to define *ratchet* according to qualities associated with those who they consider tactless, uncouth, and who have poor taste. In this sense, *ratchet* does not really have a true, singular definition. Instead, it is a word with an excess of meaning often spilling over into unresolved issues in the public and private lives of Black people. *Ratchet*, and struggles over who and what is *ratchet*, forces conversations about what it means for a Black person to be respectable, "a credit to the race," and the right kind of American. Struggles over ratchet also bring to light the racist ideological assumption that all Black people are, naturally, at our core, really just "niggas." In a white supremacist society such as ours, this racist idea haunts us regardless of our economic class, but it also affects our language practices and our understandings of Black "authenticity" and respectability.

As I argued in the previous chapter, "niggas" are Black people who purposefully act out of line with Black (and white) middle-class notions of propriety, and it is the behavior of "niggas" that is often considered to be ratchet. However, being a "credit to the race," which involves distancing oneself from behavior associated with "niggas," will often lead to an uncomfortable situation for members of the Black middle-class as they are often charged with "not being Black enough." So if you are not being ratchet, you are pretending to be something you're not. The term *boojie*, as I suggest in the definition above, is sometimes considered the antonym of *ratchet*, but the two words actually function quite similarly in attempting fix the myrid ways people can be Black (Riggs 1995) into a finite box. *Boojie*, sometimes spelled boojee, boujie, bougie, or boujee,[2] functions as both a pejorative and as an accepted designation for those whose performance of Blackness or relationships to Blackness somehow breaks from classed stereotypes of Blackness. I have identified at least three ways that *boojie* is used. The first use is in the form of an epithet related to racial authenticity. In his analysis of the relationship between class and notions of authenticity within the context of Black life, Johnson (2003) discusses the ways that authentic performances of Blackness are typically those associated with the behaviors, tastes, and cultural productions of working-class and poor Black "folk," such as blues and hip-hop (Johnson 2003, 22). Working-class performances of Blackness are often understood by

[2] I prefer the spelling "b-o-o-j-i-e" because it better approximates my own pronunciation and I believe the "j" better captures the pretentiousness intended in the use of the word.

many to be the most "authentic" forms of performing Blackness (Johnson 2011), so to refer to someone as boojie, implies that they are trying to approximate a version of Whiteness by highlighting their middle or upper-middle class proclivities. Additional epithets might be visited upon someone who is boojie, such as "Oreo," which means that a person appears Black, but is in actuality white "on the inside." In this usage of the word, a boojie person's tastes, values, behaviors, and even their speech are read as attempts to distance themselves from "real" Black people. Johnson (2003) goes on to argue that embedded within charges that educated, middle-class Black people are "not black enough" is "an assumption that educated blacks are much more likely to disavow their racial "roots" than might their poor and illiterate brothers and sisters. Although this rhetoric is problematic on many counts, one of its more disturbing aspects is that it confounds class and race such that it links racial authenticity with a certain kind of primitivism and anti-intellectualism" (Johnson 2003, 23). People belonging to the Black middle-class are often accused of "being boojie" and, therefore, turning their backs on other Black people in order to receive the benefits associated with Whiteness. This relates to the second use of the term. In this second instance, *boojie* refers to a Black person who uses various methods to mask their actual class position. They may be working-class, but behave in ways that to others may be read as them trying to "be better than" others. This is someone who drives a new Lexus, pays an astronomical amount of money for the car note, but lives with their mother in the projects. Or, which is most often the case, they are members of the *nuevo riche*. Imagine someone who lives in a mansion, but its rented and they have little to no furniture, and they eat off of paper plates and drink out of red solo cups. So, they may have enough resources to escape some of the trappings of working-class Black life, but not the knowledge to act the part of the actual (white) middle-class. To this end, they are not necessarily trying to turn their backs on Black people as much as they're attempting to escape the "authentic" place of Black people in America, the hood (see Chap. 5). If the working-class is the most authentic class position for Black people, then the "hood" or the "urban ghetto" is considered the most authentic place for Black life to unfold. In either case, *boojie* as epithet refers to someone who works diligently to not be read as working-class[3] Black. It

---

[3] For example, I abhor hotels that are less than a 4 star Micheline rating. They make me feel itchy. When it comes to hotels, I am boojie. There's nothing wrong with 3 star hotels (though I reserve the right to argue that there may be something wrong with hotels that only

is important to note that someone may take some pride in not being read as a working-class or poor Black person. They may even embrace *boojie* as a way of pointing out that their tastes, style, and behavior are different from working-class Black people. The last use of the word relates to this embracing of *boojie* within the context of the post-industrial economy. In the definition for *ratchet* that I offer, I note that the term *professional* is also an antonym of *ratchet*, and as such, is related to *boojie*. For Black people who are professionals, they may take it as a badge of their success to be boojie, because it gestures to their economic and cultural class mobility. Where their family might live in the hood, be working-class or impoverished, they no longer live in "the hood," and they work in professional jobs and have acquired new tastes and behaviors, and may even have different kinds of access to cultural capital. They may be able to enjoy theater, performance art, and fashion. There is nothing, in and of itself, problematic with pointing out one's different experiences of race based on class position, but some Black middle-class people have an uneasy relationship with claiming their "boojie-ness." In part because some Black people who make this distinction do so specifically because they want to mark that they *really are* better than working-class and poor Black people. For them, they are better than working-class and poor Black people because they do not work in the service industry, or in manual labor. They sit at desks, browse the internet in between staff meetings, and use copy machines. They have to wear professional attire rather than a uniform to work and they interact with white people not simply as customers, but as colleagues. For them, being boojie points to their ability to *transcend* the trappings of Black life. Their acquisition of respectability is what they wish to bring to bear in their usage of the term. They are keen to point out that they have an ability to get along in the "real world," not just "the hood." To this end, there are those of us who claim being boojie, but don't want to be associated with those who claim boojie as a means of pointing out that they are better than other Black people.

Brown and Young (2015) define "ratchet politics" as "policies, structures, or institutions that promote and/or result in inequality, oppression, and marginalization" (2015, 28). They consider ratchet politics to be those set of systemic and institutional forces which oppress poor women

---

have 2 stars or less), however, hotels with fewer than 4 stars simply assault my boojie sensibilities.

of color which are fueled by stereotypes of Black women as ratchet (Brown and Young 2015, 48).

> Ratchet politics is not an explicit racial, gender, sexual, and/or class-based animosity. Instead, it is the recognition that white supremacy, capitalism, and heteropatriarchy as structures, institutions, and/or policies serve as a repressive power for marginalized populations. As a hegemonic force, ratchet politics is evasive, self-reproducing, systemic, and powerful. However, as we will show through our example of Kandi Burruss of *Real Housewives of Atlanta (RHOA)* fame, ratchet politics can also be dynamic and fluid, as individuals are able to buck over-determinist approaches and challenge the proscribed ways Black women engage hegemonic power. In this way, ratchet politics is not only one-directional. It but can also be multifaceted. It provides individuals with the agency to oppose, resist, or repurpose ratchetness. Additionally, certain bodies are ratchet transgressors, in that they are able to enact ratchetness but not be fully viewed as ratchet. (Brown and Young 2015, 48)

In other words, they draw attention to the capitalist political project that maintains white supremacy and heteropatriarchy to the detriment of poor women of color. While recognizing the utility of their definition in connecting the notion of "politics" directly to institutions of hegemonic power and a scathing critique of the institution of capitalism, in this chapter, I depart slightly in my use of the concept of ratchet/boojie politics. In my analysis, I center on the "cultural" aspects of these politics. David Harvey (2007a) has described neoliberalism as the "cultural logic" of capitalism. If we are to critique the institutional nature of capitalism, then it might be prudent as well to analyze the ways in which neoliberalism exerts force on our lived experiences. Neoliberalism is a "hegemonic […] mode of discourse" with "pervasive effects on ways of thought and political-economic practices" to the point where it infiltrates our everyday, our language practices, and the "commonsense way we interpret, live in, and understand the world" (Harvey 2007b, 23). I will use the concept ratchet/boojie politics (or ratchet/boojie cultural politics) to refer to the discursive battles that occur around definitions of ratchet and boojie within contexts where we're increasingly expected to reproduce the values of capitalist accumulation through our speech, comportment, and beliefs. Thus defining the boundaries of ratchet and boojie, is rooted in defining the boundaries of what are moral and acceptable performances of Blackness in a neoliberal racist, sexist, and homophobic society where our value is often based on our consumption of the right products. White middle-class subjects are situated as the quintessential, responsible, and moral consumer citizens. White LGBT people are increasingly taking up space in the marketplace through projects of homonormativity which work to demonstrate the value and worth of gays to capitalist accumulation; however, because of the plasticity of racist ideas, Black queer middle-class subjects remain in the position of being deemed less valuable to any and all white persons, even if those white persons are LGBT. Thus, it would follow that being a Black queer subject and signaling that you are a good consumer citizen and thus a responsible and moral person might be desirable. Understanding how *boojie* functions is vital to fully grasping the way *ratchet* works. This is because one of the things *ratchet* does is point out the concerns, fears, and anxieties of the Black middle-class. When examining how ratchet/boojie politics operate among Black queer middle-class subjects, we see an additional set of anxieties beyond issues of being seen as authentic (being seen as "Black enough") or respectable (being seen by whites as worthy of respect), we also see a set of anxieties around how as Black queer people, we are supposed to represent our non-normative sexuality to white people and other Black people.

In studies of language, we refer to the act of pointing out one's feelings about a particular person, place, or idea as taking a stance. Stance taking functions as a means by which individuals relate to others (Du Bois 2007, 163). When you take a stance or a position about a particular object, you do so as a means of seeing where each of you is situated in social space. When an individual takes a stance they use a system linguists referred to as a "system of evaluation" which allows them to "negotiate emotions, judgments, and valuations" (Martin 2001, 145). According to sociolinguist Norman Fairclough "how one represents the world, to what one commits oneself, e.g. one's degree of commitment to truth, is part of how one identifies oneself, necessarily in relation to others with whom one is interacting" (Fairclough 2003, 166). Simply put, our tastes, what we like and don't, reveal a great deal about our social location. In this chapter, I focus my analysis on conversations I had with 5 different interlocutors who engaged in what I refer to as ratchet/boojie politics which animates the politics that lie within the boundary work done to contain those objects, places, and behaviors that are understood to be ratchet/boojie. They directly and indirectly addressed ratchet/boojie politics through their descriptions of the texture of the BQW's Scene in DC, marking their relationship to both Black middle-class and Black working-class sensibilities, and their investments, or not, in homonormativity. I chose to focus on these 5 informants because they shared vivid descriptions of ratchet/boojie politics as they played out within the BQW Scene, however, I also chose them because their discussions were illustrious of the kinds of conversations I had with other women within my formal sample of 40 informants. Ranging in age from their mid-20s to early 40s, they also varied in levels of education, jobs, and income. I analyze these conversations in concert with critical theories which have attempted to account for the ways that class inflect understandings of racialized gender and sexuality. I argue that how people define themselves in relation to those persons, places, things, and behaviors that are ratchet/boojie tells us a great deal about their investments in normativity. In evaluating who or what they find *ratchet*, or its inverse *boojie* (or *professional*), they mark their deservingness to be considered among who could fit within an ostensible heteronormative Black middle-class. They simply needed the Black middle-class to ease their investment in *hetero*normativity, then they too could be respectable.

Ratchet/Boojie Politics in the BQW Scene

The BQW Scene is an "unruly subject of academic investigation" (Rodriguez 2003, 8). The BQW Scene is not a place. Instead, it is a collection of social networks and the "scene spaces" where those networks gather. The Scene is most visible and best experienced through scene spaces, the sites where the Scene is instantiated. Scene spaces are temporally and geographically bound. Scene spaces reflect the diversity of the Scene itself. As one of my informants Amina told me, "There are many scenes within the Scene," and the subtle but important differences can only be understood if we recognize that each scene space has a unique texture. The Scene is not a cultural object in and of itself that can be "read," nor is it a "social production" to be deconstructed. In so far as these methods of analysis are concerned, the Scene evades detection and its complexities go unrecognized. If we are to truly understand the ways that BQW navigate the urban landscape, then we have to investigate the composition of BQW scene spaces asking in what ways these spaces embody their strategies for overcoming systemic exclusions. The subtle but important differences can only be understood if we recognize that each scene space has a unique *texture*.

Scene space is "paradoxical" space where one has the opportunity to be made to feel safe and comfortable while at the same time being exposed to risks such as social exclusion and abuse (Valentine and Skelton 2003). It is also space where forms of sexual citizenship are tied to one's level of access to resources (Binnie and Skeggs 2004; Browne and Bakshi 2011; McBride 2005; Taylor 2007; Visser 2008). The more money you have, the younger you are, and the more beautiful, the more likely you are to "fit" in the Scene and have the ability to move between the BQW Scene and the white LGBT mainstream (Binnie 2011; Binnie and Skeggs 2004; Taylor 2007). While it may be true that some BQW scene spaces conform to notions of what might be called Black homonormativity, all of them actively work against forms of normative ideologies that would position Black queer women's bodies as "out of place." It is within this context that struggles over who and what is ratchet/boojie come to affect the texture of BQW's scene spaces.

Mignon Moore's book *Invisible Families: Gay Identities, Relationships, and Motherhood among Black Women,* a sociological exploration of Black lesbian motherhood, is one of the only monographs that explore the ways that class inflects Black same-sex desiring women's gender expressions and experiences of motherhood, specifically. Moore treats homophobia and heterosexism as barriers to respectability for her interlocutors. Being a lesbian meant that they were at a greater risk of being denied access to the benefits of Black middle-class membership. One way of managing this was to keep information about their sexuality to themselves in contexts where one's safety, well-being, or respectability might be at risk. Moore (2011) borrows from Goffman and Best (1967) who discusses this strategic visibility and silence as "covering." Moore describes the covering Black lesbian mothers do in contexts of other Black middle-class people who are heterosexual, such as not discussing their same-sex co-parents or partners, as a technique for being seen as normal. Moore's discussion about respectability, covering, and class performance is about how Black lesbians manage the way they are read and treated outside of Black lesbian communities. I wish to shift the focus, however, and consider how BQW work to create the appearance of normative expressions of same-sex desire *within* Black queer spaces. This focus on the intragroup dynamics is similar to the focus of Verhawn Ashanti Young and Bridget Harris Tsemo's edited collection *From Bourgeios to Boojie: Black Middle Class Performances* (2011). In the collection's introduction Young (2011) argues that the term "middle-class" does not necessarily refer to a set of individuals with a specific socio-economic position. Discussing the way that race and class become linked in the American imagination, Young contends:

> Desegregation may have eliminated separate but equal laws, but it has not eradicated the fantasy wherein race marks class. Thus many contemporary middle-class African Americans experience a psychological dilemma: their class status is linked to a white racial identity, and their racial identity is linked to a lower-class status. To reconcile this predicament many attempt unsuccessfully to identify with only one, the white racial world, or the other, the black class world, since to repeat the familiar expression, they are caught between two worlds. Or, like the elite black bourgeoisie, the Martha's Vineyard brand, where one anonymous resident called Michelle Obama "a ghetto-girl," they try to insulate themselves from both. [...] On this basis some believe that if different groups of blacks perform class differently, "blacks can longer be thought of as a single race." (Young 2011, 16)

Young articulates the predicament that Black middle-class folk find themselves when being Black means that you are likely to be poor, unprofessional, and "ghetto," and being boojie means that you are presumed to align yourself with Whiteness. Therefore, when a language practice such as referring to people, places, and things as *ratchet* emerges, it is not a surprise that these tensions would play out in the way that people define it, use it, and work around and through it. This is especially true for Black middle-class folks who are lesbian and gay, having just reached the place where there is *public* recognition of their lives as acceptable (to some) within the Black middle-class. The word *ratchet* indexes not only poor, working-class Black behavior, but also non-normative forms of practicing sexuality. For middle-class Black queer people being ratchet could threaten their new tenuous membership within the idealized Black middle-class. It becomes especially important than to distinguish oneself from ratchet forms of behavior within BQW's spaces as a means of preserving one's status outside of it. In the next section, I analyze examples of BQW engaged in ratchet/boojie cultural politics and in so doing, demonstrate how being ratchet/boojie have material effects on the way BQW scene spaces are organized.

On That Act Right

Jay, "Everyone Didn't Get a Flyer"

During the late 1990s and early 2000s, the city was beginning to recover from the crises of violence, white flight, and economic depression set up by the general government neglect and the ill-conceived War of Drugs which ravaged the city. As young urban professionals began to move into the city center, other areas of the city became more densely populated, with higher concentrations of people living in poverty. During this time, as the city began redeveloping certain parts of the city, including U Street, several entertainment venues which attracted primarily Black clientel such as nightclubs and go-go clubs closed. And in anticipation for the redevelopment of the Navy Yard neighborhood near the Anacostia waterfront, where the Nationals Major League Baseball (MLB) stadium would be built, a collection of gay and lesbian clubs which hosted "urban" nights closed. Several other lesbian and clubs shuttered during the early 2000s including the Hung Jury in Northwest DC. While there were a few clubs still open to primarily Black LGBT clientele, including the Delta, a club neatly tucked in a shopping center near Catholic University in Northeast, the city was rapidly changing and the kinds of places where BQW could go to socialize with one another also began to shift. House parties and eventually semi-public parties hosted in lounges and bars became the norm. There was also a new crop of middle-class Black lesbian, gay, and queer women moving into DC. Many were attracted to the city because of prospects for work in the federal government, government contractors, and nonprofits, and others still because they'd heard of the promise of DC being a "Black gay mecca." As they began to meet other Black middle-class women, some of these women found that the spaces that were available to them in white LGBT mainstream and those available for BQW Scene did not live up to the classiness that could be found among those for the heterosexual Black middle-class of DC. There were collectives of Black lesbians who took to planning and organizing parties, happy hours, and events for this thriving community of lesbian, gay, and bisexual Black women.

Inspired by Sheila Alexander Reed who had formed Women in the Life, an entertainment group that produced both events and a magazine with national readership, numerous small collectives of BQW and individuals, began to organize events, parties, and happy hours for other BQW in and around the city. Since the 1990s, they would produce the primary body of scene spaces where BQW in and around Washington, DC spent considerable amounts of leisure time. During the time of my data collection, the events tended to cluster around Spring, Summer, and early Fall, but one coud count on access to the Scene all year-round because of the work that these BQW promoters did. Jay was among a group of young promoters who were looking for alternatives to the available places for

BQW to socialize in the late 1990s and 2000s. She and friends began a collective, with her as the figurehead, and threw parties in lush lounges and worked diligently to cultivate an email list and clientele who were professional and classy, and looking for nice places to drink and socialize. One of Jay's most successful events was held at Datalist, a lounge and bar in the Northwest quadrant of the city. The event was a happy hour and they called it Intertwine. When I sat down to talk with Jay, a middle-aged, middle-class Black woman from the south, asking her about the kinds of parties that she organized in the early 2000s, she drew a clear distinction between the parties that she produced and the Delta, a predominately Black gay club which was discretely tucked in a shopping center near Catholic University in Northeast DC. Some of my informants, especially those who grew up in DC, described the Delta as one of the first Black lesbian/gay clubs that they'd ever gone to. The drinks were boozy and were served in red solo cups. And there was almost always a featured performer who was stripping for tips. In the late 1990s and early 2000s, Black queer parties were often peppered with live performances by cisgender women performers would perform stripteases while lip-syncing to the latest music by Black female performers.[4]

> You're like now thrown in a room with all these beautiful, progressive, gainfully employed women it was different than what a Delta was bringing. You know what I'm saying? So it was a different type, when a woman approached you at Intertwine compared to at the Delta, **"You gon' buy me a drink?"** You know, it'll be a little bit different. [...] "No. I'm not. Mmm mm. No, I learned to stop doing that."

At this, Jay and I shared a laugh. My laughter was in some ways connected to the way that she gave voice to the woman at the Delta. She used her best approximation of a DC accent (where bolded) and used a higher pitch purposefully making the imagined owner of said voice, along with the presumption built into the question, sound annoying. Jay, describing how advertising worked for parties during this time, discussed how she and her associates would palm card, or hand out palm-sized flyers advertising their events, at other BQW scene spaces. They would often wait for "the let out," or the mass exodus of people that occur when parties end or

---

[4] This is not unlike parties that had begun to appear in the mid-2010s featuring Black "neo-burlesque" performers. The biggest difference is that the stripping taking place was not "sanctioned" vis-a-vie a trendy organizing moniker such as "burlesque."

clubs close for the night. They'd go to parties like those thrown by Women in the Life or go to the Delta, and would hand out their promotional flyers to let people know about their happy hours, and upcoming parties. Jay went on to say, "because we were going for certain type of women, everyone didn't get a flyer." I asked her to tell me more about the kind of women they were looking for. She went on:

> Definitely 24 and up. And we had a dress code. Couldn't wear jeans. And then eventually we laxed on that, to you had to pay extra to wear jeans. And that was really done to prevent the dumb girls who come up there with the pants saggin' and … you couldn't wear baseball caps. Um, so eventually we became known as the boojie crowd. Which I mean I can own it. But we did have a certain look. And in four years we never had a fight.

Jay makes clear that "not everyone got a flyer" because (1) BQW are not a monolith, and (2) not everyone was a *desirable* kind of BQW in the context of the "boojie crowd." They were selective in the type of women they invited and having a strict dress code allowed them to ensure that people were dressed in a way that would prompt their best *performances* of "beautiful, progressive, and gainfully employed." It is clear here that "gainfully employed" refers to those who have jobs associated with the professional class as described earlier in this chapter. In an effort to prevent the same kinds of crowd that might be seen at the Delta, Jay's group worked diligently to "prevent the dumb girls who come up there with the pants saggin,'" these women were presumably the source of fights, and what might otherwise be described as engaged in ratchet behavior. Further, it is the distinction between the two spaces and the set of dispositions that divide them which are most instructive here.

Jay describes the Intertwine party as a room full of "beautiful, progressive, and gainfully employed women." At the Delta on the other hand, there were the types of women who were bold enough to expect a masculine presenting woman to buy her a drink. They were young—presumably under 24—therefore, more likely to be *under*employed or in entry-level jobs. Also, they were the "dumb girls" who wore their pants sagging, a style commonly associated with young working-class Black men. According to the dress code at Intertwine, however, if one was willing to look the part of the *professional* woman, they could enter. The failure of the feminine women to act "ladylike," and the failure of the masculine women to avoid anti-social behavior such as fighting marked them as subjects who were not of the "boojie" crowd. Jay says that their parties would become known as one's for "boojie" women, and this was something that they took great pride in because they never had to deal with violence in the 4 years that the happy hour ran. Fights were something frequently discussed among informants as common occurrences in the 1990s and early 2000s. In fact, Sheila Alexander Reid of Women in the Life explained to me that one of the reasons she stopped throwing parties was because fights had become too common at her parties. The women got younger, the crowd less diverse, and the result was that a different set of attitudes and behaviors came to define the scene space she had created. For Jay, requiring *professional* self-presentation was the disciplinary practice employed to get women "on that act right,"[5] and a willingness and ability to do so would have been required to gain access to what had been created as exclusive kinds of scene space, only for certain kinds of BQW. Jay and her associates, as well as the women who were patrons at her long running happy hour, were looking for spaces where their configuration of racialized sexuality, inflected by their middle-classless was the central organizing feature.

Sade, "I Learned Quickly"

Both Jay and Sade, "learned" something about themselves and their tastes by being in BQW scene space that was organized around working-class performances. Jay describes learning not to buy drinks for the forward women who she'd met at the Delta, and Sade learned a different lesson. Sade, a middle-class Black woman from the northeast who worked in tech and was in her early 30s, used the information in the flyers, like those that Jay describes in the previous example, to determine where she fit in in the BQW Scene's scene. Flyers were (and remain) important in telling you what kind of party was being advertised. While the mode of getting that flyer may be different since most advertising for BQW parties are done on Instagram or Facebook, and Jay described palm carding at the "let out" of other parties and clubs, the image a promoter chooses to advertise their parties tell a great deal about what they value. For Sade, they taught her what kinds of scene spaces that she did not enjoy. She explained, "I learned pretty quickly that I didn't like the ratchet scene. Cause I would look at

---

[5] An AAE phrase which roughly means getting people to behave properly, respectfully, and/or as if they have decency and "common sense."

the flyers and they would just not appeal to me." I did not prompt Sade's use of *ratchet*. Instead, we were talking about her entre into the BQW Scene and the kinds of spaces that she was going to after she had moved to DC from her hometown. Sade continued making clear that ratchet places, and the people who frequented them—the ratchet scene—didn't appeal to her tastes. She went on to describe these ratchet spaces in greater detail, and where Jay only talks about what wasn't allowed in *professional* BQW scene spaces, Sade describes some of the differences in texture of between ratchet and boojie scene spaces.

> [...]it was just like strippers and it was a lot of like girls who like ... real ... it was like ... strict like strict dom-femme set up. They were real young, and like the girls were like dudes and they would be like you know imitating you know straight culture. Where as at these other events, it was more of a mixture. Where as there were woman who had, sort of, you know, felt comfortable in their skin, who were professional women. So you couldn't really wear a cap and stuff, you know, you couldn't really do all that stuff. You could still wear a tie and a bow tie, keep it professional but um, it was more *that* crowd. And that's where I felt more comfortable.

Sade describes the "ratchet scene" by pointing to the particular objects, kinds of people, and themes she associated with the individuals who comprised the scene and the scene spaces they created: "strippers," "strict dom-femme set up," "young," "girls were like dudes," and an overall sense that their "strict dom-femme set up" was an imitation of straight culture. This, she contrasts to the elements of "these other events." She is referring specifically to *professional* women's events which she describes as having "more of a mixture" of women; women who were "comfortable in their skin," while you "couldn't wear a cap and stuff," you could "wear a tie and bow tie, to keep it professional." This is where she felt more comfortable. Similar to Jay's discussion of the dress code, we see that for Sade, the performances of same-sex desire of the ratchet scene were unappealing to her tastes as a Black middle-class woman who happened to be same-sex desiring. What's interesting here is that she depicts the ratchet scene where "the girls were like dudes," as a space where women were imitating "straight culture." It should be pointed out, however, that the strict stud/dom-femme set up that she describes doesn't necessarily go away in the *professional* women's environment that she describes—at least not on the surface. In the more boojie, *professional* scene, baseball caps are replaced by bowties and jeans are replaced by nice slacks. Later in our discussion,

Sade talked about the tendency in DC for gender presentations to be polarized, a sentiment shared by many of the women in my sample. What is most interesting about Sade's evaluation of the differences between *ratchet* and *professional* here is its similarity with lesbian-feminist disparaging views of Black lesbian and gay women's feminine and masculine gender presentations, most popular in the 1970s (Moore 2006).

Similar to the findings in my sample, Moore (2006) found that class greatly influenced the way that gender presentations were discussed within the women in her study. Some middle-class and highly educated women tended to avoid labels of their gender presentation such as "femme" and "dom," and if they did not avoid the labels, they would discuss "toning it down" for work, opting to wear women's clothing even if in slightly less feminine ways. In an attempt to be viewed as more acceptable and respectable, these women lessen the effect of what might be seen as overt presentations of their non-normativity (Hammonds 1994). As Moore puts it rather succinctly:

> In the case of nonfeminine lesbians, cultural notions of black female sexuality may inhibit their freedom of gender expression in certain contexts and disrupt the image of middle-class respectability they have achieved through other symbols of their socioeconomic mobility. As black women, many feel that they have to work harder to be accepted in mainstream society, and admitting a nonfeminine gender display categorizes them as "other" in yet another way by confirming pejorative conceptualizations of the black bulldagger and other stereotypes of black female sexuality. (Moore 2006, 131)

I want to draw specific attention to the critiques shared by Sade and Jay. Both negatively evaluate femme and dom gender presentations associated specifically with hip-hop youth culture. As Moore (2006) argues, nonfeminine gender display might invite and confirm pejorative conceptualizations of their Black female sexuality. In dom gender presentations "caps," or baseball hats, and "sagging jeans," gesture to these women's appropriation of an aesthetic propagated by Black men, especially those associated with hip-hop cultures. They might have been viewed as "imitating" a kind of masculinity that was disrespectful to women (Moore 2006). Masculine presenting women, such as Jay, distanced themselves from these versions of dom which might index a misogynist ethic as well as a low-class, and otherwise unprofessional way of being. Other informants described femme presentations that were viewed as inappropriate using the following descriptions: showing "too much" skin, "too much" jewelry, "too much" weave, wearing "too many" trendy clothes at once, and wearing heels that were "too high." Excess marked femmes as being ratchet. The kinds of feminities and masculinities, those associated with Black hip-hop youth culture, fall far outside the notions of what is acceptable by the middle-class, thus they we can understand their distaste as related to their desire to distinguist themselves from ways of practicing their sexuality that confirm stereotypical images of Black female sexuality.

Timi, "Southeast Tracy"

A few months before Timi invited me to her birthday celebration where she, her friends, and I talked about ratchet music (Chap. 1), I sat down with her and asked about her experiences on the BQW Scene in DC. Like many Black people who grew up in Maryland, she was the daughter of Nigerian immigrants. Timi was in her early 30s, was first-generation American, born and raised in a Maryland suburb of Washington, DC. She owned an apartment in DC, and explained how she was able to purchase it with help from local nonprofit organizations, because upon returning to DC after living in New York City, she says, "I was broke." Yet being "broke" and needing financial assistance to purchase a home, did not stop her from identifying with the middle-class. The way that she experienced the BQW's Scene in the 1990s and early 2000s was clearly shaped by this identification. She began explaining to me how the Scene at that time was particularly ill-suited to her tastes.

> Like, that was there was always this assumption that for the queer scene, [raps knuckles on desk] boys or [raps knuckles on desk] girls, no one's going to come out unless, you know, some girl was dropping her panties on the floor. Which I found personally insulting. Which my circle of friends found personally insulting. Like, you come to party, you're looking good and you're looking sharp and **then you gotta move 'cause Southeast Tracy wants to lip sync and drop her thong**. Umm, so places like Datalist were exciting because they finally listened to us what we had been saying. Like give us a *professional* place, where all the *professional* women can meet. Laid back. Chill and know that it's about engaging and you know, *we don't have to come out and see panties droppin.*

Timi found it "personally insulting" that it was assumed that she would not attend a party unless "some girl was dropping her panties on the floor." Southeast is one of four quadrants of Washington, DC and is most noted for its large Black working-class population, high rates of poverty, over-policing, and government neglect. It also is home to one of the largest concentration of low-income housing in DC. "Southeast Tracy" is a figure Timi creates as a generalized caricature of a woman from Southeast DC. It is important to note that Timi changed the way she spoke during this portion of the interview (where bolded). She hyperbolized a Black DC accent, effectively "code-switching," to emphasize her difference from "Southeast Tracy." Southeast DC in Timi's use becomes a container for ideas about urban blight, crime, poverty, and the underclass. "Southeast Tracy" is an icon that represents a particular kind of space, DC's working-class Black neighborhoods; it's ghetto. She also raps on the desk with her knuckles to emphasize her distinction from those "girls who would drop their panties" and the women who would only attend a party to see said "girl." It is in this moment, where Pierre Bourdieu's notion of class is particularly helpful.

Bourdieu suggests that one's social location isn't just a matter of how much money, or economic capital they have. In fact, there are several forms of capital including cultural (tastes, dispositions, mannerisms), social capital (the resources found within one's relationships and social ties), and symbolic (college degrees, titles, and other forms of credentials or recognition which maintain value) which might distinguish one's class position (Bourdieu 1986). If class were viewed as *only* a matter of economic capital, then it would not follow why Timi found "Southeast Tracy" so off-putting since she "was broke," or had very little economic capital at the time. Instead, it is the volume and composition of Timi's cultural and symbolic capital which distinguish her from "Southeast Tracy." Timi was educated, resourceful, and knew how to act.[6] Her performance of both her class and her sexuality were quite at odds with "Southeast Tracy's" performance. Timi was classy and sophisticated. As you might recall (Chap. 1), she didn't like to listen to ratchet music at a party so it follows that she would not enjoy watching women strip to ratchet music while she was at a party. Even though she might have been living paycheck to paycheck, she was on the come up.[7] She had a graduate

---

[6] In AAE, "knowing how to act" often refers to having knowledge of, and behaving in ways sanctioned by the Black middle-class.

[7] "Come up" refers to experiencing a form of upward mobility. In this case, she experienced class mobility. Being on the "come up" in terms of class may come about through earning more money, or strategic investments in education.

degree, worked in a professional job, and had been socialized with different kinds of values—one's that did not glorify the naked Black woman's body in public.

Professional as Timi uses it, refers not only to the type of work that she and her friends do, but also to the kind of tastes and judgments that they have (Bourdieu 1984). *Professional* women were the antithesis to "Southeast Tracy." Timi wants to be clear that she and her friends wanted a "professional place, where all the professional women" could meet, mingle, and drink professional drinks. Timi is a *professional* woman with particular tastes. Timi contrasts the professional women who are "looking sharp," or well put together, with an image of "Southeast Tracy" dropping "her thong." In drawing such a distinction, she offers the naked body of an urban, working-class Black women in order to highlight her negative judgment of ratchet BQW spaces which offended her sensibilities. What is most important here, however, is that Timi highlights the way both *ratchet* and *professional* are situated within the optics of class distinction that came to organize the BQW Scene. She wanted to be in a BQW's scene space where her performance of Black middle-class same-sex desire was the primary organizing feature. While she doesn't use the word *ratchet* here, Timi constructs the image of "Southeast Tracy" in much the same way—as an index finger to point out what was wrong with a public, overly sexual performance of Black same-sex desire.

Renee, "Not the Best DC Had to Offer"

Renee was relatively new to the BQW Scene in DC when I interviewed her. A 20-something, middle-class woman with an advanced degree originally from the southern United States, she'd been in the city for less than a year. Like many people, she moved to DC to work for the federal government. She explained that she was still adjusting to life in the BQW Scene in DC, and often went out to find women to date and hang out with. On a few occasions, she went to a club that often hosted BQW called Fab Lounge in the Dupont Circle neighborhood of Northwest. But, as she would describe it, there was something that didn't quite work for her about the kind of women who were at Fab Lounge. She said, "I didn't like Fab, just because I felt like the women there weren't the kind of women I was looking for." I asked her to tell me more about what these women at Fab were like.

> They were a little young, a little bit ratchet. Um ... [laughs] Not that—not polished at all. Just kind of party type. And I mean I know that the kind of people who go to clubs are party types but they were—I just remember feeling like, "Uh, I prolly won't come back here cause I don't feel like this is a good kinda of like pool for me to be in." Um, even though there were some really attractive women there. There were all kinds of different women fem studs, all of that.

Renee describes ratchet women as not being "polished." It "wasn't the right pool" of women for her to be in. She says, "Uh, I prolly won't come back here" although the women were nice, some were attractive, and there was a diversity of women. She didn't see all of herself there, not unlike Sade, Timi, and Jay. A few moments later, I found an opportunity in our conversation to asking her to tell me about this word she'd used and giggled about using: *ratchet*. Here was another example of someone using *ratchet* without my prompting to describe particular kinds of BQW or the spaces that they occupied. I asked her to tell me more about what she meant by them being ratchet.

> I mean, they just didn't seem like the type of women who could ... Uh, transform into other environments. You know what I mean? And I think, yeah, I mean, that's kinda all I could say. They just didn't seem like the kind of polished, you know. [2s pause] Career ... Type of women. And, you can't really know that without talking to somebody, but I didn't get the vibe that this was the best DC had to offer in terms of lesbians.

It was clear during our conversation that Renee did not seek to denigrate these women who were ratchet outright, but she honestly struggled to find the words to describe them that didn't make *her* sound boojie, or invested in Black middle-class notions of propriety. Renee makes two evaluations which tell us a great deal about where she is situated in terms of class: (1) the scene space—Fab Lounge, and (2) her overall impression of the scene based on her assessment of the women there. Renee not liking Fab meant that unlike the women there who *did* like Fab, she was *not* "the party type," she was not ratchet, and she was able to "transform," or was able to be behave in ways that allowed access to "other environments" [read whiter, and/or *boojier* environments] with ease. This transformation is similar to Mignon R. Moore's discussion of Black gay women "toning down" their non-normativity in order to engage within Black heteronormative, middle-class communities (Moore 2006). Further, she felt that the ratchet women at Fab weren't "the best DC had to offer in terms of lesbians." The women in my sample who spoke most often about their capacity to move in and out of various kinds of *classed* social spaces were often women who were upwardly mobile—they came from a family that was working-class but had achieved class mobility through higher education, advanced degrees, and/or professional careers. What is vital here is that Renee simply wanted to be in spaces with other same-sex desiring Black women "with careers." This was the most common way that I saw women discuss ratchet scene space and social networks which comprised them, as a collection of parties and individuals that simply did not present themselves in ways that suggested that they had "careers," who were "young," and who didn't seem able or willing to "tone it down." Further, they were Black, presumably working-class, likely living in Southeast, and had less access to cultural and economic capital. While not necessarily the intent, the persons whom Timi, Jay, Sade, and Renee describe are women who occupied the very bottom of the racialized sexuality and class hierarchies, and their distancing themselves from those women does the work of making it a appear as if they have very little in common, even though as Black queer women, they too occupied a similar denigrated position in society.

Working with Ratchet

Anna, "Sometimes You Need Ratchet"

I'd be remiss if I didn't talk about working-class women's definitions of *ratchet* which also came up during my research. However, I should point out that the majority of the women I interviewed took up oppositional stances toward ratchet, or in the cases of Jay and Timi, who didn't use the word, they still took up positions within ratchet/boojie politics by discussing the differences between working-class and "boojie" or "professional" performances of Black same-sex women's sexuality. By the time I had interviewed Anna, I had heard several women define *ratchet* in much the same way, and noted in my field journal days before my interview with Anna: "Am I really the only boojie bitch in all of DC who likes ratchet shit?" It was a stance similar to the one I had taken up at Timi's birthday happy hour. Then I sat down with Anna. Anna was working-class, in her 30s, worked in retail, and was from the mid-West. She moved to DC for college and had become a producer of BQW scene spaces in DC. She had been throwing event in DC since 2004, but was far less active throwing parties by the time of my interviews with her. Her entertainment group was among those that hosted "Ladies Takeover" events, put on by a team of promoters who pooled social and economic capital to put on large, upscale events for primarily BQW. Anna was a creator of BQW scene space, and I wanted her opinion about the ways that scene space was organized around issues of class. Because *ratchet* hadn't come up, that is, she didn't engage in ratchet/boojie politics in our conversation without prompting, I asked if she'd ever heard of *ratchet* and asked if she saw it relating to the Black queer scene:

> Yeah, so. I've heard the term ratchet. I've may uttered it on an occasion or two, um. Ratchet has its place. I feel like sometimes you want to be a little ratchet. You want to go out and not care how your hair looks, what clothes you have on, or if you have a stank attitude or not. Um … I think that um … Sometimes ratchet has a longer um has more longevity in the party scene than boojie or posh or just a regular bar, because you know that the drama will probably be up. Maybe a fight or two. Somebody getting cursed out possibly. Somebody wearing something where you're like, "Ooo girl, do you see what she got on?" [Laughs] "Oh my god! How she leave the house like that?" [Laughs] Um, I mean when I think about what I would consider ratchet those are the events and parties that are still going on.

Before defining *ratchet*, Anna suggests that it is something that can be possessed—something that at certain times you may actually want. In other words, rather than *ratchet* being a static identity, it was a transient state of being. Anna goes on to describe that it is the inhibition from certain codes of behavior, specifically those associated with appearance. Sometimes women wanted to be in a place that that didn't have a strict dress code, and you didn't have to worry about "what your hair looks like, or what clothes you have on," or worry about your overall disposition: "if you have a stank attitude or not." Anna distinguishes between ratchet and boojie parties, noting that these ratchet parties tend to last longer and be more economically viable. The expectation is that these parties also have the potential to be sites of violence, both verbal and physical. The people at these parties may also be dressed in ways that may be thought of as inappropriate, like the femme and doms discussed by Timi, Jay, and Sade, prompting such sentiments such as "Ooh girl, do you see what she got on?"

My research supported this notion: parties where you don't have to worry about what you're wearing, your attitude, or behavior, tended to have a more stable following. These parties were certainly the best attended, but they were also the most likely to change locations at the last minute. They were the most likely to charge a hefty cover, and accept only cash at the door, rather than accept virtual payment in advance. Ratchet things while perhaps a bit inconvenient, even a bit dangerous, Anna implies, are necessary from time to time, as mechanisms of release. When discussing what one can expect of ratchet parties, Anna contrasts ratchet parties with "boojie parties."

> I mean, it's funny to me because everyone says they don't want to go to a ratchet party. By everyone, I mean everyone I know. Everyone I roll with. But at the same time … those are the same people who like are going to be fickle if it rains and not go out. Those are the same people who if something better comes up, if someone decides they want to go bowling instead, or … Go away to Deep Creek for the weekend, they're down for that. You have a lot of people talking about other cities' Black Pride, or Women's Weekends that are ratchet … "but you're going to them." [laughs]

Anna describes the middle-class, more professional crowd as especially fickle—making it less worthwhile to promote parties for them, precisely because they don't go out as often, were more likely to balk at the sight of rain, or were the first to do something else if the opportunity arose. While they professed not to want to go to a ratchet party in DC, they would travel to Black Pride or Women's Weekends in other cities that were deemed ratchet, muddying their own distinction between *ratchet* and *professional*. Anna would go on to explain that planning boojie parties—where expectations would be high and where the optics of middle-class values must be evident—was sometimes more complicated and costly to negotiate with club and lounge owners because nicer venues required bar minimums and might even expect a percentage of entrance fees. These kinds of parties, more upscale parties, often require lots of people to be there to make them worthwhile for both the club owner and the promoter but were often in danger of not being able to achieve the attendance. As a result, the parties were usually one-off or short-lived. Arguably, one of the reasons why ratchet parties had more longevity was because *everyone*, both ratchet and boojie, went to ratchet parties whether they aligned with their tastes or not, because sometimes they were the only kinds of BQW scene spaces available, or because they promised what people were looking for, a care-free night.

Anna and I shared laughs throughout much of our conversation because we knew that the very same people who *said* they did not like ratchet parties still went to them, or had gone to them in the past and had a good time. The real difference, it seemed, was in how one perceived themselves in relation to everyone else there. Statements like, "Ooo girl, do you see what she got on?" functioned as discursive practices that reinforced the distinction between those people, objects, and scene spaces that *were* ratchet and those individuals who did not perceive themselves to be ratchet even if they sometimes went to ratchet scene spaces. The logic goes something like this: "I can be professional and go to a ratchet party, but if I see *you* at a ratchet party, well then you're just ratchet." Seeking further clarity about the distinction between *ratchet* and *boojie*, I asked Anna to tell me what a boojie party in DC looked like. Her description is told in the form of 'advice.' She describes what I might expect in being in such a place, and in so doing describes the very same markers of middle-class status that Timi, Jay, Sade, and Renee discuss.

> Everyone's going to be coming straight from work, it'll probably be a happy hour. It's going to be networking there. Um, there's going to be some dancing but not too much because everyone still has on their work clothes. If you are dancing there, you're doing it to impress someone. It may or may not be the person you're with. [Laughs] Um ... you should probably bring business cards. You might maybe want to introduce yourself with the Ph.D. "Doctor, doctor, actually." You're definitely going to ask someone what they do ...

The first thing Anna notes is that a boojie event would most likely be a happy hour. Intertwine, which was described by Timi and Jay, was a happy hour that ended around 9 pm when the club's regular, mostly heterosexual Black patrons would come in and "re-claim" the space. Drink prices are cheaper during happy hour, but it is also around the time that one might be getting off of work therefore, they'd have the clothes to *prove* that they do indeed work in an office setting. My field notes suggest that, "What do you do?" was the most frequently asked question that I was subjected to when introducing myself to women in professional BQW scene spaces, especially those who had lived in DC for more than a year. This was a way of assessing someone's cultural and symbolic capital. In contrast, among those who had recently moved to the area and working-class Black women, I was hardly ever asked what I did for a living. Instead, people asked about where I hung out. Anna continued:

"Oh, so what do you do? Oh were you at …?" insert another boojie party or based on their age maybe, "Did you used to go to …?" insert another boojie party that no longer exists, because you stopped going to it and then they stopped having it. [Laughs] You're probably going to make sure you reference someone you might know in common who maybe has a fictional elevated status in the community to you. "So, I think I know you through …" insert that person here. [Laughs] Are any of these resonating with you?

Framed in the context of "networking," Anna felt that asking about someone's career or "what they do" was really a means of sorting out the amount of cultural capital that one might have, and sorting out the value of their connection to you (i.e. social capital). Networking appears here in Anna's discussion as a suspect form of building relationships. Anna provides an example of "networking" through namedropping and mentioning defunct scene spaces precisely because the very same people didn't go to them, and we share a laugh. Indeed, while there are differences among the kinds of parties and the ways in which they maintain boundaries of class behavior, Anna's description of ratchet parties and boojie parties displays a deep complexity in the nature of Black queer working-class sensibilities and Black queer middle-class, upwardly mobile sensibilities.

It's funny because you would think that at a boojie party you would make more money because people are trying to impress each other, but really the ratchet party is probably going to bring in more bar sales because people are going to pop bottles for no reason. [Laughs] Uh huh! You're gonna be at the bar with a bottle. You know, get Moet, for no reason except that it's Saturday, and we're alive. Yeah. Meanwhile at the boojie party, everyone's planning to pay their mortgage tomorrow. [Laughs] They're like, "Absolutely not. You know what I could do with that money?" […] It's fun. It's all fun.

At first glance it would seem that these kinds of scene spaces exist as opposites, but according to Anna, "we all need a little ratchet some times." When defining who and what is *ratchet*, oftentimes, those who understand *ratchet* as a set of immutable characteristics of those who are "young," "working-class," and "unprofessional" fail to acknowledge that there are women who are middle-class who may *also* be in a ratchet space, doing ratchet things, wearing ratchet clothes. It is precisely those women who are upwardly mobile, but whose families are working-class—that often find themselves enjoying the comfort and sense of release that comes with being in ratchet scene spaces. At boojie parties, a great amount of energy goes into trying to establish your class position in relation to others, which for some can be stressful, or unpleasant. Growing up poor, and having achieved a great deal of class mobility, I often find myself uncomfortable in those positions, even if I "fit" in. Anna's engagement in ratchet/boojie politics gives a clue as to why. As Anna points out, there are women who are middle-class who are in those spaces as well, but they may think of their *temporary* engagement in said behavior as different from those who simply *are* ratchet. While Renee acknowledges that there is no way of knowing if people are ratchet, being in those spaces might give people the impression that you are unable to "transform" and therefore, some may wish to avoid them altogether. Despite some of the prescriptions against ratchet behavior in the constellation of BQW scene space in DC, ratchet scene spaces still offer BQW the unique opportunity to engage in a practice of self-authorship outside of the normative prescriptions of "proper" behavior. They not only get to bend the rules, but they also get to bend and twist the very ground on which those normative formations are built.

Continuum

I have considered how middle-class and upwardly mobile BQW engage in ratchet/boojie politics. That is, how they define ratchet/boojie people, ratchet/boojie behavior, and ratchet/boojie social spaces. Within my sample, often definitions of *ratchet* were consistent with heteronormative, Black middle-class notions of propriety. That is, being ratchet related to appearing, talking, and otherwise embodying Blackness in ways that were consistent with what was believed to either be "working-class," "young," "unprofessional," and "stereotypical." These were individuals and places who did not *appear* to have class, and were therefore undesirable reference points for *how* BQW should be seen in public.

This is somewhat at odds with the fact that most Black middle-class notions of propriety continue to situate all same-sex desiring bodies outside of its boundaries (Moore 2011; Johnson 1998, 2001, 2003; McBride 2005). And yet, *some* middle-class BQW work very diligently to *distinguish* themselves from embodiments of Black queerness that are inconsistent with normative Black middle-class ideologies. This, they do as well as they can, since they are at the *margins* of Black middle-class propriety on account of their non-normative forms of sexuality and gender. The linguistic work that is required to distinguish oneself as a different kind of

Black lesbian, gay woman, maps onto to linguistic work done to define *ratchet/boojie* and position some Black subjects as worthy of respect and others as not.

The way ratchet was deployed in my sample was primarily along a continuum. On one side, *ratchet* was seen as a condition of youth culture, and belonging to women who were not educated, or who had tastes and dispositions tied more distinctly to hip-hop culture. As examples I offer throughout the book illustrate, women who defined ratchet in this way discussed not feeling comfortable in ratchet spaces, because they could not identify with the women in those spaces. The most conservative of this viewpoint used ratchet to refer to individuals, spaces, and behavior that were young, appeared unable to assimilate into *professional*, middle-class spaces.[8] In this use of *ratchet* we see the "homonormative strivings" (Ferguson 2000, 2005a, 2005b) of the Black middle-class queer subject.

I talked to more Black queer middle-class women with impulses to avoid ratchet performances of Black lesbian, gay, bisexual women's behavior, than those who embraced it, even temporarily. There's was a kind of homonormative script for some of them that put me in the mind of the notion of the "Talented Tenth", which holds that the most respectable of us have to be the ones that get recognized first before the most ratchet of us. Vershawn Ashanti Young argues that class has had an increasingly significant effect on the African American experience since desegregation, "yet the increased influence of class on African American identity has benefited the middle class, if not politically and socially, certainly economically, more than it has helped the poor and lower classes" (Young and Tsemo 2011, 3). In contexts where Black people predominate, class becomes rubric by which one's position gets assessed, and a filter through which they come to view their experience. Given this, it was not a surprise that in contexts with predominately Black queer middle-class people, they would be deeply engaged in discursive practices that sought to establish one's class in relation to others.

On the other side of the continuum clustered a handful of my interlocutors (four to be exact), who used *ratchet* to describe a way of being that refused the normative prescriptions of Black or white middle-class culture; ratchet spaces served as a refuge from constraints of normative structures, and offered a space of self-authoring and re-imagination of the

---

[8] Interestingly enough, if you're being your most ratchet self, you would absolutely appear unable to assimilate.

rules of behavior and the rules of hip-hop (Miller-Young 2008; Stallings 2013). Ratchet spaces for these women lacked the pretense of other kinds of BQW scene spaces. Within these women's deployments of *ratchet*, we see them actively reshaping Black sexual politics, the heteronormative strivings of which has actively negated the existence of Black queers.

The definitions of *ratchet* almost always speak to three interrelated sets of issues: optics, hierarchy, and transformation. First, individuals are concerned with a set of optics believed by the interlocutor to confirm preexisting stereotypes about the behavior and intelligence of Black women, Black femininity, and/or the working-class. As one of my informants, Kennedy, a 30 something woman who described herself as working-middle-class, put it: "Ratchet is in the eye of the beholder." *Ratchet* is, in many ways, shaped by who is doing the looking. This points to the existence of ratchet/boojie politics, and the ideological investments of those doing the work of defining the terms. Being perceived as classy, elegant, and professional, it cannot be understated, *is* important for BQW because we're not typically represented at all, let alone in ways that might be self-authored and recognizable in popular culture. While it might seem that *boojie* is a way of both looking and being seen that participates in an assimilationist normative politic, as Anna clues us into, much like *ratchet*, it is actually a technique people use to enter into certain kinds of spaces. One could be ratchet, but put on a bowtie and go to a boojie happy hour with a firm grasp of the rules of behavior and *become* boojie. The opposite is also true. *Boojie*, like *ratchet*, are techniques of managing how one is perceived (though they are certainly not the only ways); they aren't necessarily static identities, but a way of understanding a set of performances. In this way, no one is ratchet or boojie, but we could say that these categories are performative.

Some will argue that ratchet/boojie politics relates to what W.E.B. Du Bois in one of his most influential books *The Souls of Black Folk* refers to as "double-consciousness." Black people must, according to Dubois, see themselves through two opposing lenses. They see themselves as they are and they see themselves as white people see them, and must work out a sense of being a Black person in the world, in relation to both these likely opposing views. This implies, rather presumptuously, that all Black people are constantly measuring themselves against white standards of behavior and must manage their behavior in such a way as to not confirm the negative stereotypes about Black people that exist in the "white consciousness" about Black people. In the "double-consciousness" world-view, being Black *and* classy, poised, graceful are treated as antithetical and places those individuals who might be those things, in the perpetual position of trying not to confirm the stereotype of Black folks as unsophisticated and inarticulate (Alim and Smitherman 2012). However, if one believes that as a Black people, they are perfectly capable of having grace, poise, expertise, passion, as well as rudeness, ignorance, loudness, and anger, then they aren't beholden to a "double-consciousness." They don't make decisions about how to move about in the world based on what white people might think of them. Those normative assessments of their behavior ("All Black women are x.") simply do not figure into their sense of being. Black folks must deal with the material effects of how white people see them because of the systemic nature of white supremacy, but this doesn't mean that how white people see Black people serves as one of the primary lenses through which a Black person sees themselves. If a Black person exudes ratchet behavior of any kind, they are assumed to be "unable" to be a part of a racially progressive movement to change how Black folks are seen by white normative ideologies according to those members of the Black middle-class whose primary concern is acceptance into the mainstream. Unfortunately, this way of thinking is akin to blaming the victim. It follows the logic: "They treat you like a nigga, 'cause you act like a nigga." But this same logic fails to account for the true nature of white supremacy: "They will treat you like a 'nigga,' even when you don't act like a nigga, because to them, you will always be a nigga."

The second thing that definitions and deployments of *ratchet* address are issues of hierarchy. Alain Locke, believed that it was the most educated, the most wealthy, and "the more intelligent and representative" of Black folks who would solve the issue of race relations in concert with the most educated, wealthy, and intelligent white people. This same idea about educated, materially wealthy Black people being the best "representatives" of Black people fuels the contemporary belief that "Black faces in high places" will be able to (or desire to) change racists policies according to Keeanga Yahmatta-Taylor (2016). Taylor (2016) shows us that "Black faces in high places," don't always have the same interests as the Black working-class, and they also share some of the same racist ideas about working-class Black people shared by their white counterparts in "high places." So, in defining *ratchet* as "not the best" version of Blackness, it creates a hierarchal relationship among the numerous, diverse ways that one might perform Blackness (Riggs 1995). For some, *ratchet* refers to a fixed position at the very bottom of the social and cultural hierarchy. Still for others it represents a refusal to get on that "act right," a refusal to care about how white folks might see, and therefore, judge all Black folk.

Lastly, it is important to note that many definitions of *ratchet* speak to its time and place—its when and where, and one's ability to *transform* into something else when necessary. This is because ratchet ways of being are sometimes seen as a necessary and inescapable, if not permanent, aspect of Black middle-class life. You may not be ratchet, but you have a cousin who is and they always come late to the family reunion dressed like they are on their way to the club after this. However, there is a un/spoken rule that ratchet things belong in certain places at certain times. Ratchet behavior, styles of dress, or comportments do not belong in (white) middle-class or upper-class settings; do not belong on television, or in any public setting where those who might judge all Black folks based on one of us. *Ratchet*, if it at all acceptable, belongs in private, familial (Black) places where they are not going to be seen by the "wrong" people, or in "mixed company." *Ratchet*, in this sense, operates as the "dirty laundry" of Black people. Something that some wish not to expose to public viewership. Interestingly enough, *ratchet* is also the unlimited resource of "I don't give a fuck" energy that has made many Black cultural formations possible. And it is this potential that causes some to define *ratchet* as a means of escaping the confines of Black middle-class notions of propriety—even if only for a night.

References

Alim, H. Samy, and Geneva Smitherman. 2012. *Articulate While Black: Barack Obama, Language, and Race in the U.S.* New York: Oxford University Press.

Binnie, Jon. 2011. Class, Sexuality and Space: A Comment. *Sexualities* 14 (1): 21–26.

Binnie, Jon, and Beverley Skeggs. 2004. Cosmopolitan Knowledge and the Production and Consumption of Sexualized Space: Manchester's Gay Village. *The Sociological Review* 52 (1): 39–61.

Bourdieu, Pierre. 1984. *Distinction: A Social Critique of the Judgement of Taste.* Cambridge, MA: Harvard University Press. Reprint, 2000.

———. 1986. The Forms of Capital. In *Handbook of Theory of Research for the Sociology of Education*, ed. J.E. Richardson. Westport, CT: Greenwood Press.

Brown, Nadia E., and Lisa Young. 2015. Ratchet Politics: Moving Beyond Black Women's Bodies to Indict Institutions and Structures. In *Broadening the Contours in the Study of Black Politics: Political Development and Black Women*, ed. Michael Mitchell and David Covin. Brunswick, NJ: Transaction Publishers.

Browne, Kath, and Leela Bakshi. 2011. We Are Here to Party? Lesbian, Gay, Bisexual and Trans Leisurescapes Beyond Commercial Gay Scenes. *Leisure Studies* 30 (2): 179–196.

Cohen, Cathy J. 2005. Punks, Bulldaggers, and Welfare Queens: The Radical Potential of Queer Politics. In *Black Queer Studies: A Critical Anthology*, ed. E. Patrick Johnson and Mae Henderson, 21–51. Durham: Duke University Press.

Du Bois, John. 2007. The Stance Triangle. In *Stancetaking in Discourse: Subjectivity, Evaluation, Interaction*, ed. Robert Englebretson. Amsterdam & Philadelphia: John Benjamins Publishing Company.

Fairclough, Norman. 2003. *Analysing Discourse: Textual Analysis for Social Research*. London and New York: Routledge.

Ferguson, Roderick A. 2000. The Nightmares of the Heteronormative. *Journal for Cultural Research* 4 (4): 419–444.

———. 2005a. Of Our Normative Strivings: African American Studies and the Histories of Sexuality. *Social Text* 23 (3–4): 85–100.

———. 2005b. Race-ing Homonormativity: Citizenship, Sociology, and Gay Identity. In *Black Queer Studies: A Critical Anthology*, ed. E. Patrick Johnson and Mae Henderson, 52–67. Durham: Duke University Press.

Goffman, E., and J. Best. 1967. *Interaction Ritual: Essays in Face to Face Behavior*. Rochester, NY: Aldine Publishing Company.

Hammonds, Evelynn. 1994. Black (W)holes and the Geometry of Black Female Sexuality. *Differences: A Journal of Feminist Cultural Studies* 6 (2/3): 126–145.

Harvey, David. 2007a. *A Brief History of Neoliberalism*. Oxford: Oxford University Press.

———. 2007b. Neoliberalism as Creative Destruction. *The Annals of the American Academy of Political and Social Science* 610: 22–44.

Johnson, E. Patrick. 1998. Feeling the Spirit in the Dark: Expanding Notions of the Sacred in the African-American Gay Community. *Callaloo* 21 (2): 399–416.

———. 2001. "Quare" Studies, or (Almost) Everything I Know About Queer Studies I Learned from My Grandmother. *Text and Performance Quarterly* 21 (1): 1–25.

———. 2003. The Pot is Brewing: Marlon Riggs' Black is… Black Ain't. In *Appropriating Blackness: Performance and the Politics of Authenticity*. Durham and London: Duke University Press.

———. 2011. Foreword. In *From Bourgeois to Boojie: Black Middle-Class Performances*, ed. Vershawn Ashanti Young and Bridget Harris Tsemo, xiii–xxxi. Detroit: Wayne State University Press.

Martin, J.R. 2001. Beyond Exchange: Appraisal Systems in English. In *Evaluation in Text: Authorial Stance and the Construction of Discourse*, ed. Susan Hunston and Geoff Thompson. Oxford and New York: Oxford University Press.

McBride, Dwight A. 2005. *Why I Hate Abercrombie & Fitch: Essays on Race and Sexuality*. New York: New York University.

Miller-Young, Mireille. 2008. Hip-Hop Honeys and Da Hustlaz: Black Sexualities in the New Hip-Hop Pornography. *Meridians: Feminism, Race, Transnationalism* 8 (1): 261–292.

Moore, Mignon R. 2006. Lipstick or Timberlands? Meanings of Gender Presentation in Black Lesbian Communities. *Signs* 32 (1): 113–138.

———. 2011. *Invisible Families: Gay Identities, Relationships, and Motherhood Among Black Women*. Berkeley, CA: University of California Press.

Riggs, Marlon T. 1995. *Black Is… Black Ain't*. San Francisco: California Newsreel.

Rodriguez, Juana Maria. 2003. *Queer Latinidad: Identity Practices, Discursive Spaces*. New York and London: New York University Press.

Smitherman, Geneva. 1994. *Black Talk: Words and Phrases from the Hood to the Amen Corner*. Boston: Houghton Mifflin.

———. 2000. *Black Talk: Words and Phrases from the Hood to the Amen Corner*. Rev. ed. Boston: Houghton Mifflin.

Stallings, LaMonda Horton. 2013. Hip Hop and the Black Ratchet Imagination. *Palimpsest: A Journal on Women, Gender, and the Black International* 2 (2): 135–139.

Stevenson, Angus, and Christine A. Lindberg. 2018. Ratchet. In *New Oxford American Dictionary*. Oxford: Oxford University Press.

Taylor, Yvette. 2007. *Working-Class Lesbian Life: Classed Outsiders*. New York: Palgrave Macmillan.

Taylor, Keeanga-Yamahtta. 2016. *From #BlackLivesMatter to Black Liberation*. Chicago: Haymarket Books.

Valentine, Gill, and Tracey Skelton. 2003. Finding Oneself, Losing Oneself: The Lesbian and Gay 'Scene' as Paradoxical Space. *International Journal of Urban and Regional Research* 27 (4): 849–866.

Visser, Gustav. 2008. The Homonormalisation of White Heterosexual Leisure Spaces in Bloemfontein, South Africa. *Geoforum* 39 (3): 1344–1358.

Walker, Alice. 1983. *In Search of Our Mothers' Gardens: Prose*. San Diego: Harcourt.

Young, Vershawn Ashanti. 2011. Introduction: Performing Citizenship. In *From Bourgeois to Boojie: Black Middle-Class Performances*, ed. Vershawn Ashanti Young and Bridget Harris Tsemo, 1–38. Detroit: Wayne State University Press.

Young, Vershawn, and Bridget Harris Tsemo, eds. 2011. *African American Life Series: From Bourgeois to Boojie: Black Middle-Class Performances*. Detroit: Wayne State University Press.

CHAPTER 3

Being Ratchet: Undoing the Politics of Respectability in Black Queer Space

Un/Ladylike

I know you want to bite this. It's so enticing. Nothing else like this. Imma make you my bitch
—Rihanna, "Birthday Cake" (2012)

"Birthday Cake" is a 78-second song performed by the Barbadian hip-hop and pop artist Rihanna that appeared on the "Deluxe" edition of her multiplatinum album *Talk that Talk* (2012). The song nearly broke Spotify setting new records for the streaming platform, and at the time of my writing this, it has been listened to over 20 million times on YouTube and was certified Gold. Hip-hop has always trafficked in Black women's bodies, and has become one of the most popular music forms in the world while relying on the bodies of Black women. Gender hegemony is best described as the constellation of forces, social structures, and ideologies that maintain patriarchy including the belief in the gender binary, the ideas that men are naturally superior to women, that women need men, and that the differences between individuals can be understood through a prism of gender (e.g. "this person behaves this way because they are a woman"). When we consider how gender hegemony establishes itself within the context of Black sexual politics, we come to understand the ways that Black women who are "liberated," or untethered from Black patriarchy, pose a threat to its existence, because they make a lie of its core beliefs. I have argued before that hip-hop is heteromasculinist. It is organized around the putative desires of heterosexual, cisgender men, and this can be seen throughout its language practices. Typically, women are not speaking subjects in hip-hop; however, when Black women do speak up they often do so through a set of language practices that weren't set up for them to speak (Lane 2011). And yet, women speak anyway. "Birthday Cake" is a song about the desirability of a Black woman, but also her ability to "flip it, and reverse" gender hegemony, at least temporarily. Rihanna uses the metaphor of a decadent, rich cake to describe her body, and says "he want to lick the icing off" even though it's not actually her birthday—even though she doesn't "deserve" any special treat. She goes on to say, that she intends to make him her "bitch." Oftentimes when women in hip-hop use language practices reserved for men, it is read as "doing what the boys do," but I suggest reading these moments as transgressive acts where women claim the right to speak about their sexual desire and desirability. As I have argued before, the linguistic acts that women deploy to be speaking subjects within the context of a hip-hop cultural terrain are often—slightly off, an intentional break of the rules of heteronormativity—queer (Lane 2011). One of the effects of this queer language practice is that it allows this presumably heterosexual woman to take up a counter-hegemonic position within the landscape of the Black sexual politics of hip-hop which typically only makes room for men who are "improperly" masculine or women to be the "bitches" of cisgender, heterosexual men. The song does another thing as well that is of particular interest to my analysis. The reason the line "Imma make you my bitch" is queer is not just because she calls a man a "bitch" or even suggests a "reverse" in their gender roles (following a binary logic). It's queer because Rihanna is not "supposed to" desire a "bitch." Since the figure of the "bitch" is typically a feminine person, or a person behaving in ways associated with femininity, there's something homoerotic about her desiring one. This is arguably why it was one of the more popular songs played at parties during my time in the field in BQW scene space. It was, in effect, one of the linguistic sites in hip-hop where a BQW might be able to see herself, and seeing ourselves—even through the cracks of popular culture—is often difficult to do. In what follows, I aim to ask what happens when hip-hop artists linguistically deploy the queer woman's body, which happens primarily through ratchet hip-hop music, and what it means for a Black middle-class woman to see herself there especially given the way that Black women's bodies are used in American popular culture.

It is important to understand the context under which Black middle-class women see their sexualities take form in the public.

As Lisa B. Thompson explains, performing Black middle-class womanhood means conforming to a set of predetermined mandates about how a Black woman can *be* in public (Thompson 2009, 2). Thompson argues that a performance of middle-class Black womanhood "relies heavily upon aggressive shielding of their body; concealing sexuality; and foregrounding morality, intelligence, and civility as a way to counter negative stereotypes" (Thompson 2009, 2). And perhaps most important to this discussion, Thompson argues "conservative sexual behavior is the foundation of the performance of middle-class Black womanhood" (Thompson 2009, 3). Conservative sexual behavior cannot, by its nature, include nonnormative sexualities such as those which involve same-sex desire. Being a lesbian, for example, and being a middle-class Black woman is an ontological impossibility under these constraints. Conservative stands in for conceptions of "moral" and "decent," and as Matt Richardson has argued "the tradition of representing Black people as decent and moral historical agents" leads to the erasure of the variety of Black sexualities and gender performances "in favor of a static heterosexual narrative. Far from being totally invisible, the "queer" is present in Black history as a threat to Black respectability" (Richardson 2003, 64). Thus, any "queer" chink in the armor of a middle-class Black woman's performance, might jeopardize her respectability. It is not a surprise then that so many of the middle-class and upwardly mobile BQW I spoke to had such strong reactions to performances of Black lesbian sexuality that were not "sanitized." The fear of being seen as any thing other than "ladylike" was something shared by many women, femmes in particular, including those who were working-class. However, it is important to understand that being conservative or downplaying the non-normativity of one's sexual behaviors and desires is not the only strategy that BQW use to move throughout the world. In fact, being ratchet offers a compelling means of acting outside of the confines of those mandates on middle-class behavior.

> Black women did dissemble, making their interior thoughts and feelings inaccessible from public view. And they were undoubtedly obsessed with making the race "respectable." But these were not the only strategies Black women used to navigate the public sphere, in part because they were acutely aware of the limitations of making themselves invisible in a world predicated in the surveillance of Black bodies. (Cooper 2017, 3)

The politics of respectability, in particular, the call for Black women to be ladylike and to dissemble, never really protected all Black women from being verbally or physically assaulted. It should come as no surprise then that being ladylike and respectable, were never the only strategies Black women used when constructing their sense of personhood or their public lives (Cooper 2017). It is true though that when Black women self-indulgently revel in non-normativity, they place themselves in the direct line of sight of those who police the boundaries of good/bad Black behavior from both within Black life and outside of it. *Ratchet* functions as an effective technology for disciplining Black bodies, especially Black feminine, and queer bodies who refuse to act out ways of being Black that demonstrate sophistication, "morality," and cosmopolitanism. This is in part because of how norms of race/class, gender, and sexuality are implicated within the deployment of the term. How a BQW positions themselves in relation to *ratchet* ("Oh, I don't do ratchet"), or how they engage in ratchet/boojie politics as was discussed in the previous chapter, is a technique BQW use to work out their relationship to notions of what it means to be worthy of respect given their queer sexuality. The very things that could make someone queer such as masculine gender presentations, "excessive" feminine gender presentation, engaging in romantic and sexual relationships with women, or not having sexual relationships with cisgender men, have the potential to mark them as "unladylike" and therefore unworthy of respect. BQW regularly contend with cultural and societal exclusion from notions of respectability, and some go to great lengths to distance themselves from the more *ratchet* forms of enacting a Black, queer sexuality, as a way of claiming a closer relationship to (even if not having a card carrying membership in) the Black middle-class. But what if you are a card carrying member of the ratchet scene? How does one work out their relationship to respectability? And, borrowing from Brittney Cooper (2017), what other issues are they concerned with beyond respectability?

In this chapter, I consider how BQW strategically bend and reshape ratchet configurations of Black female sexuality in hip-hop, in order to press against cultural boundaries that would otherwise exclude them from the Black Ratchet Imagination as speaking, desiring subjects. I will consider the ways that hip-hop has often trafficked in the Black non-heterosexual woman's body and image. Understanding both of these is important to recognize the ways by which Black queer women's bodies circulate within ratchet cultural productions. I begin by analyzing a conversation I had with an informant named Amber who illustrated how those who found themselves *in between* the working-class and middle-class navigated what she called "the divide." For her, being ratchet was both necessary and intrinsic to who she was, and expressing that side of her was what kept her feeling like herself. I then offer reflections from the field. I examine two moments where I spent time in the ratchet scene—strip clubs to be specific. These moments in particular stood out because queer sexuality was evident in unique ways on the ratchet scene where middle-class notions of propriety were not the dominant organizing principles. The places I describe and the language practices therein exceed the boundaries of respectability, and in some ways I take a risk by putting my own body on the line, but I believe my view as a young, upwardly mobile Black woman from the south illustrates one of the very points that I wish to make clear: *ratchet* isn't just for the working-class, nor does it accurately depict the composition and makeup of these space or the people who enjoyed them. The majority of my informants identified as middle-class and upwardly mobile, and many of them described a displeasure in being in ratchet spaces, and yet, I witnessed them on occasion in ratchet places, doing ratchet things. My hope here is to demonstrate how BQW purposefully engage in ratchet behavior, and use it to engage in the work of counter-hegemonic work. I also want to illustrate how ratchet rubs against the skin even when some parts of you are boojie.

Amber, "The Divide"

Amber was in her early 30s and had moved to DC in 2008 for graduate school. When I asked Amber to tell me about places that she liked to hang out in DC, the first party she mentioned was one held at Aqua Club and Lounge (located in Northeast DC) which occasionally hosted a BQW scene space organized by a Black lesbian party promoters. Immediately after telling me that she liked to go to the party at Aqua, Amber dove into a discussion about "the divide" in which she lives. Amber makes three discursive moves that I will highlight. First, she describes aspects of Aqua that mark the space as ratchet. Then she points out those aspects of herself that mark her as someone who is ratchet. Lastly, she provides a definition of *ratchet* that points out the way it becomes an embodied form of class politics within BQW scene space.

Well, first off, if you gonna have strippers, I'm need to be able to see them. You can't see strippers on the floor." Let me say, I definitely live in this. My grandparents, my father's parents are very educated. My mother's parents are, um, I don't think my grandparents, well my mother's siblings, I don't think any of them have a college degree. So I've always lived in this divide of I see rings on every finger, and I know you're in public housing. So I've always lived just on this cusp of everything and it's kinda weird. And so I kinda still bask in that. Where I'm like, Imma go to Busboys and I'm going to have tomato soup, and I'm do a research [project] and I'm going to kick it, but in the same sense I wanna walk out here with my Jordan's on and my hat and I want to look gangsta like, per se. I've always just had this divide. And so Aqua, at moments, would give me what I need, to be like, "Okay I got enough ratchetness." People dancing and twerking sweaty and hot, you sliding on the floor. You know probably you shouldn't be there somebody probably gone fight, and there might be some gun shots but I love it. And then in the same sense, I want to go to the events like yesterday at the HRC (Human Rights Campaign) event, you know it's going to be nice, where you know people are going to behave themselves. And all those things. So I've always just ... the divide. Sometimes I just need it.

What was worthy of critique for Amber wasn't that there were strippers at Aqua, but that she was unable to see the strippers because the organizers held a dance showcase without a stage. Before continuing in her discussion of Aqua, she stops to tell me about the classed nature of her upbringing. She calls it "the divide." Amber explains that she comes from a racially segregated city and multi-classed family background. One side of her family lived in public housing and lacked college educations. On the other side, they were "very educated" and wore "rings on every finger." The divide Amber describes is very much a clash between the sensibilities of the Black working-class and of the Black lower-middle class. This same divide effects the way she understands and navigates the BQW Scene in DC. Karyn Lacy's study of the Black middle-class in the suburbs of Washington, DC is instructive here. First, Lacy (2007) explains that the Black middle-class often live among the Black working-class, and are more likely to live in neighborhoods that are predominately Black, as opposed to their white middle-class counterparts. Lacy also notes of the *spatial* practices of the Black middle-class that constant movement between white and Black "characterizes their everyday lives (Lacy 2007, 151). Based on the interviews I conducted, and the spatial practices that I observed among BQW who, because of the way spaces are normatively coded as heterosexual unless otherwise specified, had to create spaces for themselves, I would argue that the Black queer middle-class spends much of their time moving between sets of racialized and sexualized social spaces each with their own unique sets of rules for their appropriate behavior. The broader LGBT Scene in DC is segregated according to race, gender, and class. The racial, gendered, and class-based politics of LGBT spaces has been well documented (Kennedy and Davis 1993; Lorde 1982; Binnie 1995, 2004; Browne and Bakshi 2011; McDermott 2011; Visser 2008). Amber's ability and willingness to perform in a way associated with her presumably more educated, and more financially fit side of the family ("rings on every finger"), rather than the less educated and working-class side, allows her entrée into homonormative white and middle-class Black space. She cites the Human Rights Campaign and Busboys and Poets, an upscale coffee house that caters to DC's professional hipsters, many of whom are people of color, as spaces that contrast with the party at Aqua. It is her "other" side that allows her to enjoy Aqua, to wear Jordan sneakers, and a fitted baseball cap to produce a "gangsta" aesthetic all of which are linked to the negative images of working-class Blacks. After she used "ratchetness" to describe something she needed and could get from Aqua, I asked her to be more specific about how she defined *ratchet*.

> What is ratchet? Ooo. What is ratchet? Ratchet is something that can embarrass you if it was seen in the wrong context. That's what I think ratchet is. Just embarrassment. Um, at moments it can be seen as, ignorant. Ignorant behavior, or ignorant circumstances, but that just depends on who you're asking and what the moment is. Is it ratchet to have strippers at the club? Probably, if you're at a really sophisticated ball gown club you probably don't any strippers at the club, but if you're at Aqua and it's $20 to get in and its a showcase its okay to have strippers at the club. I don't know. I think we all need that though. I think that … what I've noticed, I know in Columbus that's what we did. That's where we went. There wasn't an upper, higher level of elite I guess you could say when it came to the Black lesbian crowd or whatnot. Everyone was kinda just cool with everything. Rather than here, I feel like there's, there's levels to this. Hands down. And Aqua is probably on the lower level. I don't know about Lace, but some other places I probably never been to are up here. [*Each hand held flat and parallel, one higher than the other*] I think to go to the Stadium on a regular basis you at the high level cause you gone drop some money to get into

Stadium and the people. So, I think ratchet is just something you might be embarrassed about, that you might be embarrassed if you were to tell somebody who wouldn't necessarily be in that circle. I got a little ratchet in me. I support it.

For Amber it wasn't necessarily ratchet to have strippers at Aqua. The party's cover was expensive, $20 which was a premium for most BQW scene spaces, but given that it included an exotic dance showcase this was an acceptable amount for Amber. Of Aqua, Amber says, "you know probably you shouldn't be there" because none of its features follows a set of homonormative/middle-class/white norms and thus it is purposefully organized around according to the principles of the Black Ratchet Imagination (Stallings 2013). However, there was something uniquely rejuvenating about ratchet space; not being able to see the strippers' performances, potentially being witness to a fight or worse, the dancing, the twerking, and otherwise "bad" Black behavior, would give her what she needed. Amber basks in is this divide—the ability to *act right* when necessary and to *act up* when necessary.

According to Amber, *ratchet* is located within three interconnected frameworks. First, *ratchet* is located within a set of optics. *Ratchet* is about the potential to be embarrassed if your behavior were seen out of context. This means that *ratchet* greatly depends on who is doing the looking, and where the ratchet behavior occurs. Second, there is a hierarchy of BQW scene spaces where on the bottom are spaces seen as ratchet. And at the top, at least for Amber, are spaces where one is expected to spend a lot of money, like the strip club Stadium, for example. For most of the women in my sample, the "Ladies Day Party" hosted by the same group that planned the party at Aqua would be characterized as a part of the "ratchet scene." For Amber though it constituted a space where one had to have access to money in order to properly enjoy it. This was a similar claim made by Anna (in Chap. 2), who suggested that boojie BQW spend less discretionary income in boojie scene spaces. And if they did go to ratchet parties it was because they didn't have to worry about being irresponsible. Anna also discussed how boojie BQW frequented parties that they deemed ratchet in other cities which requires extra discretionary funds to get to, but also gives the impression that they would rather go to other places to get ratchet because they wanted to avoid being seen doing ratchet things in DC. It may also point to the efforts to which they would go in order to enjoy the pleasure of engaging in behavior that others might deem irresponsible. Lastly, Amber describes *ratchet* as a necessary suspension of the rules; something that we all need. While there might be "levels," or hierarchical relations on the Scene as Amber suggests, I found that the different scene spaces, ratchet or professional did not have mutually exclusive clientele. During my fieldwork, I often saw the same people across various kinds of spaces. I would see someone at a happy hour for professional women one week, and the next week see them at Stadium. It is clear that Amber was not alone in experiencing pleasure in being ratchet because it was an opportunity to shake off the burdens and expectations of middle-class propriety.

Amber's discussion of *ratchet* and her relationship to *ratchet* implicates another important aspect of ratchet and the sexual behaviors and spaces associated with it: stripping, strip clubs, and hip-hop cultural practices. Hip-hop continually traffics in discursive practices which link women's non-heterosexuality "girls kissing girls" and "my girl got a girlfriend," to a cisgender heterosexual man's sexual prowess, and yet it was often the soundtrack for many of the parties where many of my informants talked about spending their leisure time. It is the strip club, the Black strip club from which famous former strippers such as Cardi B, Amber Rose, and Josylin Hernandez hail, that Amber cites as one of the "high level" BQW scene spaces. This raised an important question for me: how can any strip club be understood as a "high level" scene space if it is rooted in a ratchet sensibility? Was there something boojie about the strip club? Or perhaps it was that in some cases, being ratchet takes access to middle-class income. Certainly the kinds of money that one could spend in a strip club far exceeds what many would spend on an average night out. If this was the case, then the strip club was a kind of space that existed within a kind of divide on the BQW scene, and for more than one reason. The strip club was normatively coded as heterosexual space. And the club Amber mentions, and which I will discuss below, Stadium was a club whose clientele were primarily Black heterosexual cisgender men. And yet, it would become, at least temporarily a BQW scene space. Further, it would be organized around BQW's ratchet sensibilities, and ratchet hip-hop music would be one of its most salient features. How would BQW manage to achieve legible subjectivity within this space and within ratchet hip-hop music which primarily understands them as nonspeaking objects of men's desires?

"I'm 'Bout to Hit the Club and Dance Like a Stippa"

Ratchet Music

During the early 2000s, as "the strip club" became a fundamental geographic site in the world of hip-hop[1], what would come to be known as *ratchet music* began to gain popularity in mainstream hip-hop. Ratchet music is easily identifiable to those with a trained ear: a simple but melodic bass line, an infectious hook, and, if you close your eyes, you can see a booty bouncing up and down to it.[2] Ratchet music relies on the booty for it to work. It often makes references to strip clubs,[3] strippers,[4] even going so far as to mention specific names of famous strippers[5]; sometimes there is a discussion of particular sexual acts often acts that emphasize a focus on the booty.[6] There is always mention of money being thrown onto women,[7] presumably strippers (though this is not always clear) as a means of tipping them for their service, and this service may be sexual or related to one's ability to entertain more generally. These songs reference "bad," inappropriate behavior like illicit drug use, public drunkenness, and women who are *always* sexually available to men, but also sometimes have sex with women. I would argue that it is not a coincidence that songs intended for strippers to dance to or for women to dance to *like* they're strippers,[8] frequently reference women who have sex with women.

---

[1] See the 1998 film *The Players Club* written and directed by rapper Ice Cube. The film grossed over $20 million, starred Bernie Mac, Monica Calhoun, Jamie Foxx, John Amos, Terrence Howard, Faizon Love, and LisaRaye. The film was an instant "hood classic," or a film popular among Black audiences. Arguably, this film solidified the strip club as a geographic marker of hip-hop. The strip club was hip-hop's *place*.

[2] For proof, see Yo Gotti's "Rake it Up" (2017).

[3] In Waka Flocka Flame's "Round of Applause" (2012) which featured rapper Drake, Drake mentions DC's famous strip club, Stadium. Drake also mentions King of Diamonds, a club in Miami, in his song "Miss Me" (2010). That same song mentions Blac Chyna, a stripper who had achieved great acclaim for her prowess and physique.

[4] Rihanna's "Throw it Up" (2012) was about throwing money on strippers at a strip club, and still having plenty of money left over.

[5] Nicki Minaj in her verse on 2 Chainz hit "I Luv Dem Strippers" (2012) also mentions Blac Chyna, would go on to marry and have a child with Rob Kardashian.

[6] Gucci Mane's "Freak Girl" (2006) talks about a "freaky woman" performing fellatio in the front seat of a Hummer.

[7] Juicy Jays' "Bands a Make Her Dance" (2013) is an excellent song *about* throwing "bands" or large amounts of bills rolled and fixed into place with rubber bands.

[8] M.E.'s "Dance Like a Stripper" (2011).

3 BEING RATCHET: UNDOING THE POLITICS OF RESPECTABILITY...

Stripping and the strip club are important features not only to hip-hop but also to BQW's constellations of scene spaces. Recall that Timi and Sade talked about how the BQW's Scene in DC in the early 2000s was a time when many of the scene spaces included strippers and quasi-burlesque performances. Stripping is an important aspect of the BQW Scene with a healthy collection of popular acts who travel across the country performing at various queer events including stud performers such as Carter the Body. A Black Pride Celebration in Atlanta, for example, would not be complete without a tour of its most famous strip clubs, some of which "go gay" for the day to host the Black lesbians who travel far and wide—to see some of their most popular performers, some of whom are bisexual and lesbians themselves. During my fieldwork, I went to Atlanta for Black Pride, a common destination for many of my DC informants and took the obligatory tour of its strip clubs.

From field notes 8/31/13:

> After getting drinks from the bar, we found a booth that was directly across from the main stage. I took a seat next a friend of my friend, Keisha, who was tagging along. She leaned over to me and pointed out one of the strippers—Cookie—who had apparently asked for her number while we were at the bar. Keisha told me that she had given it to her. I said, "You know she's going to call you, right?" And then, Cookie approached another woman near the bar and started flirting with her. Keisha had, as she reported to me, asked Cookie to do that. And then I said, "Oh she's going to call both of you?" We laughed and joked about how that might possible go down later. Another woman who worked at the club came over, and sat next to us and started chatting with us. She said that she was brand new to the club; it was her first day on the job. Curious about why she felt comfortable approaching us, I came right out and asked her if she was a lesbian, and she giggled saying that she was.

The context of Black Pride offered an opportunity for strippers who were same-sex desiring to be visible in ways that might not happen during the normal course of business. I don't offer this bit from my field notes to be salacious,[9] but to highlight that the strip club is not homogenous and all of the women there are not heterosexual women—as many ratchet songs have alluded to, there really are strippers who are same-sex

---

[9] However, you are welcome.

desiring.[10] Describing hip-hop pornography Mirielle Miller-Young argues that it signifies "the benefits of heterosexist playerdom, proffers a sense of luxury, abundance, and sexual possibility that is consciously figured within a sexual marketplace" (Miller-Young 2008, 275). The strip club works similarly. It is a site of playerdom and one organized around a sexual marketplace of desire that presumes only certain kinds of relationships exist between men and women, men and men, and women and women. In the sexual marketplace of hip-hop, women are in competition with one another, typically vying for men's attention and that attention is paid, literally and figuratively in the form of money. In DC during the early 2000s exotic dance performances where women dance for other women typically took place in the midst of the partygoers—not on stages (Carnes 2009). This is in part because many of these parties did not take place in strip clubs. Even when erotic dance performances did take place in strip clubs, I noticed that dom (masculine presenting women), would begin their performance in the midst of the crowd making their way to the stage. They interacted with the femmes in the audiences directly, blurring the line between performer and audience members. Carnes has argued that exotic dance performances, where Black same-gender-loving women dance for other Black women, produce a particular kind of relationship between the performer and the audience effectively queering the "traditional" relationship set up in a strip club where women perform for a heteromasculinist gaze on a stage. Where Carnes was interested in how Black same-gender loving women queered erotic dance, I am interested in how BQW put ratchet music to work in the practice of their sexuality and sensibilities in scene spaces. I am interested in asking what happens to hip-hop and its attendant discourses when it comes into BQW scene space? What happens when BQW attempt to make space for themselves in Black cultural spaces where they are presumed to not to be?

---

[10] We need only tune in to an episode of Love & Hip-Hop on VH1 and find Joseline, a former stripper now reality television star. My favorite Joseline moment was an appearance she made on the show *The Real* in January 2017 where she revealed a longtime crush that she had on one of the co-hosts, Tamera Mowry-Housley. Tamera, married and the frequent voice of Black female respectability, reacts with an "Oh my god!" Joseline wasn't even above propositioning her, "You're welcome [to join us] if you'd like?" she says to Tamera after discussing liking threesomes that included both a male and female partner.

Ladies Day Party

In March 2013, I went to party at the strip club Stadium in DC. One of the more 'upscale' strip clubs in the region, it played host to a "Ladies Day Party" organized by Onyx Entertainment, once a month. When I walked in, I noticed two women behind a glass counter on my left. There were velvet ropes at the entrance preventing anyone from walking directly into the space. There was also a separate entryway to the VIP section. One of the two women had a head wrap on and a familiar DC accent. She said, "Oh my god." She went on as I pulled out my cash, "You are so pretty. And little like me." I thanked her and asked if they were the ladies that organized the event. She responded that they were a part of the crew, but indicated a couple other people were better to talk to and she told me that they'd be back to the front later if I wanted to come back. I assured her that I didn't want anything weird, but she said, "I have an open mind." We laughed and I paid the $15 entrance fee and changed out $20, getting singles. I walked in, about 8 pm at this point and the strip club was packed with women patrons, the vast majority of whom were Black and brown.

After securing a drink from the bar, I migrated from one side of the club to the other. I walked around getting a sense of the space. There were four poles. The one at the center of the club was the main stage. There were two bars on either side of the main stage, and on the other side of the two bars there were two smaller stages. Not only were there traditional stripper poles on each of the stages, there was also a network of poles built into the ceiling above the main stage just above the bars and above the two smaller stages which accommodated more acrobatic performances. The DJ booth was a nest facing the main stage. The DJs had a birds-eye view of the entire club. There was also a stage to the right of the DJ booth directly in front of a U-shaped booth, presumably set up for small parties. On the other side of this booth was a door leading to a back patio area with outdoor furniture used for smoking. The VIP areas were situated behind the bars, main stage, and its two smaller stages. There were also even more private spaces with approximately $4'1/2''$ partitions behind the VIP area, presumably the club's "Champaign rooms" for private lap dances. Seating areas with tiny square-shaped end tables lined the perimeter of the club facing the stages.

As I moved around, I spoke to people that I knew. I made small talk when possible and moved along when it was not. Most people had come with friends and/or partners. I was one of few people who seemed to be alone. There was a noticeable mix of women paying careful attention to the women dancing on stage, and those who were only passively participating in watching the dancers. In addition to the club's regular performers, the party featured erotic dance performances by visiting performers some of whom were doms. These were masculine-presenting women I noted that some women were closely watching the performance, some were tipping, some were not, others were chatting and flirting, drinking, trying to get the attention of the bartender, and a few people are dancing.

A person might shift from one mode of engagement to another based on the woman on stage, or the song that plays. What was apparent was that not everyone was comfortable with there. Not everyone was there for the same reason. Not every woman there had come to spend hard-earned cash on dancers, and not everyone there seemed especially at ease with watching the women strip naked. Some appeared to be there because their friends implored them to. On this particular night, there was not any other public party or event being hosted on the BQW Scene that I knew of. This means that if someone had plans to go out and visit with friends in a scene space with other BQW, it was likely they would be attending that party whether they were "into" strip clubs or not, or whether they had the discretionary funds to spend on tips for the dancers or not.

About halfway through my time at the club, something happened. I was perched somewhere between the small stage on the right and the small stage next to the DJ booth. Crowd favorite Sparkle left the stage, and staff members quickly sanitize it so that the next performer can take her place on the main stage. As she took the stage the DJ played the remix of Chief Keef's 2012 song "I Don't Like." The moment the beat dropped, the entire club took on a new character. Nearly everyone stopped what they were doing, including myself, paying more attention to their own internal groove than the dancers on stage.

> A fuck nigga, that's that shit I don't like
> A snitch nigga, that's that shit I don't like
> A bitch nigga, that's that shit I don't like
> Sneak disser, that's that shit I don't like

The content of the song expresses various visceral dislikes specifically about certain kinds of men. In the hook, Chief Keef, says he doesn't like people who are generally uncool, think here middle-class "boojie," ("fuck"), people who tell your business, usually to a third party who holds some kind of power ("snitch"), *men* who are not properly masculine ("bitch"), or people who will talk about you behind your back as opposed to bringing their concerns to you directly ("sneak disser"). Then the DJ skipped right to Kanye West's verse. At this point, almost everyone in the club was singing along, and the DJ cut the volume to the song as the whole club rapped louder than the music that was coming out of the speakers:

> Girls kissin' girls,
> cause it's hot, right?
> But unless they use a strap-on
> then they not dykes
> They ain't about that life
> they ain't about that life
> We hangin' out the window
> it's about to be a Suge Knight

The DJ brought the music back when Kanye says, "We hangin' out the the window," and cut it back to the hook just as the gunshot sound effect in the middle of Kanye's verse bumped at the end of bar "it's 'bout to be a Suge Knight." I was left with the sensation that something had just occurred that could have only occurred in a ratchet BQW scene space. Technically, the song wasn't even playing and BQW had just wholesale appropriated an entire Kanye West verse in the middle of a strip club—one of the most important sites for hip-hop heteromasculinist playerdom—arguably to say something about what it means to be a same-sex desiring woman in the context of hip-hop.

Kanye does several interesting things in the verse that makes it well suited for appropriation by BQW at a ratchet party. It starts with his shift in intonation from "girls kissing girls" to that which he uses in the line "cause it's hot right?" He shifts into what might be read as a linguistic representation of a "white girl," slightly altering his tone and saying what otherwise could be said as a statement, as a question. This is a parody of the stereotypical way that white "Valley girls" are perceived to make statements—in the form of questions. This parodying of a "Valley girl" allows us to read what follows against the normative framework within the sexual economies of desire within hip-hop. Within hip-hop, as in many places within American popular culture, "girls kissing girls" are positioned as sexual "freaks" whose main interests are in gaining men's attention and satisfying men's putative desires. Kanye distances himself from "girls kissing girls, cause it's hot, right?" by literally changing from his voice to another's, and drawing a distinction between these "girls kissing girls" who feign sexual interest in other women because they believe a man will find this attractive, and those women who engage in actual erotic and sexual encounters with women because they want to. In other words, Kanye, in his way, recognizes the sexual agency of women who "use a strap on" rather than simply kiss another woman because a man believes it to be "hot." I emphasize Kanye's recognition here of female sexual agency because it is different than the way that most women who have sex with women are treated within hip-hop, and also because outside of the context of a strip club, occupied by BQW, Kanye's lyrics could very well be read according to the way that *most* "girls kissing girls" are treated in hip-hop, or ignored altogether, because it doesn't fit within the normative discursive frame of hip-hop. For example, Atlanta rapper, Gucci Mane's song "Freaky Girls," is framed around an imagined conversation with a "freaky girl."

> Don't be conceited, girl.
> I know you'll eat a girl,
> I know your secret, girl
> But I'm gonna keep it, girl
> Oh, you's a college girl?
> Come be a Gucci girl
> Oh, you's a Gucci fan?
> Let's go to Gucci land
> You diggin Gucci man
> Cause only Gucci can
> Drop a stack, pop your back with a rubber band
> You diggin Gucci, Gucci
> Let's do the oochi-coochi
> Oh, that's your girlfriend?
> Why don't you introduce me?

Gucci Mane's "freaky girl" is a college girl, who secretly has sex with women ("I know you'll eat a girl, I know your secret, girl"), but really wants to have sex with him ("You diggin Gucci Gucci, let's do the oochi-coochi")—presumably for money ("Drop a stack, pop your back with a rubber band"). His reference to dropping "a stack" of dollar bills implies that she is a stripper, or at least dances like one. He also references that she has a girlfriend ("Oh, that's your girlfriend?") who implicitly will also want to have sex with him ("Why don't you introduce me?"). In this case, this girl likes girls, but *really* wants Gucci Mane. Gucci constructs a one-sided conversation wherein we learn everything we need to know about the "freaky girl" through his questions and replies to her. She doesn't actually speak, but is spoken for as is her sexuality which is constructed to be in service of his pleasure and desire. When "girls kiss girls" in hip-hop, it is almost always for the pleasure of men. And for heterosexual women who aren't sexually attracted to women, the implication that they have to oblige having sex with women in order be sexually attractive is obviously problematic, but also common throughout the sexual marketplace of hip-hop. For example, Usher's "Lil' Freak," is rather pointedly about a woman who would feign interest in another woman for the pleasure of the male protagonist, presumably Usher himself.

> If you fuckin with me
> Really fuckin with me
> You'll let her put her hands in your pants
> Be my lil' freak, yeah

Here the only way a woman could demonstrate interest in Usher is to let another woman touch her sexually. Her only value to him is in her willingness to enact a queerness, at least temporarily. One of the few ways that BQW's bodies have been incorporated as legible subjects in hip-hop, a recognizable topic of conversation that makes sense within its linguistic milieu, is for those bodies to be positioned in relation to men's gazes and their putative desires for women who are also attracted to other women, but only insofar as their attraction to the woman is for the pleasure of men. Women who act out of their own pleasure and desire within the framework of hip-hop are acting outside of the racialized gender scripts of hip-hop, and yet the song has a contradictory message, or at least a *slippery* one. In the song, Usher is telling a woman that the only way that she can be with him is if she agrees to have sex with him, and also an other woman, but that woman is Nicki Minaj, a rapper, who brings up her sexual desires and pleasures in the context of the lyrics of her rap. Minaj, who is featured on the song and in the music video adaptation speaks and acts of her own accord, with notable limitations. The song opens with Minaj saying, "you want me to get you something daddy?" This clues us in to the fact that Minaj is the "her" in the line "you'll let her put her hands in your pants."

However, I would argue that Minaj's lyrics makes this song's racialized gender and sexual politics queer. She dances ambiguously between acquiring the "lil' freak" for the protagonist, Usher, and keeping the "lil' freak" all to herself.

> Excuse me little mommy,
> but you could say I'm on duty.
> I'm lookin' for a cutie,
> a real big ol' ghetto booty.
>
> I really like your kitty cat,
> and if you let me touch her
> I know you're not a bluffer
> I'll take you to go see Usher.
>
> I keep a couple hoes
> Like Santa I keep a Vixen
> Got that Dasher, Dancer,
> Prancer,
>
> Dixon, Comet,
> Cupid,
> Donner, Blitzen.
>
> I'm hotter than
> A hundred degrees
> A lot of bread
> No sesame seeds
>
> If I'm in yo' city
> I'm signin' them tig-o-bitties
> I'm plotting on how I can take Cassie
> a-way from Di-ddy
>
> Them girls want a Minaj/ménage?
> Yeah, they wetter than the rain then!
> Usher buzz me in!
> Everybody loves Raymond!

Minaj complicates a reading of this verse as simply her performing her "duty" for the pleasure of the Black male gaze where she asserts that she's "plotting on how she can take Cassie/a-way from D-iddy." Cassie, was the longtime girlfriend of hip-hop mogul, Puff Daddy (P. Diddy). In the music video accompanying the song, Minaj points decidedly at Usher as she makes the statement about "stealing" away a man's woman. Minaj further complicates matters by inserting a series of boasts about herself. She begins by drawing upon a common metaphor used throughout American popular culture: *women are objects*. She asserts that she "keeps a couple hos." "To keep" in what H. Samy Alim calls refers to as "hip-hop national language," or HHNL is to not only possess something—generally an object of desire and often times a woman—but it also means to maintain possession over that thing or those things for use any time you want. She adds that she "keeps a couple hos/like Santa, I keep a vixen." This line is complicated because not only has she drawn on simile to compare herself to Santa Claus, a white male pop-cultural icon, but she also collapses one of Santa's reindeer into a HHNL term for a video model, a video *vixen*. Thus, Minaj's deployment of the verb "to keep" here refers to her ability to have, control, discard, and replace a woman strictly for the purposes of sex. The connotation is not that she *shares* these women with men, or that she "keeps" these women specifically for the male gaze. On the contrary, she keeps them for herself and enjoys marking them for her own consumption by signing their breast ("If I'm in yo city, I'm signin' them tig-o-bitties"), a gesture often associated with white, male rock-n-roll artists of the 1980s. In effect, Minaj, like Kanye, points out the sliver through which an authentic same-sex desiring woman *could* claim authority in hip-hop.[11] Such a move is important in considering what the BQW in my ethnographic encounter did with Kanye's lyrics in the strip club.

Conclusion

There were close to 200 Black lesbian, bi, femme, bois, doms, and queer girls rapping these lyrics, and Kanye was effectively silenced as the DJ cut the song to allow the voices of the women to be heard in its full tenor. Laura Ahearn has argued that the focus of linguistic anthropological analysis should not necessarily be on searching for definitive interpretations of

---

[11] Nicki Minaj has made clear that she is neither a lesbian nor bisexual. In these and other lyrics we see her "queering the mic," a practice where Black women say what might otherwise be thought of as queer in order to make claims of authenticity as rapping subjects. It is a practice that I demonstrate can be found in many Black female rappers' work.

social practices, texts, and contexts, but rather our goal should be to "look for constraints on the kinds of meanings that might emerge from an event" (Ahearn 2001, 112). The context of the ratchet scene itself, the strip club full of BQW being ratchet, engaging in ratchet behavior—whether they were middle-class or working-class—set up the constraints for the interpretation of Kanye West's lyrics. I asked Mim, who had been the DJ that night, her opinion about why hip-hop, with its clear misogyny, sexism, and homophobia could be a major facet of Black lesbian social life. She explained that being in the club, drinking, having an otherwise good time while surrounded by BQW allowed you to "let go" and created the necessary conditions for suspending critique of some hip-hop songs. Far from not recognizing that hip-hop music rarely allows for BQW to be fully realized subjects, what Mim argues is that being ratchet allows for a relinquishing, at least temporarily, of both the norms of Black female respectability and a sense of the always already injured Black female subject that Black feminist critiques of hip-hop sometimes hinge upon (Morgan 2000). In other words, being ratchet did not require that you feel any particular way: you could just be. When I hear Black women who view themselves as middle-class refer to being ratchet sometimes, I see them tapping into the Black Ratchet Imagination—taking a moment out of their lives to be irresponsible, bad feminists and bad respectable women. Far from slumming, engaging in ratchet behavior is about "tapping into the subconscious to unleash the power of the imagination." This is the very reason why Mim can say that when you're in the club space, you let go of what in other times you would hear (consciously) and be offended by.

The BQW who were singing along, "They ain't about that life! They ain't about that life!" arguably, were temporarily suspending any reading of Kanye West's lyrics that would either negate their existence, or place it within the realm of cisgender, heterosexual men's putative desires for "freaky girls." They were using his lyrics to argue that living a life structured around being Black, female, and queer marked an experience that was completely different from one simply attempting to please men. They were distinguishing themselves from the heterosexual women who feign sexual interest in women in order to be seen as "hot" by heterosexual men.

There is still something especially *sweet* about hanging out in the margins. One of the reasons I understood this moment to be so profound was because I had heard this song dozens of times before, but had never before had occasion to hear it in this way, and a different interpretation of the lyrics was made possible. When Kanye says, "We hanging out the window it's 'bout to be a 'Suge night.'" Kanye is referring to Suge Knight, a hip-hop mogul who founded Death Row Records, spent time in prison for armed robbery, and was the subject of rumors around the deaths of Tupac and Biggie. Thus, hanging out the window, might refer to a metaphorical "drive by" shooting. However, as is often the case in hip-hop lyrics, this lyric could have an additional meaning. In Alice Walker's book *The Color Purple*, later adapted for film by Steven Spielberg and starring Whoopi Goldberg as the protagonist Celie Harris, Shug Avery who plants a delicate, powerful kiss one night on Celie's lips which provides this important moment of sexual awakening for Celie who before then had never had access to this wealth of erotic power. I like to think about this moment at the club as one where Kanye didn't say "Suge Knight," but a bunch of BQW at a strip club said "Shug night," referencing Walker, and a powerful moment of eroticism between two Black women.

Shimizu argues that "the bondage of hypersexuality in representation need not be reviled, because if normalcy signifies the rigidity of the status quo, perversity may be the opportunity to critique normative scripts of race and sexuality in representation" (Shimizu 2007, 57). Indeed, the perversity of BQW stripping for other BQW who were singing along to a song where a cisgender heterosexual man references strap-ons and dykes marks a critique of and an *undoing* of the politics of respectability and homonormativity (Stallings 2013; Halberstam 2011). If as Stallings argues, the Black Ratchet Imagination is a performance of failure in the face of normative constructions, then it is a space of "unmaking, undoing, unbecoming" (Halberstam 2011, 2) proper versions of Black women. *Ratchet*, like perversity, creates the potential for escaping the bondage that Shimizu suggests is at the center of hypersexuality (Shimizu 2007). For some, this song might easily be discarded by those who see a popular rap song disparaging "fuck niggas," boojie Black people, and other "fake people" and lyrics by Kanye West about "girls kissing girls" as an affront to their sensibilities, but the Black Ratchet Imagination makes it possible to creatively remake a rap song about "fake" people and "girls kissing girls," into a statement about the presence, authenticity, and power of BQW to *make* space for themselves. I've argued that there are few avenues for women to achieve legibility and subjecthood within the context of hip-hop. They are almost always defined according to their relationship to men: side-chick, main chick, strippers, hos, sluts, and freaks, where freaks are women willing to do anything to give men sexual pleasure. In hip-hop, Black women's compulsory heterosexuality remains a complex fiction that stands alongside her willingness to engage in sex with other women. And that has typically been the tiny sliver through which Black queer women have been able to enter mainstream hip-hop—as "freaky women." "Freaky women" are "hypersexual" and emblemized as strippers and usually lesbians and bisexual women willing to have to have sex with men. Shimizu argues that "instances of hypersexuality alert us to limited definitions of sexuality, race, and representation" (2007: 5–6). Where Shimizu's work departs from most readings of racialized hypersexuality is that it challenges the conception of the normal and the moral by going beyond the work of Patricia Hill Collins (1990) and her notion of the controlling image. Shimizu suggests that while sexual trauma and exploitation are bound up in notions of "hypersexualization," so too is there a considerable amount of power in hypersexuality to point out the limits of normative ideas. For some Black queer women on the scene in DC, they work hard to distinguish themselves from "freaks" and other kinds of "bad" behaving, "hypersexual" women like strippers. They do so to establish their practice of same-sex desire as sanitized, proper, and "normal." Not only do they not have sex with women for men, but they also would never be caught in a strip-club, listening to or dancing to ratchet music. And then there were women who enjoyed the strip club and purposely occupied their position as "bad" women. Rather than distinguishing themselves from "freaks," they distinguish themselves from "fake" freaks. Queering the mic is when Black women take possession of the mic (the object which gives one the authority to speak in hip-hop) and purposefully operate outside of the normative scripts of proper Black femininity, saying and doing what women, especially Black women, are not supposed to say or do in a public. They disturb the boundaries of race/gender/sexuality—articulating themselves in excess of the borders around who and what is supposed to be acceptable (Lane 2011). Similarly, we see the BQW in a strip club who take up Kanye's lyrics for themselves—in fact, they mute his voice completely—and they say, "but unless they use a strap on then they are not dykes." I wish to argue that they do so as a way of self-authoring their authenticity as actual same-sex-desiring women who don't have sex with women to please men, but do so for their own (non-guilty) pleasure. Further, they stake claim to their right to occupy hip-hop spaces—such as the strip club, to be a part of hip-hop and not only as objects there to please men. While I do not claim to know exactly what kind of moment this was, I know what it wasn't. This wasn't some moment where these women were colluding in the maintenance of the gendered heteronormative scripts of Black womanhood; this was to the contrary. The BQW who were singing along were making a claim that living a life structured around being Black, female, and queer marked an experience that those "girls kissing girls" would have no knowledge of—"They ain't about that life"—and that's that shit they don't like.

References

Ahearn, Laura H. 2001. Language and Agency. *Annual Review of Anthropology* 30: 109–137.

Binnie, Jon. 1995. Trading Places: Consumption, Sexuality and the Production of Queer Space. In *Mapping Desire: Geographies of Sexuality*, ed. David Bell and Gill Valentine. London: Routledge.

———. 2004. Quartering Sexualities. In *City of Quarters: Urban Villages in the Contemporary City*, ed. David Bell and Mark Jayne, 163–172. England & Burlington: Ashgate Publishing.

Browne, Kath, and Leela Bakshi. 2011. We Are Here to Party? Lesbian, Gay, Bisexual and Trans Leisurescapes Beyond Commercial Gay Scenes. *Leisure Studies* 30 (2): 179–196.

Carnes, Michelle M. 2009. *Do It for Your Sistas: Black Same-Sex-Desiring Women's Erotic Performance Parties in Washington D.C.* Ph.D Dissertation, Department of Anthropology, American University.

Cooper, Brittney C. 2017. *Beyond Respectability: The Intellectual Thought of Race Women*. Champaign: University of Illinois Press.

Halberstam, J. Jack. 2011. *The Queer Art of Failure*. Durham, NC: Duke University Press.

Kennedy, Elizabeth Lapovsky, and Madeline D. Davis. 1993. *Boots of Leather, Slippers of Gold: The History of a Lesbian Community*. New York and London: Routledge.

Lacy, Karyn R. 2007. *Blue-Chip Black: Race, Class, and Status in the New Black Middle Class*. Berkeley and Los Angeles: University of California Press.

Lane, Nikki. 2011. Black Women Queering the Mic: Missy Elliot Disturbing the Boundaries of Racialized Sexuality and Gender. *Journal of Homosexuality* 58 (6–7): 775–792.

Lorde, Audre. 1982. *Zami: A New Spelling of My Name*. Trumansburg, NY: Crossing Press.

McDermott, E. 2011. The World Some Have Won: Sexuality, Class and Inequality. *Sexualities* 14 (1): 63.

Miller-Young, Mireille. 2008. Hip-Hop Honeys and Da Hustlaz: Black Sexualities in the New Hip-Hop Pornography. *Meridians* 8 (1): 261–292.

Morgan, Joan. 2000. *When Chickenheads Come Home to Roost: A Hip-Hop Feminist Breaks It Down*. New York: Simon & Schuster.

Richardson, Matt. 2003. No More Secrets, No More Lies: African American History and Compulsory Heterosexuality. *Journal of Women's History* 15 (3): 63–76.

Shimizu, Celine Parreñas. 2007. *The Hypersexuality of Race: Performing Asian/American Women on Screen and Scene*. Durham: Duke University Press.

Stallings, LaMonda Horton. 2013. Hip Hop and the Black Ratchet Imagination. *Palimpsest: A Journal on Women, Gender, and the Black International* 2 (2): 135–139.

Thompson, Lisa B. 2009. *Beyond the Black Lady: Sexuality and the New African American Middle Class, The New Black Studies Series*. Urbana: University of Illinois Press.

Visser, Gustav. 2008. The Homonormalisation of White Heterosexual Leisure Spaces in Bloemfontein, South Africa. *Geoforum* 39 (3): 1344–1358.

CHAPTER 4

Representing Ratchet: Screening Black Lesbian Sex and Ratchet Cultural Politics

SCREENING RATCHET/BOOJIE POLITICS

I have thus far discussed the layers of cultural and sexual politics that revolve around the word *ratchet*, the way BQW utilize the Black Ratchet Imagination to remake Black cultural spaces for the expressed purposes of honoring their own pleasure, and what it means for BQW to *embody* ratchet ways of being as middle-class and class mobile BQW subjects. In this chapter, I hone in on the way BQW create representations which are situated within the ratchet/boojie politics of the Scene. How do they engage in the production and dissemination of cultural artifacts that might represent BQW *as* ratchet/boojie? And what is at stake when those representations position BQW as ratchet/boojie? In the previous chapter, I discussed a strip club transformed into a ratchet scene space for BQW. BQW *queered* hip-hop aesthetics, Black youth culture, and explicit Black female sexuality, effectively transforming the structures of feeling such that it was Black female same-sex desire that reigned in contexts (the strip club and hip-hop songs) where BQW's desire is typically foreclosed. Just as BQW have found ways of reorganizing space and *queering* Black cultural formations in ways that allow them to be seen and heard on their own terms, I consider another tool BQW employ to make themselves both seen and heard: YouTube.

In this chapter, I will demonstrate that as BQW become more visible within American popular culture, their representations become embedded within a cultural field which compels their active engagement with distinguishing the *kind* of Black queer person they are. These distinctions do not only play out in the form of the politics of respectability but also in and through a politics of authenticity. To frame this discussion, I will analyze the YouTube web series *District Heat*, created, directed, written and produced by Shanovia McKenzie. Set in DC and its surrounding suburbs, the DMV, *District Heat* follows the lives and loves of an ensemble cast of Black lesbian and queer women. I am interested in *District Heat* because its central conflict in the first two seasons is among Black lesbians who might be characterized as *ratchet*—sagging pants, hip-hop, baseball hats, gangsta, drug dealing, gender non-conforming, masculine, and *un*professional Black women. In particular, I am interested in reading how McKenzie engages in ratchet/boojie politics through her evocation of Black lesbian gender politics, ratchet/boojie representations, and her deployment of explicit sex between Black women.

Black Lesbians on TV

There are Black lesbian, bisexual, and queer women on television now. There aren't many, but they are there. Some of the most popular over the past decade have been Bette and Tasha on Showtime's *The L Word*, and Kima and Snoop on HBO's *The Wire*. Lena on FreeForm's *The Fosters*. Nova on OWN's *Queen Sugar* is a complex and rich character who engages in romantic relationships with both men and women. The high powered, murderous lawyer Annalise Keating of *How to Get Away with Murder*, played by Viola Davis, also has had romantic relationships with both men and women. Crazy Eyes and Poussey have important roles on Netflix's *Orange is the New Black*, and M-Chuck provides comic relief on Starz's *Survivor's Remorse*. There's also Lena Waithe, an out Black lesbian, who won an Emmy for comedy writing and was featured in the show *Master of None*. In 2017, Spike Lee adapted his film *She Gotta Have It*, into a television series for Netflix. Nola Darling, the main character, would describe herself as a "sex positive, polyamorous pansexual." In the cases I've mentioned, BQW aren't throw-away characters, but central to the plot. Analyzing the depictions of the Black queer characters in *The Wire*, Jennifer DeClue (2011) argues that while their depictions can be said to expand representations of the sexuality of Black people and Black queer people specifically in mainstream television, the increased visibility of Black queer characters allows a show and its creators to demonstrate their progressiveness. It also allows them to situate their projects within an aesthetic that

Robert J. Thompson calls "Quality TV." Quality TV is a phrase meant to capture both the increased importance of television in American popular culture as well as the set of shared aesthetic characteristics of television shows considered in any given time period to speak to a young, urban-dwelling, well-educated sensibility. Quoting Robert J. Thompson, DeClue defines Quality TV as that which "tends both toward controversial subject matter as well as realism" (DeClue 2011). To put it simply, DeClue argues that the appearance of Black queer characters can make a show appear more "edgy," "realistic," and therefore, of a higher quality. *The Wire*, DeClue argues, by including representations of Black queer sexuality engages in a discussion of "black sexual taboo," and thus appeals to the target audience of "Quality TV" who would be at least tangentially aware of such taboos. The concern it seems is no longer the invisibility of fictional depictions of BQW in the mainstream. Instead, we might ask *how* they are represented.

On *The L Word*, Bette is a fair-skinned, highly educated art patron and power-lesbian while Tasha, darker-skinned, is a barely making it, war veteran. In *The Wire*, Kima is a good police detective and a terrible, cheating spouse. Snoop, on the other hand, is a soldier for a drug king pin. M-Chuck, in *Survivor's Remorse* is a formerly working-class, panty-chasing, high-femme who taught her brother to ball and is enjoying the fruits of that labor. And Nola Darling of Lee's *She Gotta Have It*, only begins to date a woman when she goes on a self-imposed "dick hiatus." Where Cheryl Dunye's film 1996 *Watermelon Woman* troubled the impossibility and invisibility of Black lesbians within American cinema (Sullivan 2000), over the past decade and a half, television has seemed to take up the figure of the Black lesbian, bisexual, and otherwise queer woman and the new question is: what versions of Black queer female sexuality show up in these fictional accounts?

What consistently rings true across most depictions of BQW in mainstream, "quality TV" is that the characters almost never have other BQW around them (Moore 2015). For example, on *The Wire*, Kima is a cop and spends all of her on-screen time in the company of other cops, save for the one time she went to a lesbian bar and found a woman to cheat on her partner with. And on *The* (notoriously white) *L Word* Bette's circle is comprised entirely of white women and her Black, slightly darker sister, played by Pam Grier. Nola Darling only engages in a romantic relationship with a woman when she gets upset with her boyfriends. Annalise Keating has only had an on-screen sexual relationship with a white woman and is too busy trying not to go to jail to spend much time in the company of anyone other than her co-conspirators. I could go on, but the pattern is clear: BQW in the mainstream, while included, are often depicted as singular, individual anomalies who simply braid themselves into the fabric of mostly white, straight people's worlds (Moore 2015). However, this is quite at odds with the lives and experiences of the BQW in DC I studied. For many of these BQW, being in a community of other Black women, queer people of color, and/or BQW, was of the utmost importance in their personal lives. Whether they found those communities and were able to connect with them, or not, it was on their mind because even if they didn't consider themselves a part of it, they knew that such a thing as the BQW Scene existed. And over the past decade, particularly in the virtual space of YouTube, BQW have been working diligently to make these Scene's visible.

Black Lesbians on YouTube

Independent, Black queer filmmakers are actively producing stories that center on the lives of BQW. YouTube, a social media video streaming site where user-created content forms the basis of the interactions, has been especially important to this group of storytellers (Johnson and Boylorn 2015). Social media platforms such as YouTube, as well as streaming services such as Amazon Prime and Netflix, make it possible for BQW to share their stories with broad audiences. One of the first YouTube webseries revolving around the fictional lives of Black lesbians was Charmain Johnson's *The Lovers and Friends Show* (2008–2010). Set in Miami, the melodrama followed the lives of a group of young friends and their lovers. The success of *The Lovers and Friends Show* and others like it, which highlighted the unique circumstances of predominately Black same-sex desiring women in specific locales, would lead to the emergence of other shows which followed a similar concept including *Lipstick: The Series* (2016–2018) a Black lesbian webseries set in Los Angeles, *Skye's the Limit* (2014), set in DC, and Studville TV (2013–2018), set in Atlanta and following the lives of studs, or masculine Black lesbians. The webseries hasn't been the only format in which these stories have been told. Coquie Hughes and Milon V. Parker's *The Lies We Tell, The Secrets We Keep* (2011) is the first film in a series of 3 which tell a complex and multilayered story about Black men and women's sexual and romantic misfortunes. Milon V. Parker continues to make short films, many of which are available to stream on Amazon Prime. One of the most-watched LGBT YouTube webseries to date is Michelle Daniel's *Between Women* which premiered during the winter of 2011. The show is set in Atlanta and pivots around the experience of masculine Black lesbians and their high-fem partners and former partners. Daniel would spin the success from *Between Women* into a production company Between Women TV Network that produces other Black queer webseries, and charges on a per-episode basis for a reboot of *Between Women* that features new characters and storylines.

BLACK LESBIAN GENDER POLITICS AND RATCHET/BOOJIE POLITICS

Amber Johnson and Robin M. Boylorn (2015) closely examine the lesbian webseries *Between Women*'s first two seasons and argue that while the show is important in that makes visible the experiences of Black lesbians, its hyperfocus on Black lesbian stud/fem relations seemingly reproduces heteronormative ideologies. This, along with its portrayal of hypermasculine Black lesbians who participate in discourses of hegemonic masculinity, "did not expand representations and/or create nuanced depictions of black women, but rather recycled problematic and stereotypical images of blackness adding a layer and lens of sexuality" (Johnson and Boylorn 2015, 21). Considering the mainstreaming effects of Black same-sex desiring women's cultural productions in the age of social and digital new media, Marlon Rachquel Moore, reading the show through its 3rd season, argues that *Between Women* does important work in the field of representation of masculine Black lesbians by offering a variety of versions of Black female masculinity. She argues "in addition to situating minority characters within their communities," the "storylines involve more realistic portrayals of the personal, social, or political problems lesbians face" (Moore 2015, 212). Moore recognizes that *Between Women* is situated within a set of intragroup sexual politics where hegemonic masculinity actually plays a role, as does versions of female masculinity that break with a patriarchal paradigm, "the paradigm that often informs the much-maligned butch/femme framework of lesbian romance" (Moore 2015, 210). Where Johnson and Boylorn (2015) are suspicious of the representation of stud/femme (butch/femme) framework of Black lesbian life, Marlon Moore recognizes that the representation is rooted in real-life scenarios of Black lesbian socializing. Further, Marlon Moore's reading of *Between Women* reads the representations of masculinity as falling along masculinity on which these masculine Black lesbian gender performances as based.

It is incomplete a reading to understand Black lesbian gender performances strictly in terms of "parroting" heteronormative formations. In reality, it is much more complicated.

In her study of gender presentations across working-class and middle-class lesbians in New York City, Mignon R. Moore (2006) argues that while lesbian-feminists distanced themselves from butch/femme gender presentation in the 1970s, Black lesbians continued to use gender performance as an organizing feature of social life and community (Moore 2006, 114–115). Since the 1970s, there has been a reconfiguration of the old butch/femme dichotomy such that now there are at least three different kinds of gender presentations among Black gay women as opposed to the dichotomous "butch-femme" that most often was assumed to be norm in Black gay women's cultures. The first, femmes, or feminine presenting women, are described as wearing dresses and skirts, form-fitting clothes, low cut shirts, blouses that reveal cleavage, jewelry, and high heels. They wear make-up, and wear their hair in the latest styles for Black women. The second type of gender presentation was the gender-blender, who as the name suggests borrows elements from both masculine and feminine styles to create unique looks (Moore 2006, 124). Sometimes labeled "soft-studs" in DC, they preferred to wear women's clothing but in less feminine ways. Alternatively, they might opt to pair men's wear with less masculine or form-fitting pieces. In some cases, these women might wear a little make-up. While related to androgynous gender presentations, Moore (2006) draws a distinction between minority women's "gender-blender" styles since the point is not to de-emphasize gender, but to highlight specific parts of a woman's masculinity and femininity in ways that are unique to her. Within the mainstream, these women may not be read as lesbians, due to the increased variation of women's dress. They may simply look like "tomboys" or women who are simply less feminine. Lastly, Moore (2006) describes what she calls a "transgressive" gender presentation. The women who were transgressive tended to wear men's clothes, shoes exclusively, where their hair close-cropped, dreadlocked, or braided in cornrows. They purposefully transgressed notions of femininity. In DC, these women would be called "masculine of center," "doms," or "studs." Further, Mignon Moore makes clear that the physical presentations of gender do not necessarily speak to the personality traits or gender ideologies assumed to correlate with transgressive or femme gender performances. Moore makes clear that when she uses "femme" she means only to discuss the way women presented themselves aesthetically. That is, being femme did not mean one was passive, submissive, or took on traditionally feminine roles in their relationships (Moore 2006, 124). Similarly, Mignon Moore finds that for transgressive women "while some [...] identify a masculine style as well as an assertive, dominant personality as components of a transgressive presentation of self, this link with personality is largely a reflection of how women within that category believe they *should* behave" (Moore 2006, 126). That is, they believed that they should act and perform more masculine, active, aggressive roles in their relationships, but that didn't mean that they did. Instead, gender presentation did more to structure social interactions, romantic and otherwise. One dressed in a particular way so that they could attract a person who possessed the desired complementary gender presentation (Moore 2006, 129).

> However, the structure imposed by these norms also grants women a certain agency or freedom to present themselves in a gendered way if they so desire, and that is different from the expectations in many lesbian-feminist social circles that encourage a look that is not overtly feminine or masculine. In black lesbian environments, [some] lesbians [...] feel liberated by these categories of gender display, especially the gender-blender identity, because they allow for a way to express a nonfeminine gendered self and to have that identity valued by other gay women. (Moore 2006, 129)

As already discussed, class greatly influences the ways that gender presentation was discussed on the BQW scene. BQW who were thought to be ratchet exuded a gender presentation, whether dom or femme, that was rooted in working-class and hip-hop aesthetics. For failing to reproduce middle-class standards, they were seen as outside the boundaries of homonormative gender presentations. Homonormativity is more interested in fitting into already established systems of gender rather than destabilizing the gender order. However, it is important to bear in mind that those who engage in ratchet ways of being may also participate in shoring up the boundaries of what are acceptable and authentic performances of Black female masculinity and lesbian femininity. While middle-class BQW might avoid labeling their gender presentations altogether, for working-class BQW, those labels can offer an important set of principles that organize their erotic and social lives. I draw attention to these debates in my analysis of *District Heat* and the discourses about lesbian sex and gender that surround the show. Understanding the complexities of gender performance in Black lesbian communities helps when considering what is and is not at stake in the representation of BQW and fictional accounts of Black lesbian life.

Like *Between Women* and other Black lesbian webseries, *District Heat* revolves around a group of BQW and its main protagonist is a dom, but what sets it apart is that it is situated within the Scene in DC. *District Heat* deals with a variety of issues: money, sex, drugs, family, betrayal, crime, intimate partner violence, and infidelity. The show features an ensemble cast with a variety of gender presentations, though the central tension of the show revolves around a love triangle between two femmes, one middle-class and the other working-class, and a dom, a working-class drug dealer trying to go legit. Where Johnson and Boylorn were interested in how issues related to the intersections of race, gender, and sexuality informed the plot of *Between Women*, and Marlon Moore was interested in how *Between Women* participated in the mainstreaming of Black lesbian life, I enter the conversation in this analysis of *District Heat* by considering the way that it depicts sexual encounters (between women), and how viewers describe their reactions to those fictional sexual encounters. I consider sex because as Jennifer Nash and Mirielle Miller-Young have demonstrated, representations of Black women engaging in sex can be an effective and rich site for grappling with ideological constructions about Black women's bodies (see Chap. 3). Black women having explicit sex with other Black women is the one thing that is often lacking in mainstream depictions of Black lesbians, as has been the analysis of those depictions. In the mainstream, when sex between Black women occur, the characters are often both middle-class and femme or gender-blending (but leaning more toward femme). I would argue that this because middle-class femme and gender-blending depictions of Black lesbianism are far more palatable for mainstream audiences. Palatable because while the women have sex, they are not completely *transgressing* the boundaries of acceptable Black female presentation or behavior. Thus, when the first sex scene in *District Heat* is between a drug dealing, hypermasculine Black dom and two nameless Black femmes, it is clear that *District Heat* is not interested in appealing to the "masses." It's also clear that *something* ratchet is going on and worthy of our full and undivided attention.

District Heat

The opening credits for *District Heat* include a theme song which introduces the main characters. The song is a hip-hop song and the lyrics are performed by a rapper, and plays over shots of DC from the perspective of the passenger seat of a car. The car makes its way around the entire city, through each quadrant of 68 square mile city. The car is moving through a DC neighborhood on a bright, sunny day. Houses and small shops wiz by as the credits slide onto the screen. Abruptly, the Capitol Building from the perspective of the Capitol Reflecting Pool comes into view, and then a shot through the windshield of the car of a Metropolitan Police Department police car lights flashing with two white-shirts[1] talking to a patrol officer. The car continues to move again past a carryout until we stop again at the 19 ft. "Big Chair" in Anacostia in Southeast DC. Suddenly, we're looking at DC's Union Station, and then at North Capitol Street from the Northeast side, which divides the city into east and west. Finally, at the corner of 7th and F St Northwest, there's a shot of the Gallery Place-Chinatown Metro station sign as the car cruises down 7th street until the screen fades to black.

As the shots of the city fade, an opening monologue plays over shots of what appear to be a series of drug buys. A masculine presenting woman with locs and a fitted blue Nationals baseball cap makes an exchange with a figure in a dark hooded jacket, as the door of a multi-family apartment shuts behind her. Another woman with locs, baggy jeans, and a white tee stands on the stoop of an apartment building making an exchange with another person. We see, four people holding money in their hands participating in a game of craps, and then more exchanges taking place indiscreetly through daps. Then we hear the words:

> When I was a younger, I though life was a puzzle. As I got older, I realized life is nothing but a blue print, already predesigned. Everyday that goes by, my finger is on the trigger. With one bullet left, Russian Roulette is the game that I play with every decision I make. As you see how my life unfolds, it's only two ways out. "Take my finger off the trigger, or I'll keep pullin."

District Heat (2017) follows Ali, a dom, living in Washington, DC, who sells drugs in a crew with 3 other women, two of whom have a quick

---

[1] In DC, "white-shirts" refer to ranking officers.

temper and whose violent ways do not sit well with Ali. As Ali tries to pull away from the group, two of the others devise a scheme to get rid of her. The drama of her life as a drug dealer unfolds as Ali courts a woman named Wyllow who is "out of her league," a real estate agent and CPA, who we later learn is the sister of one of her drug crew partners, Wayne (Wynetta). Meanwhile, Ali's best friend Tinka, a hair stylist, is coming to grips with the fact that she's in love with Ali. A host of other minor characters whose lives intersect with Ali, Tinka, and Willow round out the show and revolve around the main conflicts between Ali and her love interests and Ali and her drug crew. Torn in different directions in her "professional" life as well as in her personal life, Ali serves as an interesting and thoroughly fascinating character for this crime and love triangle melodrama.

District Heat aired for the first time in 2014. At the time, there was another lesbian webseries on YouTube set in DC called *Skye's the Limit* created by Blue Telusma that following a newly single Howard University-educated writer named Skye, as she sought both love and a rewarding career. The characters met for coffee, worked out in the gyms of their fancy apartment buildings, met up in Miami for SweetHeat and stayed in a nice hotels. *Skye's the Limit* ended after one season. Through much of 2014, *Skye's the Limit* could be accessed for pay through the creator's website, but as of 2015 that was no longer an option. *District Heat* remains the only running Black lesbian webseries set in DC and as of my writing this chapter in 2017, is enjoying a popular second season. Its characters meet up for coffee, but they also met at the strip club, in public parks late at night, and in their lightly furnished apartments with drug paraphernalia. Its main character is a dom, drug dealer who was only single for the first episode. Both shows featured explicit sex scenes, but from the beginning it was clear that *District Heat* would feature *more* and that those scenes would take place outside of normative frameworks of partnerships. In contrast to the careful framing of sex within the context of *Skye's the Limit*, in *District Heat*, we may not always know the names of the characters involved, and the sex scene might not contribute to the overall plot of the story.

Representing Sex in District Heat

The first sex scene in *District Heat* was not romantic. It was not between loving partners whose lives we'd get to see unfold across later episodes. It was quite simply "fucking." The scene featured Wayne, a stud[2] (masculine presenting) military vet and compatriot of Ali, and two femmes, who are both nameless and essentially faceless, as they are neither major nor minor characters in the rest of the show. The scene follows a narrative arc common in most pornographic threesomes with two women and a man. The two women are having an okay time and then a dick arrives. Wayne, who is mostly clothed throughout the scene in boxer briefs and a tank top[3] equips a strap-on, and then the two femmes *really* enjoy themselves. People's reaction to the scene in public comments seem to suggest that most people (who commented) enjoyed it. Beyond mere excitement, however, some people talked about the *realism* that this particular scene employed.

Shannon Finnicks: "I think they have the most realistic sex scenes out of all the webseries on youtube"

mixon270: "damn in that sex scene she was really eatin up the pussy huh?"[4]

The show seemed to revel in the fact that it wasn't always clear whether or not you were watching simulated or *real* sex. In fact, the lines were often blurred. Because those lines were so blurred, and because "reality" and representing the "real DMV" were discourses featured so prominently within the comments section and in the promotional material of the show, it is worth taking a moment to interrogate it further. The accouterments of the working-class abound within this first sex scene, a threesome: a small apartment, a drug dealer, red solo cups, two femmes "too many" tattoos, "too many" piercings, and "too much" weave. It is not a stretch to say that the sex, while very likely simulated, is filmed with careful attention to give the viewer a sense that the sex is in fact happening. It is explicit, and this is in part what Shannon Finnicks and mixon270 are responding to in their comments. The insistence on the "real," paired with the working-class sensibilities in the scene, and the show, however,

---

[2] I want to note here that I'm using the language that is used in the show and the comments sections. Masculine women are referred to as either studs/doms, and feminine presenting women as fems.

[3] Or, as it is colloquially known, "wife-beater."

[4] These comments from Season 1, Episode 1 of *District Heat*. Using the computer program NVivo, I was able to pull all the comments from all 10 available episodes of *District Heat*, code and analyze them.

should not in and of themselves lead us to a suggestion that *District Heat* is somehow more "authentic" a representation of BQW life in DC than *Skye's the Limit*. Too often what has been considered the most "authentic" representations of Blackness have been cultural objects and behaviors associated with the "folk," the "hood," and the "street" (Johnson 2003). Therefore, when I distinguish *District Heat* from *Skye's the Limit*, I do not bring this distinction up in order to argue that one was more "real" than the other. Instead, I want to point out that *District Heat*, unlike many other lesbian webseries, centralizes the very things about Black same-sex desiring women that makes them incompatible within the politics of respectability: that they have sex with each other, often; and, that sex does not always take place in the context of loving, monogamous partnerships. In fact, plenty of the sex is simply gratuitous.

Dalia Milani: "THAT LESBIAN SEX SCENE, YAAAAAAAAAAAAAAAAS"
Sldainfamous: "That sex scene though … get that shit, bro."
Kayla_D: "Chiiiiile that sex scene had my eyes like two capital O's"

It is that no-holds barred approach to sex that made Kayla_D's "eyes like two capital O's" after viewing this scene. In total, there were 13 sex scenes in the first 10 episodes[5] of *District Heat*. I counted any scene where there was clear evidence of a sexual encounter or where sex was implied, even if not fully screened. That excluded two scenes: one where the sexual activity was interrupted and another where a character got a lap dance and was teased, but there was no sex implied. I base my discussion that follows on these 13 scenes. *District Heat*'s purposeful lack of discretion when it comes to screening sex between Black women is what marks it as ratchet, and the depth of that indiscretion is what I will analyze in the remainder of this chapter.

Black Lesbian Hypermasculinity

In her ethnographic study of Black lesbian female masculinity in South Carolina, Laura Lane-Steele analyzes the expressions and historical constructions of Black female masculinities (Lane-Steele 2011). She argues for

---

[5] Available for analysis at the time of this analysis and writing.

understanding Black masculinity as a "protest masculinity," formed under the conditions of economic, cultural, and social oppression (Lane-Steele 2011). Lane-Steele suggests that one kind of Black protest masculinity "is characterized by hypermasculinity: taking certain characteristics of hegemonic masculinity (homophobia, misogyny, dominance, and the policing of gender) to more extreme levels. This protest-hypermasculinity serves as a tool to protect Black men, and the Black community that they are expected to protect, from racism, violence, and discrimination" (Lane-Steele 2011, 483). Lane-Steele suggests that Black female masculinity in the context of Black lesbian spaces, is rooted within this Black protest masculinity allowing gender-nonconforming Black lesbians to strategically shape their masculinity in terms that will allow them to avoid mistreatment on the basis of their gender (Lane-Steele 2011, 483). What makes the process "strategic," is that the aspects of hypermasculinity that studs "adopt function in ways that give these women privilege and power despite their subordinated position as lesbian women in a heteronormative, patriarchal culture" (Lane-Steele 2011, 483). Consider that *District Heat's* main plot revolves around a hypermasculine Black female character, Ali, who sells drugs. Drug dealing is typically considered to be a male-dominated domain and enterprise. However, taking on masculine characteristics and being able to blend in, "being one of the boys," in this domain would offer considerable access and power to move about the domain of the street (Lane-Steele 2011, 486). There are other studs in the main cast of *District Heat* including Choppa, Jay, Wayne, Lyric, Syn, and Kryst. Only two are not engaged in selling drugs, Syn and Kryst. Syn has a job working in an office—a professional, but Kryst is chronically unemployed, living off any girlfriend willing to put up with her chronic infidelity. In one especially revelatory scene, Kryst visits her father who tells her she needs to be better at putting her women "in check." Each stud character differently configures their masculinity, but what is relatively consistent is the way that gender performance organized the way that they had sex. Lane-Steele explains something crucial to our understanding of the way sex was screened in *District Heat*.

> There are ways in which these studs do not follow traditional male scripts in their sexual relationships, however. In general, during sex the femme's sexual pleasure is prioritized over the stud's. While the stud is still in control during sex, the femme's sexual needs come first. In fact, some studs do not like to be sexually stimulated at all. This does not follow the heterosexual

script that places men's sexual desires ahead of their female partners, and in fact, it is exactly the opposite. While these studs' masculinities still require dominance in the bedroom, they are expected to satisfy their partners, with their sexual desires coming second or sometimes not at all. (Lane-Steele 2011, 486)

Lane-Steele finds that the stud/femme dichotomy organized the sexual scripts of Black lesbians such that the sexual pleasure and stimulation of studs was not central to the sex act. This is quite at odds with heterosexual scripts, particularly in the field of representation. In visual media such as hard-core pornography, for example, the "money shot," or the man's ejaculation functions as narrative signal of an ending of the scene (Williams 1999, 93). No such signals appear in the context of lesbian pornography. In considering the nature of the first 13 sex scenes in *District Heat*, only 2 of 13 scenes did not feature a stud. To put this in perspective, I've already discussed the first: before Wayne enters the room, there are two nameless femmes who are in a bed engaging in a sexual encounter. It then becomes a threesome with a stud. The other was a fantasy of Ali's, a brief sequence between the two women with whom she is romantically involved, Tinka and Wyllow. In other words, in the two instances where there was an opportunity to demonstrate femme-for-femme desire, the desire and fantasies of hypermasculinity were privileged instead. The two scenes are especially interesting given the fact that the show does not treat any femme-on-femme romantic relationships in the first 10 episodes.[6] Arguably, the two femme-on-femme sex scenes are used to authenticate a certain kind of Black female hypermasculinity in *District Heat* situating both Wayne and Ali as particular kinds of masculine subjects—one's who subscribe to a version of Black protest masculinity that grants them power and privilege in spite of their lesbian identity (Lane-Steele 2011, 483), specifically in the visual field. Being active partners in sexual encounters, having one's fantasies fulfilled and privileged is one way that studs take up positions of power within the context of representations of Black lesbian sexuality.

---

[6] Or "stud-on-stud" though that is considerably less likely in general given the way that such relationships are generally frowned upon in Black lesbian communities. See Mignon R. Moore (2006), Laura Lane-Steele (2011), and the 2015 documentary *The Same Difference* by Nneka Onuorah which address gender roles and performances in Black lesbian communities.

I counted 9 of the 13 scenes as explicit. By explicit, I refer to scenes that either showed characters having orgasms, giving, or receiving oral sex, or being penetrated. Of the 9 explicit scenes, all except for 1, featured a character that was a stud. Femmes were exclusively partnered with studs (except briefly in the case of the threesome). This also means that femmes were overrepresented in the sex scenes. In 15 instances femmes were represented whereas in 12 instances were studs. Of the 8 explicit scenes that featured a stud character, in 5 of those cases, the stud was represented as only being in an active sexual position. That is, we primarily see stud characters giving sexual pleasure, but not receiving it. In the 3 instances where the stud was in a receptive role, one includes a scene where the stud character was in a non-normative sex position which placed her in both the active and passive position.[7] Contrasted with the stud roles during sex, most scenes featured feminine women in passive, or receptive positions. Only 1 scene included a feminine woman, Tasha, fucking her stud partner, Syn, and viewers had much to say in the comments section on the episode. When I collected the comments in 2016 for this particular episode where this scene between Syn and Tasha takes place—Episode 1 of Season 2—I was struck by the negative sentiments about Syn and Tasha's scene—where Syn, the stud, is "bottoming" were these:

Niko Negrita Diabla: "… Why was one of the studs being stuck with a strap …. Just saying? The leg was up WTF"
Gina Hickerson: "I see femininity written all over the fake studs"
AG Lokster: "Man studs don't really be with the shits like this …."

It was clear that some found that the way *District Heat* screened the sexual behavior of one of its stud characters, Syn to be inauthentic. By showing Syn in a receptive role it represented her female masculinity in a way that, unlike Wayne and Ali, did not foreground her as the partner who exclusively gave sexual pleasure to her femme partner. For Niko Negretia Diabla, a stud "getting stuck with a strap" was off-putting: "WTF."[8] For Gina Hickerson, however, the scene seemed emblematic of larger problem with the way that the show portrayed female masculinity, a point echoed

---

[7] Colloquially referred to as a "69" position.
[8] Internet lingo for "What the Fuck?"

by AG[9] Lokster. For each of them, being a receptive partner for a sexual act other than oral sex, marked Syn as "too feminine." Others responded to these negative comments challenging the idea that studs could not be receptive partners during sex.

Starlight: +Niko Negrita Diabla There was no strap involved. It's called: Tribadism

Veronica: Ones complaining about Cyn and Tasha's sex scene, Cyn is still a woman. There should be no rules with your other half in the bedroom. Everyone doesn't conform to gender roles, so if you think the masculinity defines what can be done in the bedroom, your sex life probably sucks and you're small minded. I love submissive studs, get you some!

Terri Smith: I have to agree with you. When that seem came on I was proud that they showed that side of us. A stud that can be submissive in the bedroom has awesome awesome sex. We exist and we're cherished. More scenes showing that will be ok with me.

The policing of gender barriers within Black lesbian communities in DC was primarily an issue I saw among women who dated or were involved with working-class women. What it meant to be a "real" stud or femme, were persistent sources of tension within interpersonal relationships among Black lesbians. These discussions of who or what was stud/femme was typically discussed disparagingly among middle-class and upper-class women, who did not think of themselves as participating in the policing of the boundaries of gender performance in the same way. However, recall in Chap. 2 my informants who did not like the strict "stud/dom-femme" set up simply replaced the baseball caps with bowties, sagging pants with slacks, basketball shoes with nice loafers. It wasn't that the gender dichotomy disappeared, but that it looked different.

---

[9] A Black queer colloquial way of referring to an "Aggressive" woman which is another way of saying "stud" or "dom."

If we look to *District Heat*'s portrayal of femininity and masculinity in terms of class politics, the two main characters, for example, Wyllow and Ali demonstrate both the politics of gender performance and class within Black lesbian cultural politics in DC. Ali is a drug dealer and masculine presenting. Her performance of masculinity is steeped in hip-hop culture. Loose-fitting jeans that sag, baseball hats, sneakers or combat boots, visible tattoos, one on her face, carries a gun, deals in cash—in one scene, we see her counting a stack of bills, uses DC's version of African American English; references to self and other masculine presenting women as "bruh," "brother," and "nigga." Ali's masculinity could be considered ratchet. Wyllow on the other hand, works as a CPA, speaks in Standard American English.[10] She wears a modest amount of make-up, fashionable high-femme clothes that aren't gaudy. She's the epitome of the "progressive, beautiful, and gainfully employed" woman who might have frequented an Intertwine Party that Jay discusses in Chap. 2. She is a professional woman with the accouterments of a middle-class lifestyle. A home, a desk job, and good weave. When Wyllow and Ali get together, Wyllow encourages her to go back to her "day job," as a welder. Skilled, high-paying work, but manual labor. Ali complies, but does not give up her "night job." Wyllow's gender performance as femme and her middle-classness restrict her movement and prevents her access to certain spaces, particularly those where her partner has great freedom of movement. In fact, Wyllow's sister, Wayne is involved in the same gang as Ali, and Wyllow doesn't even know that the two know one another. Both Wayne and Ali work diligently to keep Wyllow "in her place," at home or at work. The masculine characters might be seen in the street and at the club, but Wyllow is only ever screened in the context of an office, at home, on her way home, or on her way to the office. Initially, Ali and Wyllow's class differences seemed an insurmountable barrier to their getting together, however, the two become seriously involved quickly. Now that they are together, it's the ratchet aspects of Ali's life—her drug dealing and Tinka, her "homegirl" who exudes a working-class femme gender expression—that threatens to break the two of them up.

---

[10] Oddly, she very rarely uses contractions which might demonstrate a "forced" Standard American English. In other words, she may be using SAE as a means of masking her actual class position, and thus engaging in boojie behavior.

Quare Work of District Heat

"I know you want to bite this. It's so enticing. Nothing else like this. Imma make you my bitch."—Rihanna, "Cake, Cake, Cake" (2014)

"Yoncé all on his mouth like liquor like like liquor. Like like liquor, like like liquor."—Beyoncé, "Partition" (2014)

"So, lick it now, lick it good, lick this pussy just like you should. My neck, my back, lick my pussy and my crack."—RaSheeda, "My neck, my back (Lick it)" (2001)

Black women have been daring us to consume them from the inside out, evoking ratchet ways of being to do so. *Ratchet* grants one the power to evoke a particular kind of sexuality—one that is unabashed, unbothered, tempting, bacchanalian. By evoking ratchet, Black women are able to unapologetically represent a kind sexuality that does not require permission to exist and which centers on their pleasure. That is, being ratchet activates opportunities to represent oneself in a way that is not concerned with prescriptive dictates as to what constitutes "classyness." Representations, therefore, of Black women within the context of *ratchet*, have the potential to expand the boundaries around that which is possible for all Black women while also calling out and critiquing the delicate sensibilities of middle-class Blackness. We can see this most clearly within the context of hip-hop, where Black women artists regularly evoke the ratchet—sultry basslines, unabashedly sexual lyrics, and images that highlight their bodies and their sex.

As Miller-Young (2014) beautifully illustrates in her book *A Taste for Brown Sugar: Black Women in Pornography* there have always been Black women who've disregarded respectability politics, cultures of dissemblance, using their bodies, and their sexualities to make space for themselves and to make money. Charges of "hypersexuality" often abound in ratchet representations of Black women's sexuality. Hypersexuality is only useful insofar as it points out the boundaries and borders of respectability. However, claims about black women's "hypersexuality" is frequently used to disregard their "play" at the boundaries of acceptable, appropriate, morally pure Black womanhood. I will always be suspicious of the term "hypersexuality." *Hyper* in relation to what? Using hypersexuality to describe individuals, their behaviors, or representations, is, as I've argued before, problematic (Lane 2011). In fact, I think "it might be another way to call black women hoes" (Lane 2011). A ratchet sensibility doesn't simply exploit boundaries, it explodes them offering a way of experiencing and representing anything that is outside of normative logics about racialized sexuality, masculinity and femininity, and class ideologies. In other words, we might read *District Heat* as using female masculinity to demonstrate the true source of Black femme pleasure, and it doesn't necessarily mean that such is true for all femmes. Similarly, a stud might like to be fucked by her femme partner, and that also doesn't necessarily mean that such is true for all studs.

District Heat is ratchet because it questions the notion that there is a proper way for Black women's bodies to engage in sex. Even when we are sure that it is telling only one kind of story, one that centers on the experiences of female masculinity, it reminds us that the rules are still malleable by having Syn "bottom" in the first episode of the long-awaited second season. It also sits in contradistinction to a Black homonormative ways of thinking, a way that many of my informants, mostly middle-class, highly educated, and upwardly mobile Black lesbians tended to buy into that Black lesbians should strive to display their gender and sexuality ways that (1) do not "parrot" heterosexuality (the first sex scene in the show is a play-by-play of a porno 2 girl, 1 guy threesome); (2) should not offend the sensibilities of the white or Black heteronormative middle-class (the main character is a dom drug dealer with a tattoo on her face); and (3), that even if you engage in ratchet behavior occasionally, you should be able to "transform" into environments that are not tolerant of Black working-class ways of being. At this last point, I should note that while Ali is in a relationship with Wyllow, she "transforms" into a respectable line of work (at least part time), but it is still manual labor. In this way, her transformation is incomplete.

District Heat does not attempt to fit within a normative framework. It is not glossy. It is not made by professionals. Its actors are not members of the Screen Actors Guild. They make the show through ratchet means. By representing and showing Black lesbians—unclothed, naked, strapped, and unstrapped—*District Heat* engages in a purposeful act of ratchetness. The sex scenes reflect the ongoing ideological debates about normative and non-normative forms of gender and class actively taking place within Black lesbian communities in DC. Robin D.G. Kelley's *Race Rebels* reminds us that working-class acts of resistance are often framed as "lazy," "inarticulate," or ways of "setting the race back." I, like many other lesbians, have found YouTube to be one of the few places where I can find shows where people who kinda look like me will be loving, fighting, and fucking each other. And it is in these ratchet representations where the most interesting kinds of loving, fighting, and fucking often take place.

References

DeClue, Jennifer. 2011. Lesbian Cop, Queer Killer: Leveraging Black Queer Women's Sexuality on HBO's The Wire. *The Spectator* 31 (2): 53.

Johnson, E. Patrick. 2003. The Pot is Brewing: Marlon Riggs' Black Is… Black Ain't. In *Appropriating Blackness: Performance and the Politics of Authenticity*. Durham and London: Duke University Press.

Johnson, Amber, and Robin M. Boylorn. 2015. Digital Media and the Politics of Intersectional Queer Hyper/In/Visibility in Between Women. *Digital Media* 11: 1.

Lane, Nikki. 2011. Black Women Queering the Mic: Missy Elliot Disturbing the Boundaries of Racialized Sexuality and Gender. *Journal of Homosexuality* 58 (6–7): 775–792.

Lane-Steele, Laura. 2011. Studs and Protest-Hypermasculinity: The Tomboyism within Black Lesbian Female Masculinity. *Journal of Lesbian Studies* 15 (4): 480–492.

Miller-Young, Mireille. 2014. *A Taste for Brown Sugar: Black Women in Pornography*. Durham: Duke University Press.

Moore, Mignon R. 2006. Lipstick or Timberlands? Meanings of Gender Presentation in Black Lesbian Communities. *Signs* 32 (1): 113–138.

Moore, Marlon Rachquel. 2015. Between Women TV: Toward the Mainstreaming of Black Lesbian Masculinity and Black Queer Women in Community. *Black Camera: The New Series* 6 (2): 201–216.

Sullivan, Laura L. 2000. Chasing Fae: The Watermelon Woman and Black Lesbian Possibility. *Callaloo* 23 (1): 448–460.

Williams, Linda. 1999. *Hard Core: Power, Pleasure, and the "Frenzy of the Visible"*. Expanded ed. Berkeley: University of California Press.

CHAPTER 5

Coming Out Ratchet and Whole: Black Women and the Struggle to Just Be

SELLING BQW'S SEXUAL STORIES

Black women's bodies and lives are subject to particular, daily forms of scrutiny in American society. This scrutiny happens at all levels of Black women's existence and happens in both "private" and "public" domains. The realm of reality television and the vlogs, Tweets, and gossip blogs which revolve around the lives of their casts, offer a glimpse into the way that scrutiny is commodified. Combining the melodrama of soap opera with the potential for ratchet verbal jousting and even violent encounters, VH1's hit "unscripted" (reality) television series *Love & Hip-Hop* based in New York, and its spin offs *Love & Hip-Hop: Atlanta, Love & Hip-Hop: Hollywood,* and *Love & Hip-Hop: Miami,* feature casts that are almost entirely Black. In 2017, during what *Business Insider* referred to as a "ratings resurgence," VH1 attributed their success to its slate of unscripted shows including *Love & Hip-Hop: Atlanta* and *Love & Hip-Hop,* which secured the top two spots in the Nielsen ratings for unscripted shows.[1] The executive producer of the *Love & Hip-Hop* franchise, Mona Scott-Young, is a Black woman who, through her success, has demonstrated that ratchet portrayals of "Black love" are extremely profitable. Each center on the love lives of prominent members of their respective city's local hip-hop scene as well as ancillary figures in the Hip-Hop Nation such as managers, radio personalities, DJs, bar tenders, video vixens, strippers, ex-strippers, and

---

[1] Nededog (2017).

fashion designers. The shows typically revolve around complicated love triangles, intimate betrayals, break-ups, and reconciliations between husbands, wives, boyfriends, girlfriends, exes, best friends, and side pieces.

Collectively, the Reality TV shows which feature predominately Black casts including the *Love & Hip-Hop* franchise, as well as Bravo's *Real Housewives: Atlanta* and VH1's *Black Ink Crew* and *Basketball Wives*, are referred to as "Ratchet TV." What makes them ratchet is not only that they display Black folks who might otherwise be read as boojie because while they are upwardly mobile and middle-class according to their income, they still engage in behavior that is assumed to be "authentically" Black (they use African American English, they are loud, rude, and many retain an affiliation with "the hood" through their associations or tastes and judgments). In other words, they no longer live in the hood, but they still act hood (Chap. 2). This is especially true of the casts of *Love & Hip-Hop* because hip-hop artists, whether they come from working-class backgrounds or not, are expected to be close to "the street" and "the hood," the imagined geographic epicenter of hip-hop. Further, the cast members might be rich, or at least are able to pretend to be, but they are acting ratchet by willingly talking about their sexual practices in public. This act of "putting their business in the street" is a clear violation of Black middle-class codes of behavior. The shows tend to focus on Black women who are already characterized as (un)naturally aggressive, unreasonable, and more prone to the emotional outbursts which are, as Rachel E. Dubrofsky describes, the "money shot" of Reality TV (Dubrofsky 2009). Dubrofsky follows Laura Grindstaff who considers the way that talk shows work to produce an emotional outburst in the guests that it can then exploit. Grindstaff argues that for the producers of these shows "the more emotional and volatile the guests and audience members, the more "real" (and the more "ordinary") they are" (Grindstaff 2002, 20). Dubrofsky applies this insight to Reality TV arguing that "the "money shot" is not simply about expressing emotion: it is about expressing emotions so overpowering they are beyond a person's control, and about expressing them in a way that is unexpected and breaks social norms" (Dubrofsky 2009). What makes each of their descriptions of "the money shot" so important to our consideration of Ratchet TV is that having emotional outbursts that break social norms is seen as an ordinary aspect of Black women's character.

In an American visual emporium that is both obsessed with being them, and obsessed with hating them, multimedia conglomerates, marketers, *and* Black women have found ingenious ways of capitalizing on those seemingly private sentiments about Black women. The popularity of these shows and the wide circulation of opinions about the Black women featured in them, demonstrate the American public's disgust, rage, and/or "guilty pleasure" at watching Black women *be* "Black women" and tell intimate stories of their sexual lives (Nash 2014; Miller-Young 2014). But what does it mean to *be* a Black woman, that is, what does it mean to fulfill the promise of Black womanhood in the mass mediated American popular sphere? And moreover, what does it mean to tell one's sexual story as a Black woman on Ratchet TV?

In this chapter, I consider the discourses that circulate around the framing of "coming out" narratives of BQW, paying particular attention to those who disclose their sexuality on the Ratchet TV show *Love & Hip-Hop: Atlanta* (*LHHAtl*). I perform a critical discursive analysis of "coming out" storylines of Ariane Davis, Mimi Faust, and Joseline Hernandez featured throughout *LHHAtl*, as well as the reactions to these storylines on popular blogs that follow the cast members throughout production and the airing of the episodes. I focus on *LHHAtl* primarily because Atlanta, like DC, is considered a "Black Gay Mecca." Given how *queer* hip-hop is (McCune 2014, 80), it is not a surprise that members of Atlanta's thriving Black LGBTQ Scene would end up on *LHHAtl*. Atlanta's Black queer folk have dense multi-city social networks. During my ethnographic research, I traveled to Atlanta for its Black Pride Celebration, as it was a common destination for many of my informants over Labor Day. I've since gone to Atlanta's Black Pride thrice more, and on each trip saw members of the *LHHAtl* cast including Joseline Hernandez, Ariane Davis, and Mimi Faust. My examination of *LHHAtl* is rooted in a desire to understand how the producers of *LHHAtl* screen the same-sex desire of its cast members in the context of a show revolved around the telling of "authentic" sexual stories of Black heterosexual men and women.

"Coming out (of the closet)" is a phrase used in popular discourses to describe a particular kind of speech act associated with revealing something *queer*, or not quite heteronormative, in one's sexual identification or behaviors. The phrase holds particular significance in the age of neoliberal identity politics and middle-class normative formations which require people to reveal more and more of themselves: Tweet their inner thoughts, take a picture of every meal that they eat and every pound of weight they lose, and "Go Live" for the important moments in their life and the most mundane. "Coming out" is often treated as a finite, singular speech act that happens once during a linear process of a LGBTQ subject's "coming of age." Once complete, you are officially in a state of being "who you 'really' are" and can be counted among the modern gay subjects living their "truth." I contend here, however, that the Black queer (quare) work of ratchet cultural politics destabilizes notions of an authentic, modern gay subjectivity. In part because even when "coming out" narratives are used to fix Black queer identities into neat, bite-sized morsels, the actual work of *being* Black and queer (quare) often necessitates living in excess of homonormative or heteronormative logics.

I argue that the framing of Black women's "coming out" stories demonstrates a desire to contend with the fact that "real" narratives of Black life infrequently feature stories of Black women who are not sexually available to Black men. While hip-hop artists often claim to have "girlfriends who got girlfriends," those claims are situated within a "heteromasculinist" Playboy "fantasy where those women *remain* available to men (Chap. 3). Trying to frame "real" stories of Black women who partner with women on *LHHAtl* is complicated given the sexual politics of hip-hop. In the blogs and comments reacting to "coming out" stories on *LHHAtl*, another set of related anxieties emerge about Black women telling sexual stories, especially those stories which don't involve men. Following Mireille Miller-Young (2014) who examines the "natural marriage" of hip-hop and porn, I consider the commodification of sexual stories by Black women on Ratchet TV. I end by discussing the way Black women's disclosure of their sexuality is framed more broadly in the mainstream, and consider the way that one of my informants, Maegan, decided to manage the disclosure of her sexuality with her colleagues at work. This chapter utilizes all the arguments I've tried to make throughout this book. I will argue that the discourses which circulate around Black queer women deciding to "come out" in public including those related to notions of authenticity, the politics of respectability, the commodification of Black bodies, and conservative Christian morality demonstrate a great deal about the struggle Black women face collectively when simply attempting to *be* who they want to be, a struggle that happens inside and outside of ratchet cultural spaces.

#LHHAtl and the Commodification of Ratchet

The telling and retelling of what Kenneth Plummer (1995) refers to as "sexual stories" is incredibly profitable. Racialized stories, like sexual ones, are just as lucrative in Reality TV (Hasinoff 2008). *LHHAtl* capitalizes on both vis-a-vis hip-hop. Few American cultural institutions are considered as authentically Black as hip-hop. And, as Miller-Young (2014) has noted, the "pornification" of hip-hop has solidified the genre's link to commodified sex. In particular, the "soft-core" hip-hop music video typically relies on Black women in the role of "video vixens" or "video hos" being the sexual object who "drops it like it's hot" at the whim of the hip-hop "player." While *LHHAtl* does not typically show sex, it does rely on the insinuation of sexual situations. For those who have sexual relationships, they are often filmed lying in bed together, bathing together, entering into rooms with closed doors, going out on dates, and sharing other intimate moments. These moments are filmed with purposeful intent to appear and "feel" like real intimate moments and make the viewer forget that there is an entire production crew present. *LHHAtl*, and other reality television shows, promise audiences a glimpse into "real" intimate moments and genuine emotions that give rise to those moments (Aslama and Pantti 2006; Dubrofsky 2009). But more specifically, *LHHAtl* traffics in the promise of giving the audience a glimpse into the "real" romantic and sexual lives of Black people.[2]

Within hip-hop there are very few opportunities for Black women to create sustainable, lucrative careers. With few exception,[3] many of the women on *Love & Hip-Hop* were or currently work as "video vixens," sex workers including strippers, models, or aspiring artists. As one of the most notorious and popular sources for images of Black ratchet behavior—fighting, cursing, drinking, partying, and sassy meme generation—Ratchet TV has become a site where Black women who perform in the "illicit erotic economy," including video vixens and strippers, have been able to flourish in the post-industrial American economy which increasingly values (shameless) self-promotion[4] and entrepreneurship. Mireille Miller-Young (2010), studying Black women in pornography, formulated the concept of "illicit erotic economy" to describe Black women's participation in U.S. porn industry.

> Encompassing a range of informal and intimate labors, illicit erotic workers employ their sexual capital, talents, and knowledges to perform sexual service work on 'the margins' of an economy increasingly focused on the commodification of intimacy. (Miller-Young 2010, 6)

---

[2] Especially those who always seem to have things that cost money—fly bags, fresh weave, body augmentation, the latest fashion—but, seemingly, never work.

[3] Rasheeda Frost and Trina both had successful careers as local hip-hop artists in Atlanta and Miami.

[4] Such as "leaked" sex tapes which are purposefully sold to adult entertainment companies by the individuals featured in them.

Some Black women who are members of the Hip-Hop Nation use illicit erotic labor as means of supplementing their income, or as means of furthering their careers. This is most certainly true of rapper Cardi B, who was a stripper in New York before becoming a cast member on *Love & Hip-Hop: New York* and then, after several mixtapes, struck platinum multiple times with her record "Bodak Yellow." *In Touch Weekly*, an entertainment and gossip publication, posted the salaries of the top earners on *LHHAtl*. Joseline Hernandez earned $400,000 per season before her departure in Season 7, Rasheeda Frost earns $300,000, and Tommie Lee about $270,000 (Hernandez 2018). It pays to be ratchet. Ratchet TV represents one of the few places in American popular culture where one can see a range of Black women, including those who are not heterosexual, engaged in intimate, sexual relationships and getting paid to do so. I would argue that being on Ratchet TV is a form of illicit erotic labor. The Black women on Ratchet TV *sell* their racialized sexual stories, and much of the discourse surrounding their decisions to do so mirror those used to discredit and disparage Black women who are engaged in other forms of sexual labor.

As I mentioned earlier, *LHHAtl* is also one of the few mainstream sources for representations of Black queer folks. Arguably, however, even as the bodies and sexual stories that are screened become increasingly diverse, the commodification itself tends to flatten Black women and their lives into neat[5] narratives that fit episodic melodramatic arcs. For example, a cast member "coming out of the closet" presents a particular kind of storyline. It is rooted in the ethos of "keeping it real," and related to living "authentically" after previously living "inauthentically." Interestingly enough, in the context of conservative Black cultural life "coming out" can often represent moving from one backward identity to another: "in the closet" to "outwardly flaunting" one's sexuality. Following Jennifer Nash (2014), I'm not interested in focusing exclusively on how *LHHAtl* restricts or confines Black queer women's sexual stories. I'm actually interested in how they create opportunities to articulate a version of their "truth" on their own terms. I'm also interested in how discourses circulate about BQW's articulation of their non-normative sexualities within the context of *LHHAtl* especially given its hyperfocus on the commodification of "authentic" race and intimacy. How does the show balance por-

---

[5] By which I simply mean to flag how the producers edit complex and otherwise messy storylines to ensure that we're able to follow the convoluted reality of cast members lives.

traying "realistic" versions of non-heteronormative Black female sexuality in hip-hop when *in reality* Black female sexuality in hip-hop is under so many constraints linked to the assumption that all Black women are always sexually available to Black men?

#LHHAtl's BQW's Coming Out

In the first season of *LHHAtl*, we are introduced to Oluremi Fela James (Mimi Faust) who is the longtime partner of Steven Jordan (Stevie J), a four-time Grammy award winning record producer best known for his work in the 1990s under P. Diddy's Bad Boy record label. Mimi is the mother of (one of five of) Stevie J's children, Eva, and entrepreneur who ran a small housekeeping service. While Mimi and Stevie weren't married, they were in a relationship intended to be monogamous. Stevie meets a young(er) Puerto Rican woman named Stenellica Juneann Bettencourt (Joseline Hernandez) at a strip club who rocks the foundation of his relationship with Mimi. Joseline had become a well-known erotic dancer with a large following who had set up shop in Atlanta which has a thriving strip club and hip-hop scene attracting rappers, professional athletes, and the "everyday man" looking to see performances by top acts in exotic dancing. Stevie J enters into a business relationship with Joseline, helping her transition into a new career as a rapper. And in true melodramatic fashion, what the audience thought would happen, does indeed transpire: the two end up having an affair. Mimi finds out and the two women spend the first season jousting with one another, and with Stevie, who refuses to choose between the two women. Mimi's longtime friend and confidant Ariane, a mixologist,[6] is there every step of the way. In addition to their heated arguments and petty jabs, each of these women expresses same-sex desire in the show. For Ratchet TV, the more one's sexual life deviates from what is considered the "norm" in both mainstream (white) American life and in Black middle-class life—that is, the more ratchet one's life and behavior can be—the more those sexual stories promise to both disgust and excite the viewer, and the greater the potential for profit. Their "messy" sexual identities create unique storylines, and activate ratchet/boojie cultural political struggles over what it means to be a morally upright, positive representation of Black womanhood.

[6] A boojie way of saying, "bartender."

Ariane Comes Out for K. Michelle

Ariane is a supporting cast member on *LHHAtl*. As a supporting cast member, her value rests on her ability to bolster the storylines of other cast members on the show. She is typically characterized as the supportive, but somewhat "messy," friend of Mimi who often maintains friendships with other people on the cast who are sometimes at odds with one another. Conveniently, she also creates opportunities for feuding people to be in the same space where she often asks them to "be nice." This is valuable in the context of Ratchet TV, because of the potential for these moments to go wrong, and thus produce the "money shot." During Season 2, Ariane proved her value by ensuring K. Michelle and Mimi, who two feuded throughout much of Season 2, stayed in close proximity. Ariane added additional value by being the first member of the *LHHAtl* cast to share on camera that she was not heterosexual. Her willingness to have the moment she tells K. Michelle—not her closest friend on the show, Mimi—about her non-heteronormative sexual identity is an important moment to consider in part because it reveals the way that Ratchet TV capitalizes on the stories of lesbians and bisexual women while not radically shifting the conversations about them within hip-hop or Black cultural spaces.

In the context of the show, what makes K. Michelle ratchet is her Southernness and accompanying Southern accent, her surgically augmented butt, her willingness to *start* physical confrontations, and her penchant for dishing out verbal lashings on anyone bold enough to challenge her. During a meeting with her record label, we witness representatives from the label tell her that she needs to "change her image," because her fan base did not approve of her (ratchet) behavior. She's told that she needs to "tone it down," not only on camera, but also on Twitter, and other places where her "mouth" might land her in the middle of drama. It is one of a handful of moments where we witness a cast member be self-reflective about their ratchet behavior and performance. For K. Michelle, her self-reflection is directly related to her ability to make money outside of what she makes on *LHHAtl*. She agrees to "do better" and to not let her fans down. From that moment on, we see a noticeable shift in her behavior, or at least in what is captured by the cameras. She doesn't get into any further fights and she even apologizes to Mimi for hitting her during one of their arguments. Nothing changes about her sexual behavior, because like Ariane, K. Michelle is not, to the audience's knowledge, engaged in any serious dating relationships during the show.

The reason for this, she explains in the first episode of Season 2, is because her "pussy is broken." Her inability to enjoy penetrative sex, as she explains it, as well as the demands of her burgeoning music career, including needing to "behave," provides a reason for the noticeable absence of her love life being screened on the show. K. Michelle's willingness to talk openly and frequently about not having sex, however, makes her "broken pussy" storyline valuable throughout the show that relies on telling "sexual stories" of one kind or another. Over the course of the season, K. Michelle tries various things to "wake up" her vagina. "It don't even like people," she says before getting her vagina "bedazzled" at a spa. She even takes cameras with her when goes to a medical specialist to talk about her options for "fixing" the issue, her inability to naturally produce lubrication since ending things with her previous partner. Ariane, on the other hand, seemingly had no love life, but there was no stated reason. And Ariane's career as a mixologist seemed stagnant. She'd expressed an interest in becoming a singer, but it did not materialize after failing at an open audition to become one of K. Michelle's background singers for her then upcoming tour.

With only two episodes of the show's second season remaining, Ariane and Mimi visit K. Michelle's apartment who tells them she's moving to New York to be closer to her management team, record label, and recording studio as the next step to get more serious about her music career.[7] K. Michelle hopes the fresh start and new city will also help her find love. Mimi and Ariane wish her well, and Ariane adds, "I'm really happy for you. You know, I'm still pursuing those things I'm passionate about. My music, mixology, women." Mimi, looking confused, but certainly not surprised, responds, "What?"

After some playful banter including a snippy, "I didn't stutter" from Ariane, K. Michelle asks, "What you mean you *want* women? Where?" To which Ariane responds, "In my bed." The three women laugh and K. Michelle asks "Y'all wasn't gon' tell me?" Again, Mimi, looking more stunned that she chose to tell K. Michelle than surprised at the news, asks Ariane, while gesturing and looking back and forth between she and K. Michelle asks, "Are you sure *this* what you want to be doing?" The question doesn't appear to be related to whether or not Ariane wants to be with women, but instead whether she was sure that she wanted to disclose this information to K. Michelle and to the audience at home. Ariane

---

[7] *Love & Hip-Hop: Atlanta*, Season 2, Episode 13.

and Mimi clearly had a conversation about her sexuality, but it was not clear, at least to Mimi that Ariane intended to share that information with the world or K. Michelle, who had exhibited homophobic behavior toward several people on the show up to that point.

K. Michelle previously referred to the marriage between Kirk Frost and rapper Rasheeda (a woman whom she had earlier thrown a candle at) as a "lesbian relationship," and posited that his "three earrings" were proof that he "wasn't right." Later, during a music video shoot for hip-hop artist Johnny and Mimi's boyfriend Nikko, K. Michelle comes to set and asks loudly, "Why is Johnny rapping about women? He like men!" She and Ariane discuss rumors each of them had heard about Johnny, just as Johnny and Nikko walk in having heard K. Michelle's loud exclamation. The three engage in a heated argument that gets broken up by security. As she's being escorted out, K. Michelle insinuates that something was going on between Nikko and Johnny because they shared an apartment. Something, in her mind, was "suspicious" (i.e. seemingly gay) about the two cohabitating, and about them *not* having a gang of "video hos" for their video. How could they be living "baller" lifestyles? To her, something simply "wasn't right."[8] K. Michelle collapses their sexuality, like Kirk's, onto notions of authenticity and uses "gayness" as a way of calling out something in them that she found to be "fake" about their racialized and gendered performances of Black hip-hop masculinity. While she regularly claimed to not have a problem with gay people, K. Michelle parrots the homophobic "down-low" discourse about Black gay and bisexual men that remains fairly common within Black sexual political conversations. When the episode aired, K. Michelle got in front of the potential backlash and reached out to B. Scott, a popular gossip blogger, echoing her sentiment from the show which B. Scott posted on her blog.

> I don't have a problem with anybody being gay, but I have a major problem with someone being on the down low and misleading other people. I've been through my situation with a girl in the past and I was very honest and

---

[8] In August 2014, Johnny said in an interview with gossip blogger Jamari Fox that Nikko wasn't as flush with cash as he wanted to appear on the show. Johnny says that he paid for the luxury two-bedroom apartment in Atlantic Station, a new development near mid-town Atlanta where the two stayed during the show's filming. He also paid for the music video the two made, and he was in creative control of the project. Fox, Jamari, "Interview: Johnny Crome 'Lies and HipHop'." Accessed July 19, 2018. http://insidejamarifox.com/interview-johnny-crome-lies-and-hiphop-atlanta/.

open about it. I don't want people to think I was being insensitive to his sexuality, because that's not the case. We're in a society now where we're open. If you know that you're gay, then you need to be that and own it ... that's just my opinion. There's nothing wrong with being gay. At the end of the day, I wasn't trying to ruin Mimi's love life. I was just trying to be a friend and let her know about some things I had heard out of concern for a friend. I would never call anybody gay for no reason and I'm not a judgmental person.

K. Michelle's "issue" isn't their sexuality, she explains. Her issue is with these men potentially being on the "down-low." As C. Riley Snorton has explained, melodrama is often a vehicle for "dramatizing moral code" (Snorton 2014, 4). She invents, in melodramatic fashion a rumor about Johnny's sexuality, and then implies that they are living together in some "down low bachelor pad." Then, she says that men who are not willing to be "open" about their sexuality given how "open" society is, are *dangerous*. Their potential threat warrants her "concern" for her friend, Mimi. K. Michelle positions herself as an expert and as one who couldn't possibly be homophobic because she herself had a romantic and sexual relationship with a woman and told people about it. It was her opinion that other people should do the same since there's "nothing wrong with being gay." However, as Marc Lamont Hill explains, questions about a Black man in hip-hop's sexuality can have disastrous effects (Hill 2009). Big Daddy Kane suffered permanent damage to his career after untruthful rumors were spread about his HIV status and sexual orientation. E. Patrick Johnson argues that homosexuality in Black men in particular has been used to mark Black gay men as *in*authentic and improper Black male subjects. Black men who engage in homosexual behavior, who express desire for other men are treated as not Black enough, and have certainly been cast as not hip-hop by the likes of people like Busta Rhymes and Lord Jamar. K. Michelle's public questioning of these men's sexuality within hip-hop culture is precisely the kind of down-low melodrama that "recirculate racial, gender, and sexual myths that produce down-low men as either morally corrupt predators or victims of a pathological culture (i.e., blackness) that repudiates queer identities" (Snorton 2014, 4). It also begs the question: *how* would she respond to Ariane?

Once the laughter dissipates, K. Michelle says "I like girls too. During the holidays." To which Ariane responds, "Oh, well, Labor Day is 'bout to be here, you want to find you one?" The three women share a hearty laugh, and Ariane's (and K. Michelle's) "coming out" is neatly wrapped in levity. Ariane says during her confessional taped after the show filmed, "It wasn't anything new. I just wanted her to know. So, there it is. Still same ol' Ariane." Ariane's disclosure to K. Michelle, was not *insignificant* even though the producers and perhaps Ariane, attempt to frame it as such. The moment was significant, because it was unclear how K. Michelle would react given her casual use of homophobic discourse in the case of Johnny, Nikko, Kirk, and Rasheeda. The way that the moment is framed—casual, whimsical even—and in K. Michelle's home during a "private moment" shared with friends, allows us to read the disclosure as an opportunity to "prove" who she really is: *not* homophobic, though it also had the potential to be scene that produced Ratchet TV "the money shot." This moment also demonstrates the difference in the way non-heterosexuality in men and women is treated in hip-hop. For men in hip-hop, accusations of homosexual behavior or identity, can damage their careers. For women, as long as they maintain their sexual availability to men, their non-normative sexuality can be permitted. K. Michelle's reaction to Ariane, including her own disclosure that she likes women, follows this discursive pattern. More importantly, however, Ariane's "coming out" moment wasn't for her. It was a way of offering K. Michelle a way to recuperate her image.

Joseline Comes Out for No One

Joseline's career as an exotic dancer was well established before meeting Stevie J, but she had ambitions of becoming a music artist and started working with Stevie J to help realize those dreams. The show works to cast her *singularly* in the role of the exotic, home-wrecking "freak" opposite Mimi's role as wholesome, home-making baby mama. In Season 2, we learn that Joseline is not heterosexual and enjoys having sex with women. What is interesting about Joseline's disclosure is that even though producers attempt to frame her sexuality as *only* being in service of Stevie, their attempts consistently fail. She is unruly. And that unruliness makes her a perfect subject for Ratchet TV, but it also means that she consistently exceeds the boundaries of a narrative that attempts to fix heterosexuality onto her or onto stories of "love" within hip-hop. Arguably, there is something extremely homoerotic about hip-hop (McCune 2014), and Joseline consistently exposes the homoeroticism implicit in the ways Black women relate to one another within hip-hop contexts (Chap. 3).

In the last episode before the finale of Season 2, K. Michelle has a dinner with the women from Atlanta whom she was directly or tangentially connected to throughout the season including Ariane and Joseline. Despite Joseline and Mimi's contentious relationship, K. Michelle met and liked Joseline and the two began a friendship (as Mimi's friend, K. Michelle might have avoided developing a friendship with the woman who "stole" Mimi's man). At dinner, K. Michelle informs the women that she's moving and Ariane uses the opportunity to "come out" to the larger group. She receives wide-eyed responses from the women and then Joseline responds, "Oh, I mean. I like *bleep* [pussy] too, but I *need* *bleep* [dick]." Her emphatic *pussy* and *dick* were replaced with a "bleep" for the home audience, but incited laughter and playful banter from the women at the table. Joseline highjacks Ariane's moment to *perform* the proper way of being "honest," and morally upright as a Black lesbian or gay person. No matter the consequences or the risks that your disclosure may pose, you must tell everyone in your social circle that you're not heterosexual and allow them to the chance to ask questions and comment. Joseline treats "coming out" as perfunctory and unnecessarily performative. Where Ariane's "coming out" is framed as proof that K. Michelle and the other main cast members (and by extension the show's producers) are "fine" with gay/lesbian people, Joseline's unexpected, ratchet disclosure simply confirms she is a "freak."

One of Joseline's most notorious stunts on stage during her time as a stripper included engaging in lesbian sex on stage with fellow strippers. She'd simulate licking their vaginas for the crowd in various positions and simulate other sex acts with both men and women. Filmed anonymously at one of her performances, a video of her act was uploaded to WorldStarHipHop.com in August of 2014. WorldStarHipHop.com is a user content driven gossip website. The release of the video coincided with the airing of Season 3 of *LHHAtl*. The edited video featured Joseline engaging in (simulated?) oral sex with another stripper, and giving a lap dance that included simulated oral sex with a man. It also showed her backstage holding a large clear trash bag filled with bills of various denominations and telling someone off-camera named "Pop," that she'd count it after she was done dancing. For the rest of Joseline's run on *LHHAtl* we learn that she regularly has sex with women with and *without* Stevie J. She admits on multiple occasions that she had sex with women when she and Stevie were "on breaks." During Season 4, we learn that a new cast member, Jessica Dime had a sexual relationship with Joseline. And during

Season 5, Joseline propositioned another cast member, Tommie, while cameras rolled. She would later claim to have had sex with Tommie when the cameras stopped rolling.

In January of 2017, after Joseline and Stevie break up and after the birth of her first child (Stevie's sixth), she appeared on the daytime talk show *The Real*. She and the hosts discuss motherhood, and life apart from the reality show. Unlike the context of *LHHAtl* where Joseline is exclusively a "freak," *The Real* attempted to also frame Joseline as a "new mom" her consistent evocation of ratchet topics of conversation prevented the hosts from using this; she was a "freak" as well. One of the co-hosts, Tamera Mowry[9] says that she is suspicious of bisexuality and expresses her uncertainty about whether it could even be a legitimate formation for one's sexual desire. Echoing homophobic discourses that posit that people who engage in sex with both men and women are self-indulgent, she says "I'm trying to understand how you can say you enjoy sex with a man, but still want to have sex with a woman." Joseline expertly deflects, and instead of responding to the homophobic and bi-phobic remark framed as a question, she says that she's had a crush on Tamera since she was a child, and if Tamera was confused about it, she would be happy to just "show her." She added, "and you don't have to worry about anyone else in the bed, it would just be me." Tamera displays both surprise and embarrassment at Joseline's proposition.

Marc Lamont Hill argues that there is difference in the way men and women in hip-hop are treated when rumors circulate about their non-heterosexuality. He argues that it is *not* because "women occupy a privileged position within hip-hop culture. On the contrary, women are merely beholden to different controlling images, such as the temptress, the mammy, the whore, or the baby momma, all of which delimit possibilities for identity development and performance within the rap world" (Hill 2009, 31). The controlling images related to Black women in hip-hop assume that they are always sexually available to men (even if they like girls). These particular controlling images work to constrain the possibilities for their participation in hip-hop and "these discursive strictures inform and reflect a broader public pedagogy that calls into question the very notion of a fully human Black female subject" (Hill 2009, 31). This

---

[9] Tamera Mowry was a child actor staring in a show with her twin sister Tia called *Sister, Sister*.

is an important distinction to parse out, but it does not account for the differential ways that homophobia is applied to women in hip-hop.

It is precisely because Ariane, K. Michelle, and Joseline's sexuality and gender performance do not break too far from cultural expectations—the temptress, the freak, and the baby mama, that they can talk about "liking girls" but also why doing so is simply understood to be evidence of their ratchetness. It is also why K. Michelle can be "happy" for her girl friend who "comes out" to her, but use "gay" as an epithet to discount Black men's masculinity and hip-hop "realness." The comments section of Bossip.com for this episode would suggest that the fear that many Black women express about the portrayal of Black women on Ratchet TV is not unfounded. Users regularly comment on Black womanhood when opining about individual storylines of the shows. One of the enduring themes across the comments sections on Bossip.com where the women cast members talk about their lesbian or bisexuality are commentators who suggest similar sentiments to users below.

> **Wepo1:** It seems like the majority of black women are gay nowadays!
> **MiMiSo:** MAJORITY OF BLACK WOMEN ARE NOT GAY! DONT LET THE IGNORANCE OF TV FOOL YOU INTO THINKING MAJORITY OF ANY RACE IS GAY (THEY ARE A SMALL GROUP) DESPITE WHAT BRAVO, RATCHET TV IS PUTTING OUT THERE! THEY WANT YOU TO DISAPPEAR AND WHAT BETTER WAY TO DO THAT …. BY LIVING A FOUL LIFE STYLE AND TRUST ME! DONT BELIEVE THE SMOKING MIRRORS, HOLLYWOOD IS UP TO NO GOOD BUT THE MAJORITY OF EVERYBODY RACE KNOW EXACTLY WHAT IS GOING ON! NO SCIENCE TESTING WILL STOP A DOMINATING RACE![10]

MiMiSo's comment is rooted in an ideological investment in Black patriarchy, and reads not unlike the anti-gay discourses of the 1960s, 1970s, and 1980s that were inspired by Black Nationalism and the Black Arts Movement. In the 1980s, the HIV/AIDS epidemic was decimating Black gay communities and independent, single Black women were being demonized in Reagan-era Conservative politics and policies. It reads as a discursive artifact of the homophobic conspiracy theories such as that

---

[10] Comment section, "Joseline (LHHA) Talks Being Bi, Stevie J Being Gay, And More [Video]" Published May 9, 2013. https://bossip.com/771110/joseline-lhha-talks-being-bi-stevie-j-being-gay-and-more-video/.

which was espoused by Eldridge Cleaver, that Negro homosexuals had a "death wish," and the homophobic idea that gayness was introduced to Black populations by white people as a means of "destroying" the Black race (Johnson 2003a, 62). According to MiMiSo, Ratchet TV is a part of the "smoke and mirrors" act that makes people believe that Black women are gay. *Ratchet* functions for MiMiSo as a way to articulate the kind of Black woman who refuses to "behave": the foul, petulant women who act out of selfish desire. They participate in Hollywood's attempt to make Black people "disappear" and their gayness points to their refusal to "reproduce the race."

Joseline does not identify as "gay," but Wepo1 and MiMiSo both are indifferent to Joseline's *bisexuality*. In fact, they both are only interested in what they find as abnormal, her sexual desire for women. Bisexuality is erased as a legitimate form of eroticism altogether. This is not uncommon. In fact, stereotypes about people who are bisexual are not unlike those leveled at people considered to be ratchet more generally: they are promiscuous, incapable of monogamous relationships, and are "hypersexual." Another important bi-phobic stereotype that may be at play is that bisexuality is a "phase" toward an actual gay sexual identity (Walker 2014). Bisexuality in women, especially in its increasing visibility on Ratchet TV, has come to stand in for the epitome of ratchet Black female sexuality. Part of the fear that Black women express around the representation of Black womanhood on Ratchet TV is connected to their sexuality. It is absurd to assume that the *majority* of Black women are gay, or even bisexual, but what Wepo1 is reacting to might very well be the way that Black women's homoeroticism is built into hip-hop, and how hip-hop has attempted to capitalize off of Black women's non-heteronormative sexualities.

Black women's same-sex desire is often exploited in hip-hop (Chap. 3), and thus public discourse about that same-sex desire is often posited as being purely a "performance" for men, as opposed to authentic. Consider that twerkin', poppin', dippin', droppin',[11] and other dance moves which emphasize the isolation of one's hips and butt, are often associated with Black women's ratchet behavior. In fact, Gaunt (2015) discusses how the comments left on YouTube videos of young Black girls who twerk, pop, dip, and drop for the camera often feature commentators who refer to the girls and/or their behavior as ratchet. Young Black women in this context are ratchet because of their self-presentation of sexuality for public con-

---

[11] See Beyoncé's song "Check on it" from her 2006 album *B'Day*.

sumption. *Ratchet* is used as an attempt to discipline their self-representation. However, as Gaunt (2015) instructs us, this form of play—twerking, dipping, poppin' for others—is not particularly new for young Black girls, nor does it necessarily relate to (hetero)sexual desire. Twerking, dippin, and poppin are "games" young Black girls play, typically in homosocial settings. What was new was that they recorded them and posted the videos to YouTube where they exist in a digital repository that can be viewed by anyone, anywhere—losing their original context as forms of play and self-discovery. The result is that a game young girls once played in semi-private settings, with a few girlfriends, gets designated as ratchet by people who understand very little about growing up as a little Black girl. These games, whether seen in the context of the girl's bathroom in a middle-school (where I played) or on YouTube, are treated as proof of Black women's inherent "hypersexuality"; proof that they are "ghetto," and in need of proper middle-class values and training to correct their behavior. In both cases, old and new, however, what remains constant is young Black women's desire to exercise their mastery of their bodies. Kyra Gaunt (2015) uses the term "auto-sexuality," borrowed from anthropologist Dan Miller, to describe one important feature of the phenomenon of Black girls who make twerking videos on YouTube (Gaunt 205, 249). "Auto-sexuality … [is] the self-presentation of sexuality in social occasions, particularly for women, that does not require the attention of a male gaze or male interactions nor is it necessarily an act of lesbianism. Its self-expression of erotic displays" (Gaunt 2015, 249). In her definition, Gaunt (2015) emphasizes that this particular form of self-presentation need not be for the expressed purposes of the 'male gaze,' nor an act of lesbianism. While this is true, I want to call attention to the homoerotic nature Black women's auto-sexuality implied by the fact that these expressions are done typically in homosocial environments. This practice could be extended to Black women hip-hop performers such as Nicki Minaj, whose song "I Endorse These Strippers," or Rihanna's "Throw it Up" were celebrations of women enjoying other women's erotic labor at a strip club.

I draw attention to this aspect of the practice of auto-sexuality, because so many women and girls are denied access to means of expressing homoerotic desires. Stallings argues that "the ordering of black female bodies and the attempt to silence their voices and make absent their desires happens through one specific means: language" (Stallings 2007, 33). Whether twerking for other women, going to a strip club and making rain, or grabbing your best friend's ass, instructing her to "throw it in a circle," constitute acts of lesbianism or not, one can still argue that it is embedded within a network of homoerotics. Homoeroticism, defined simply and loosely here, refers to the explicit or inexplicit sexual relations and performances between two individuals of the same gender. Recognizing the homoeroticism in these acts allows us to place what these Black women do for their girls, within a historical context of Black women using homoeroticism to make particular claims about their sexuality.

Blues women of the early twentieth century offer the most compelling evidence of the ways that Black women have utilized homoeroticism as a means of exercising sexual freedom. Black women blues artists such as Gertrude "Ma" Rainey and Bessie Smith maintained sexual and emotional relations with both men and women, and they sang songs that dared people to question their sexuality (Carby 1998; DuCille 1993; Johnson 2003b, 2014; Davis 1998). It wasn't just that their Blues lyrics were deeply invested in repositioning Black sexuality and Black sexual freedom within the realm of the public sphere, on front street, but that their actual lived experiences and practices of non-normative sexuality offered a means of excising from normative protocols about Black women's need to be sexually and morally upright—even though being morally upright was not a protective factor against white supremacist patriarchal violence against women—a representation of Black women's sexuality that could be controlled exclusively *by* Black women. Blues women were seen as inappropriate, disdainful, and downright sinful by the morally upright women of the day, club women and other middle-class good Christian women for engaging in this raucous, lustful behavior and then having the nerve to get on stage where they made a living, and *talk* about it.

Blues women would prepare the way for the appearance of Black women such as Rihanna who can sing about going to the strip club with her friends,[12] Nicki Minaj "endorsing" strippers,[13] and Joseline openly talking about her bisexuality. In turn, these figures make it possible for the contemporary Black queer women to see themselves within the context of hip-hop, boldly claiming hip-hop as a sensibility that has room for the lesbian, bisexual, and queer woman. And, while people may hate her and "what she represents" for Black womanhood, Joseline is not doing anything particularly different than other Black women who have tried to use their voices to make their desires legible in hip-hop.

---

[12] Rihanna's "Throw it Up" (2012).
[13] Nicki Minaj, "I Endorse These Strippers" (2010).

Mimi Comes Out for Herself

In 2013, a "sex tape" emerged featuring Mimi Faust, and her then boyfriend, Nikko London. Steve Harvey, on his nationally syndicated radio program chimed in on Mimi's sex tape. Admonishing her as a woman and single mother for choosing to participate in the filming of pornography for "fame" and money. He goes on to offer a "lesson" to the young women listening: "This thing every man got to have: your body. Your precious jewel. You're sitting on a gold mine. Please act like it, young ladies. Act like you're sitting on a gold mine, because it is what every man is after. And we will pay dearly for it." As Terrell Jermaine Star on Newsone.com correctly points out, Harvey does not talk about Nikko, the man whom Mimi is having sex with. He doesn't mention any damage to his reputation. Harvey reserves his judgment for Mimi. What's so fascinating, however, is Harvey's recognition of what Mireille Miller-Young refers to as "brown sugar."

Harvey's critique of Mimi and other Black women who engage in sex (before marriage? for money?) is wrapped up in discourses of capitalist heteropatriarchy. Harvey, and others like him, don't hear or see their hypocrisy. Black women are "sitting on a gold mine," something that "every man is after," and something that they "will pay dearly for." This language actually objectifies Black women's vaginas. It metaphorically turns it into a mine, a place for mining a precious resource. Black women are not supposed to be able to benefit from this "gold mine," except where access to it can be exchanged for heterosexual marriage (or a big diamond). Every man will "pay" for access to a Black women's body, and yet, Black women are not supposed to actually *sell* that access, because doing so would make you a ho. The logic goes that Black women are supposed to give "it" away to the *one* man who really "deserves it."

Oretha Winston of Elev8, a Christian "entertainment" blog says:

> When young ladies aspire to be strippers and can be seen "twerking" at school dances we haven't just jumped the shark we have fallen back into the plantation fields. When you allow your sexual exploits to be "entertainment" whether for personal pleasure or public consumption, you place yourself on a stockade. You take away the intimate portion of what is supposed to be a loving human act and make it merely physical, animalistic behavior.

Lisa B. Thompson in her book *Beyond the Black Lady: Sexuality and the New African American Middle Class*, argues that "it is a privilege for a black woman to occupy the role as the virgin mother or even pampered homemaker" (Thompson 2009, 84). Thus, Black women who appear in public who even resemble that image are saddled with a great deal of responsibility for maintaining said image that is rooted in Black middle-class (Christian) heteronormative values. When we're introduced to Mimi, she is packaged as the next best thing to a "virgin mother" and "pampered homemaker." She is the longtime, faithful girlfriend of Stevie J who owned a cleaning service. She was the working mother who was waiting for the father of her child to "do right" so that they can live as a "family." Winston's admonishment of Mimi takes the form of an "open letter." She wags her finger at Mimi for participating in the sex tape because she's a *mother*, a *Black* mother at that, in a seemingly privileged position. Mimi is famous (at least well-known in the realm of Black entertainment) and a Black mother engaging in ratchet behavior for profit. Indeed, staging a sex tape and selling it to one of the most successful adult entertainment companies in the country, Vivid, is not the kind of behavior one would expect from a "Black lady." Neither is sexual relationships with women.

During Season 5 which aired in 2016, Mimi's first scene is shot in Duluth, GA at K1 Speed, an indoor go-cart race track. Over romantic music, Mimi steps out of her race cart and off the track. Flanking her is someone wearing a race car helmet, their face obscured. Mimi, in her monologue explains: "It's my boo's birthday and we are celebrating all weekend long. That's right. I gotta new boo and *they* are **nothing** like Nikko. After all the lies and manipulation, I didn't know if I was ready for a new relationship. And then, I meet Chris." Over dramatic music, "Chris" takes off their helmet. Chris appears to be a masculine of center woman. The two talk over drinks near the track.

Mimi: I do have something planned. I'm throwing you a birthday party, and I'm inviting all my friends.
Chris: Are you nervous?
Mimi: No.
Chris: About coming out as a lesbian?
Mimi: I don't feel like I'm coming out as anything. This is what I want to do, and I really don't care who feels what about it.
Chris: That's the sexiest thing about you, is you don't really care.
Mimi: *blurred gesture* *Bleep* [Fuck 'em]

Mimi says she doesn't feel like she's "coming out" as a lesbian, but the show certainly frames her as "coming out" as lesbian for the audience by dramatizing Chris's gender reveal. And later, at the birthday where Mimi invites all *her* friends, not Chris' friends. In anticipation for meeting Mimi's boo, the cast members comment on how they hope the new man/he/him/his is better than Nikko. Mimi walks into the club where the party is held, her arm locked with Ariane. They are flanked by two men who wear white suits. Over, light, playful music, Mimi's friends look on. She takes the microphone and thanks people for coming out. She says, "I want to thank all you guys for coming out. I'm throwing a birthday party for my boo, Chris. Kept it on the low, 'cause you know, you put shit out there it kinda gets fucked up so. I'm ready to just share. I'm just happy, and I haven't been happy in a long time." The music pauses, for dramatic effect, and then there are cheers. Tommie, a new cast member says, "Oh, shit. I thought it was a dude!" The camera pans to Rasheeda who looks stunned. Then she turns away. A man with them, turban wrapped around his head, continues to look on, like, "no, she didn't." In a cutaway to Rasheeda's monologue, she explains her reaction, "Like, really bitch? It's a female. You always pulling some shit out the bag. I never had a clue." In the post-show confessional Mimi says, "I done dealt with a lot of shit in my time. And guess what? I'm happy right now. That's why I got a girlfriend, okay.[14]"

Chris explains in the confessional, over shots of her getting a lap dance by a stripper and Mimi talking on the microphone at the party, "So Mimi has finally stepped out of the closet after a year of secrecy. I'm not mad, I

---

[14] LHHAtl treatment of Mimi's "coming out" is very much in contrast to the later treatment Miles Brocks, a cast member on Love & Hip-Hop: Hollywood. In 2017, following the episode titled "The Truth," Miles Brock, a Los Angeles producer and rapper "comes out" on Love & Hip-Hop: Hollywood during its second season, they aired a special, one-hour program called Love & Hip-Hop: Out in Hip-Hop during which they talked about "LGBT issues" within the Black community broadly, and the hip-hop community specifically. Miles is a Black man who has had sexual and romantic relationships with both men and women, however, this is unrecognizable within the representational framework of hip-hop. Instead, they wrapped Mile's sexual story within a familiar frame: the closeted, "down-low" (DL) brother finally "comes out" (Eguchi et al. 2018). Part of what this framing does is allow for the audience, primarily heterosexual Black women, to be gratified by their "support" for him being "honest." It is clear, however, that their support is conditional and is "less about [Miles] being who [he] 'really' is" and more about him revealing himself for the world to see and judge (Eguchi et al. 2018). Arguably, the franchise Love & Hip-Hop (LHH) has reproduced problematic discourses about "authenticity," "honesty," and "morality" of Black lesbian, gay, bisexual, as well as trans men and women.

know she went through hell and back with Nikko. She didn't want people in her business. So, it's official now. Happy birthday to me." Mimi does not use lesbian or any other word to describe her sexual identity, but the show dramatizes the "reveal" of Chris around their presumed gender and thus Mimi's presumed sexual identity, lesbian.

Mimi's sexuality is further complicated by the fact that we later learn that Chris does not identify as a woman, but as trans, something that seemingly unfolds during the filming. The first time we see Chris, they ask Mimi how she's feeling about coming out as "a lesbian," implying that they are in a same-gender relationship. But in the very next episode, when we see Chris and Ariane, Mimi's best friend, talking for the first time, Ariane takes an uncharacteristically hostile posture toward Chris that is clearly rooted in transphobia. Throughout their conversation, Ariane purposefully misgenders Chris, calls them by their given name rather than Chris, and even suggests that they're in the middle of an "identity crisis," questioning the legitimacy of their trans identity.

The responses on Bossip.com to Mimi's "coming out" are rooted in charges of her using her sexuality as a means of staying on the show (a charge that is often leveled at cast members who are not heterosexual or gender conforming).

jenn: Nikko turn all his old bytches ghey!

Tray: Wasn't she happy in the freaky flick? Like I said anything to stay on that show. Disgrace and has a child. It should be illegal to claim you're born gay and keep flip flopping... How you ask for all these rights and then keep changing your mind. Wish I could [t]urn my black on and off especially when I go to the bank.

Janey (disqus_0m8Ak1z5ON): What if she's happy though?

Emjay: I wonder how much Mona paying her......

Tray: Exactly!!!! She has no dignity! That poor child of hers. How about be so tired of men and just focus on your child for a while.

Iamsheeee: Mimi is down for ANYTHING just for some type of storyline it's pathetic ☹.[15]

[15] "#LHHATL (Love & Hip Hop ATL) Season 5 Ep.1: Mimi's New Girlfriend, Scrappy's Assistant, And More [Video]" Posted April 5, 2016. Last accessed on August 1, 2018. https://bossip.com/1299723/lhhatl-love-hip-hop-atl-season-5-ep-1-mimis-new-girlfriend-scrappys-assistant-and-more-video/.

Tray responds, "She has no dignity! That poor child of hers." For Tray, Mimi's "flip flop" of her sexuality is related to being "tired" of the men she's previously dated. This is a common myth of lesbian and bisexual women rooted in the gender hegemonic ideology *women need men*. When applied to issues of women's non-normative sexualities, it presupposes that all women's sexual behaviors are connected to men in some way. They are having sexual relationships with women because: they haven't had the "right" man; they are "tired" of men; or, in the case of commentator jenn, their sexualities are the direct result of men's ability to "turn them" as if there's some switch some men have access to change someone's sexuality. Interestingly enough, this critique of Mimi was frequently paired with questions of Mimi's ability to parent. Tray in two separate comments mentions Mimi's child three times: "disgrace and has a child," "poor child," "just focus on your child for a while." Again, we see her Black motherhood here as something that *should* tether her to both men and morality, but they do not, because she's ratchet. Another user, Janey cuts in to ask what if she is actually happy. Throughout the "coming out" moments, Mimi talks about "finally" being "happy." But Tray said, as a response for Mimi's insistence that she's happy, "Wasn't she happy in that freaky flick?"

The charge here is that since Mimi has been in a pornographic film, she is willing to "do anything" to make money including faking being gay. If she would do porn, of course she'd admit to being gay. Tray goes one step further by suggesting that bisexuality should be made illegal. Not only is bisexuality treated as immoral and at odds with motherhood, but it is treated as a money driven "choice" that can be "turned on and off." Ignorant to the actual economic conditions or legal status of LGBTQ people who can legally be fired from their jobs on account of their gender or sexual identity because federal law does not prohibit private employers from discriminating against people based on gender identity or sexual identity, Tray wishes they could "turn off" their Blackness when they go to the bank. The implication here is that being queer is as economically advantageous as being white. Tray, of course, fails to recognize the irony here. Mimi is queer *and* Black.

In August 2015, followers of *LHHAtl* learned that longtime rivals and adversaries Mimi and Joseline had previously had sex around the time they met prior to the airing of the first season of the show.[16] According to Stevie, he was "asleep" in the bed where Joseline was "eating Mimi's pussy," or engaging in oral sex with her. Stevie woke up and asked her to move aside so that he could penetrate Mimi. However, their sexual encounter did not have the effect of creating an amicable relationship between the three, and when Joseline talks of the encounter during Season 5, it inspires numerous interviews about the topic. Mimi went to Bossip.com to give an interview to discuss what had been referred to as a "threesome." Mimi does not agree with this particular description in large part because she says that she didn't reciprocate. She asks, "Does anyone know the definition of a threesome? Someone eating your vagina is not considered a threesome. It's just someone eating your vagina." As one might imagine, people had a lot to say in the comments section of the YouTube video posted by Bossip.com and on the twin posting on their website.

> **eyesontheprize:** These are soulless, scandalous, immoral hoes that provide the white media every racial stereotype given to the negro woman. These sh!t stained soulless servants of the devil are an embarrassment to our race.
> **Vanessa Atkins:** This women MiMi like to come across as a classy woman, her actions say something totally different. How can she consider herself as being a good role model to her daughter If she is doing s*x tapes and doing s*x acts on women and threesomes! This woman have no credibility what so ever and is a total disgrace!

For many commentators, Mimi's sexual behavior constitutes a breach in the moral code and the reasons for said breach are not unlike what Steve Harvey had to say about Mimi's sex tape. First, as illustrated by eyesontheprize, that Mimi plays into racial stereotypes about Black women on "white media," she's "soulless, scandalous and immoral." By talking about her non-normative sexuality within a (white) public, all Black people now look bad because of her behavior. Second, as illustrated by user V. Atkins (who self-censors the word "sex" but not "threesomes"), Mimi's sexual encounters with women mark her as being unable to be a "good role model" to her daughter. The slippage between engaging in lesbian behavior while

---

[16] For video of Mimi talking about the incident as well as the comments discussed below see Bossip.com, August 27, 2015 "Don't Be Scared: Mimi Faust Details How Joseline Hernandez Ate Her Box [Video]". Accessed October 2, 2019. https://bossip.com/1208584/dont-be-scared-mimi-faust-details-how-joseline-hernandez-ate-her-box-video/.

being a mother and being immoral is not accidental. And for many users, Mimi's lack of morality is directly related to the fact that she is *talking openly* about this kind of sex, and Black women "role models" for children apparently should not talk about sex, especially sex with women. Similar to Winston's critique of Mimi, because she is a Black mother, sexuality is not something that she should be talking about, or profiting from. Mimi is a walking, talking breach in the Black middle-class Christian standards of morality, and it is on a video where Mimi openly discusses her disregard for heteronormativity that she is referred to as "shit stained soulless servant of the devil." Indeed, it is when Mimi decides to discuss being a partner in a lesbian sex act, allowing a woman to go down her, that she receives the most comments rooted in racist, sexist, and homophobic ideas. Black women engaged in illicit erotic labor and those who engage in sex with women are positioned in opposition to Black middle-class values of racial uplift. Recall that Winston suggested that Black women and girls who take control of their sexuality and use it for their own pleasure and/or financial benefit, "fall back into the plantation fields." It is as if Black women asserting control over their sexuality is not control at all. Instead, it is the equivalent to living under the condition of enslavement, setting the race back, and/or worshiping the Devil himself.

Hyperbole aside, the ratchet/boojie politics of Ratchet TV suggests that there are those who believe that Black women should not engage, discuss, or be sexual in public nor tell their sexual stories at all, and that doing so is the opposite of progressive racial politics. In their estimation, to talk candidly about sex, especially sex that is non-normative, is akin to picking cotton or paving the way for the anti-Christ. For Black women, "coming out" on Ratchet TV places them in the middle of hyperbolic, conservative Black sexual politics, and capitalist heteropatriarchal logic that seeks to profit from their non-heterosexuality. Bossip.com makes their money from generating views on content about Ratchet TV, and by keeping users on their page (and thus exposed to ads) through their comments section. They quite literally benefit from Mimi being called a "ho." Coming out (w)hole or w(ho)le (apologies to Evelynn Hammonds and her brilliantly titled 1994 essay "Black (W)holes and the Geometry of Black Female Sexuality") in public for Black women is difficult even on Ratchet TV because even though the Black Ratchet Imagination creates space for new formations of Black female sexuality, ratchetness—acting outside of the normative boundaries of Black middle-class behavior—doesn't occur in vacuum. It happens within the context of neoliberal structures which intend to extract any and all potential value from Black bodies making it difficult for any Black woman to "come out" *for* herself.

"TIGHTROPE"

Marlon B. Ross contends that the closet paradigm has been used by scholars of queer theory, and arguably, in public discourse more generally, in ways that cast Black narratives of non-heterosexuality as backward and primitive (Ross 2005). Narratives of "coming out" tend to presume that a kind of "becoming" happens to the person *revealing* their sexual identity in public. One "becomes" a modern LGBT subject when they escape "the closet." The "closet" is an imagined space of confinement and shame, and only those who are firmly "out" can experience "freedom" and a real sense of *being* themselves. Ross argues that the "closet paradigm has been such a compelling way of fixing homosexual identification exactly because it enables this powerful narrative of progress" (Ross 2005, 163). Ross argues that (white) queer theory's "fixation on the closet function as the grounding principle for sexual experience, knowledge, and politics […] diminishes and disables the full engagement with potential insights from race theory and class analysis" (Ross 2005, 162). I wish to extend Ross's critique of the closet paradigm in the following analysis of Brittany Spanos' cover article in the April 2018 issue of *Rolling Stone* magazine featuring Janelle Monáe who had just released her latest album *Dirty Computer* to critical acclaim. Spanos writes:

> "Being a queer black woman in America," she says, taking a breath as she comes out, "someone who has been in relationships with both men and women—I consider myself to be a free ass motherfucker." She initially identified as bisexual, she clarifies, "but then later I read about pansexuality and was like, 'Oh, these are things that I identify with too.' I'm open to learning more about who I am."

Spanos' addition of "taking a breath as she comes out" frames Monáe's disclosure and attempt at self-identification as a "coming out" narrative filled with the melodrama of disclosure of an inner truth. The article's headline, "Janelle Monáe Frees Herself" implies that up until this point, Monáe had been shackled, tethered to some lie, or at least to some half truth about herself. Following the publication of Spanos' cover article, "think pieces" and Tweets proliferated about "what this means" now that another Black woman was "out." People congratulated her for "going public." People worked to fit her into a neat box. Was she saying that she was "bisexual"? People worked to "ship" her, or speculate about who she was in a relation*ship* with. Gossip about her dating Tessa Thompson, the co-star of her short film *Dirty Computer* which serves as a narrative vehicle for the music videos shot for the album, grew even stronger. The public discourse, and most importantly the *Rolling Stone*'s headline demonstrated the public's fixation on gay, lesbian, bisexual, and transgender people "coming out of the closet." The cover article goes on to describe Monáe's insecurity about her identity as an artist, her perfectionism, and her obsession with being "flawless." Spanos consistently blurs the lines between Monáe's progression as an artist of renown and of her public disclosure of her sexuality. For Spanos, the two are related—Monáe's eventual "coming out" and her assent to super-stardom (and eventual Grammy nomination for Album of the Year). Spanos never really lets Monáe's speech act be what it is, though. She said during an on-record interview for a major publication that "*being* a queer black woman in America" allowed her to consider herself "a free ass motherfucker." For those who had been listening to her music throughout her career this reads more as an acknowledgment of what some might have assumed to be true all along: she considered herself to be a "free motherfucker."

Spanos' story attempts to fix a narrative of progress onto Janelle Monáe's life: from rags to riches, "pop anomaly" to "pop star," from "android" to "real girl," and from "the closet" to "freedom." This she does even though Monáe's acknowledgment that she isn't heterosexual did not fit the typically narrative of "coming out" that posits that individuals reveal their sexuality as a means of escaping some imagined space of shame so that they can live "openly" and "proudly." While it is a convenient narrative that people understand, Monáe has always used her music to push back against politics of respectability—all while wearing a suit and tie. One of her first singles, "Tightrope" featured lyrics that dealt with struggles with familiar politics of respectability, particularly those associated with the Black church.

> Some callin' me a sinner
> Some callin' me a winner
> I'm callin' you to dinner
> And you know exactly what I mean
> Yeah I'm talkin bout you

There are many ways for the Black church to excuse "sinful" behavior, but the label "sinner" is often reserved for those whose very identity cannot be divorced from their sinful behavior such as those who are gay, lesbian, bisexual, or otherwise queer. Conservative Christian ideology would also hold that a young woman wearing what appears to be men's clothing is living "out of step" with God's dictates for women, and going against God's dictates for your gender performance is also a sin. Whether Monáe was referring to her sexuality, or her gender non-conformity, she touches on an experience that many Black queer people have experienced, especially those growing up in or around "church folk." And it is Monáe's consistent use of language that captures the experiences of Black queer folk that made it possible for some to read her as a member of the *family*.[17]

Monáe even says, "If you listen to my albums, it's there" (Spanos 2018). She never actually hid the information. It could be argued, that her matter of fact revelation "express[ed] instead a strong sense that it is impossible *not* to know something so obvious among those who know you well enough. In such a context, to announce one's attraction by "coming out" would not necessarily indicate a progress in sexual identity, and it would not necessarily change one's identity from closeted to liberated as conceptualized in the dominant closet narrative" (Ross 2005, 180, *emphasis mine*). The way that Monáe decides to disclose her non-normative sexuality, through her music, isn't good enough for those who want her story to fit neatly within the narrative of modern LGBT subjectivity of progress. It was done for people who didn't know her "well enough." The discursive framing that accompanies her disclosure to Spanos is relevant to our discussion of politics of respectability and Black women's non-heteronormative sexualities, because Spanos frames Monáe's attempt to self-identify as a queer Black woman, which even then required further explanation "someone who has been in relationships with both men and women," in a more convenient, easy-to-understand type of sexual story: a "coming out" narrative. It is as if there is no sexual story that could exist where a Black woman could simply exist in a state of "being" queer. Spanos ultimately transforms what is a non-linear process, telling people that you're not heterosexual, into a bite-sized, easily digestible headline that imagines Monáe as having arrived, as finally setting herself free between

---

[17] Family is a term sometimes used by Black LGBT people to refer to those who are members of the Black LGBT community.

the pages of *Rolling Stone*, which you can own for $9.99. Consider what Monáe actually says about her sexuality:

> *Being* a queer Black woman
> someone who *has been* with both men and women
> I *consider* myself a free ass motherfucker
> If you listen to my albums, it's there

Monáe's *being* queer was framed as a story of *becoming* so that *Rolling Stone* could be the first to break her "coming out" story. But this isn't her "coming out story," it's just the moment she decided to tell a bunch of people who don't know her. But this is a common refrain in Black women's struggle to represent themselves and their sexuality, the use of our sexual stories for someone else's benefit, and why some women decide to keep their sexual stories to themselves altogether.

"They Probably Know"

Maegan, an informant who works in a predominantly Black office in the federal government, said the following when I asked her if the people that she worked with knew that she was a lesbian.

> The funny thing is at work I don't um, *they probably know*, but that's not something I like *advertise*. You know what I'm saying. I don't talk about being with men. I don't talk about having kids. There's no ring on my finger. But it's not something I have to say, like "Oh by the way, you know I'm gay, right? [...] So it's not something that I advertise. And I notice that about myself because I don't want to be treated any differently just because I'm gay. I want everyone to see me, "This is Maegan. This is what Maegan brings to the table professionally. Maegan is so super cool." If you ask me, I'll tell you, but I'm not going to advertise it. So later on, it's like you already know me outside of my sexuality.

Like many Black middle-class women, it could be argued that Maegan performs her sexuality according to silence and concealment, what Lisa B. Thompson refers to as the "hallmarks" of Black middle-class performances of respectability (Thompson 2009, 98). Since Maegan refuses to confirm what it is her colleagues "probably" know, her desire not to "advertise" her sexuality could be understood in the literal sense. She is not interested in attempting to "sell" them the idea that she is capable, and cool *even though* she does not organize her sexual life in terms of heteronormative behavior. Maegan says her colleagues, whom she would later describe to me as "Bible thumpers," "probably know." That is, she presumes that they *know* that she is a lesbian, but she's never directly talked about it with them. This, I would argue, is not necessarily related to an attempt to hide, cover, or downplay her sexual difference, but to resist the active forms of surveillance enacted on Black women's bodies, especially by individuals and institutions—such as the Black Church—which are invested Black heteronormativity.

Black queer middle-class women who actively seek acceptance within cultural institutions dominated by Black middle-class normativity find themselves in a difficult position. If simply *being* queer is a violation of Black middle-class (and heteronormative) behavior, then how could they ever achieve the "benefits" associated with inclusion into the Black middle-class? Thus far, I've demonstrated that one way that they do this is through distinguishing themselves from ratchet performances of Black queer sexuality. Through the linguistic performance of distinction, they mark their behavior as normative, but for that one thing: their same-sex desire (Chap. 2). Mignon Moore (2011), has argued that another way that Black lesbian women gain access to the benefits of Black middle-classness is through the act of covering (Goffman 1967). Where performances of distinction and covering are two ways of describing a kind of strategic navigation of the complicated position middle-class BQW find themselves, it is important to note that both of these acts are situated within a politic of representation, and related to the ways in which Black queer sexuality is represented in popular culture (Chaps. 3 and 4). Covering imagines that Black queer middle-class women *can be* nearly indistinguishable from straight women. That is, by downplaying their sexuality, they can't be identified—not with certainty, anyway—as queer, or morally suspect as demonstrated in the analysis of LHHAtl above. It is a strategy of optics. Similarly, distinguishing oneself from ratchet versions of Black queer women's sexuality, often involves pointing out the bad behaviors of young, working-class, Black women who lack class or an ability to move about in spaces that are shaped by Black middle-class hetero/homonormative ideologies such "Southeast Tracy" (Chap. 2). Typically, "those women" can serves as a foil for one's "professional" or "boojie" performance of Black queer sexuality.

Maegan's unwillingness to "advertise" her sexuality even though her colleagues probably already know might better be understood within a framework of the "glass closet." C. Riley Snorton argues that "Black sexuality [...] is figured within a "glass closet," a space [...] marked by hypervisibility and confinement, spectacle, and speculation" (Snorton, 2014, 5). This "glass closet" is what makes LHHAtl work. For those already considered to be outside of the normative cultural formations—BQW—their very presence destabilizes the fictions of Black heteronormativity as the only "reality" and true way of being Black. It also provides numerous opportunities for the spectacle of the revelation that there really *is* something "wrong" with Black people's sexuality. As I suggested in Chap. 3, *ratchet* does a particular kind of work that allows for queer (or quare) forms of interpretation and ways of being to emerge. However, being ratchet doesn't mean that one escapes the surveillance that pervades Black life in America (Snorton, 2014). The "glass closet" metaphorizes for Snorton the condition of Black sexuality in representation (Snorton 2014). Some might understand Maegan as being "in the closet," and by not telling them she's a lesbian, they'd presume she's chosen the "closet." However, Maegan's *refusal* to talk about her sexuality in public, with those who work to regulate notions of respectability in service of Black heteronormative and gender hegemonic ideology—Black women who are "Bible thumpers"—is its own kind of Black queer work.

When we examine Maegan's narrative, we see another potential strategy that might be at play in the everyday lives of BQW who spend considerable amounts of time under Black heteronormative surveillance: *refusal*. At this point, she hadn't told her colleagues outright, so she had no reason to distinguish herself from Black lesbian figures that they may be familiar with. And while she downplayed her sexuality, an act that might be read as "covering," I believe her refusing to discuss her sexuality works in a much more interesting way. When used in conjunction with Black (middle-class) heteronormative performances of ignorance (Snorton 2014), we see how the refusal to disclose information about one's sexual or intimate life is in some ways related to the way that in the neoliberal age, there are often subtle, unspoken *demands* for Black women to divulge information about their sexual lives. However, lesbian, gay, bisexual, and trans people consistently engage in strategic non-disclosure when in the presence of those who would use their openness about their non-heteronormative behavior as a means of demeaning or ostracizing them.

Ratchet involves a kind of movement in the world that is unbothered by other people's notions of what is and is not respectable, but it also involves strategic manipulation of both refusal and ignorance. If refusing to play by the rules is in and of itself the philosophy of ratchet, then Maegan not advertising her sexuality to her willfully ignorant colleagues (who probably know, but haven't said anything because they know better), is in line with the Black queer work of ratchet. Others may want to read Maegan's refusal as an acquiescence to heteronormative forms of surveillance. She seeks acceptance; therefore, she doesn't tell them something that would cause colleagues to discredit her. But this argument lacks an acknowledgment of the fact that neoliberal homonormative logic often *requires* you to tell your business, even if it offers *you* no immediate or long-term strategic or monetary gain. Therefore, I read Maegan's navigation of her homophobic colleagues as a *refusal* to give people permission to talk about her in any other way than what she wants. She manages to bursts the bubble of homonormative "coming out" fantasies wherein lies the logic of: "If we all come out, then they'll have to give us equal rights." Black women know better than that. So instead, Maegan doesn't tell them anything and in so doing, disarms them—effectively *daring* them to say something sideways. And it's that control that she refuses to relinquish by telling her sexual story, unsolicited. Not all middle-class and upwardly mobile Black queer women are seeking acceptance within cultural institutions shaped by Black middle-class normative ideas. Some, like Maegan, simply want to create the space to *be*.

Jennifer Nash offers a compelling close reading of theories of representation in the Black feminist theoretical archive. She delineates four different approaches which circulate: representation as pedagogy, representation as epistemology, representation and temporality, and recovery work. She argues that the Black feminist theories of representation have, historically, "presume[d] that dominant representation injures black female flesh and that black women's pleasure in representation comes through self-representation focused on restoring black women's wholeness, or through and active resistance of dominant representation's violence" (Nash 2014, 57). Nash then offers close readings of racialized pornographic images which feature Black women in an attempt to gesture toward the possibility to "transform this archive into a home not just for locating and healing wounds, but for naming and claiming desires, for speaking about the complex ways that pleasure—both racial and sexual—move under our skin" (Nash 2014, 58).

Jennifer Nash's reading strategy, racial iconography is about how race and sexuality, and specifically how racialized forms of sexuality are expected to be represented (Nash 2014). When treating *ratchet*, we are concerned both with representations and embodiment. When *ratchet* is used as a disciplining technique—it is both used as a means of pointing out those individuals who are acting in a way that would "represent" the whole group of African Americans (or Black non-heterosexual) women as being "of low taste." It is concerned with embodiment in so far as it will "reflect" poorly upon oneself. In this way it is primarily concerned with injury. Acting ratchet, being ratchet, poorly represents the way that Black women "really" are.

What racial iconography offers us, according to Jennifer Nash, is a strategy for seeing the supposed difference which Black women's bodies can reveal within specific contextual moments. Nash describes racial iconography as a reading practice which "grapples with the multitude of meaning-making purposes that black bodies perform in the visual field in a panoply of social, historical, and technological moments, and the complex and multiple interpretative frameworks that spectators deploy to interpret these racialized meanings" (Nash 2008, 53). Nash argues that one of the issues with "typical" Black feminist approaches to the analysis of visual culture is that they lack an ability to account for "black pleasurable spectatorship generally, and black pleasurable pornographic spectatorship specifically" (Nash 2014, 60). Let me translate that: Black feminists have often assumed that if a Black woman sees a video vixen, she immediately sees herself in opposition to said image, because she knows that the video vixen is a ho and is meant to imply that all Black women are hos. Nash is suggesting that that's a problem. First because it offers little in the way of addressing how and why a Black woman might actually enjoy seeing a video vixen while either agreeing that said video vixen is a ho, or is not a ho. Second, it imagines that there is can be no pleasure outside of an oppositional stance to images of sexualized Black women.

To put it plainly, racial iconography doesn't presume that an image of a ho is meant to convey one, linear idea about all Black women, or justify only one particular form of Black women's mistreatment. Racial iconography allows us to understand how and why other Black women, sex workers or not, might see Joseline Hernandez and think, "That bitch bad." Spectators deploy various, sometimes competing frameworks, for understanding particular images that for some only exist as negative. Racial iconography can serve as a one way of understanding how Black queer women's bodies within hip-hop and the strip club, exist in ways that are in excess of what they are supposed to be.

Any performance of non-heteronormativity and gender variance within Black cultural spaces triggers discourses rooted in the politics of respectability. Therefore, it is difficult to *be a* BQW without engaging in discourses about what *kind* of non-normative subject you want to be both within and outside of Black cultural spaces. There is no better place this is illustrated than in the realm of reality television that seeks to portray the "true" lives of those who create Black culture. Despite the fact that the hip-hop industry's massive profits tend to flow upward toward the bank accounts of huge multimedia conglomerates that are run exclusively by white men (Rose 2008), hip-hop's face remains Black. It is also important to make sense of the way that hip-hop relies on Black women's bodies to tell its stories of heterosexual men's success.

How "being" Black and a queer woman is represented in the age of "tell-alls," "gossip blogging," and reality television is an important point of rupture. The real question that this chapter has attempted to ask is: What does it mean to "be yourself," especially when you are not in control of the narrative placed around the circumstances of your life? And my answer: it feels like *being* a Black woman in America. Ratchet TV places in front of us the *reality* that Black women continue to occupy a place on the margins of even the most "glamorous" regions of Black life in America. The story remains the same—Black women are profitable, but, they aren't worth a damn. Black women get money, but only because they're willing to sell sex for it. And yet, the most Black women who strategically utilize ratchet ways of being, doing, and moving about the world, could care less what *you* think, because they are *living their best life*.

References

Aslama, Minna, and Mervi Pantti. 2006. Talking Alone: Reality TV, Emotions and Authenticity. *European Journal of Cultural Studies* 9 (2): 167–184.

Carby, Hazel. 1998. It Jus Be's Dat Way Sometime: The Sexual Politics of Women's Blues. In *The Jazz Cadence of American Culture*, ed. Robert O'Meally. New York: Columbia University Press. Original edition, 1986.

Davis, Angela Y. 1998. *Blues Legacies and Black Feminism: Gertrude "Ma" Rainey, Bessie Smith, and Billie Holiday*. New York: Pantheon Books.

Dubrofsky, Rachel E. 2009. Fallen Women in Reality TV: A Pornography of Emotion. *Feminist Media Studies* 9 (3): 353–368.

DuCille, Ann. 1993. Blues Notes on Black Sexuality: Sex and the Texts of Jessie Fauset and Nella Larsen. *Journal of the History of Sexuality* 3 (3): 418–444.

Eguchi, Shinsuke, Nicole Files-Thompson, and Bernadette Marie Calafell. 2018. Queer (of Color) Aesthetics: Fleeting Moments of Transgression in VH1's

Love & Hip-Hop: Hollywood Season 2. *Critical Studies in Media Communication* 35 (2): 180–193.

Gaunt, Kyra D. 2015. YouTube, Twerking & You: Context Collapse and the Handheld Co-Presence of Black Girls and Miley Cyrus. *Journal of Popular Music Studies* 27 (3): 244–273.

Goffman, Erving. 1967. *Interaction Ritual: Essays in Face-to-Face Behavior*. Chicago: Aldine Publishing Company.

Grindstaff, Laura. 2002. *The Money Shot: Class, Trash, and the Making of TV Talk Shows*. Chicago: University of Chicago.

Hasinoff, Amy Adele. 2008. Fashioning Race for the Free Market on America's Next Top Model. *Critical Studies in Media Communication* 25 (3): 324–343.

Hernandez, Emma. 2018. The 'Love & Hip Hop: Atlanta' Stars Can Afford Their Lavish Lifestyles Because They Make Bank. *In Touch Weekly*, April 10.

Hill, Marc Lamont. 2009. Scared Straight: Hip-Hop, Outing, and the Pedagogy of Queerness. *The Review of Education, Pedagogy, and Cultural Studies* 31 (1): 29–54.

Johnson, E. Patrick. 2003a. *Appropriating Blackness: Performance and the Politics of Authenticity*. Durham and London: Duke University Press.

Johnson, Maria V. 2003b. "Jelly Jelly Jellyroll": Lesbian Sexuality and Identity in Women's Blues. *Women & Music* 7: 31.

Johnson, Imani Kai. 2014. From Blues Women to b-Girls: Performing Badass Femininity. *Women & Performance: A Journal of Feminist Theory* 24 (1): 15–28.

McCune, Jeffrey Q. 2014. *Sexual Discretion: Black Masculinity and the Politics of Passing*. Chicago: University of Chicago Press.

Miller-Young, Mireille. 2010. Putting hypersexuality to work: Black women and illicit eroticism in pornography. *Sexualities* 13 (2): 219–235.

Miller-Young, Mireille, ed. 2014. *A Taste for Brown Sugar: Black Women in Pornography*. Durham: Duke University Press.

Moore, Mignon R. 2011. *Invisible Families: Gay Identities, Relationships, and Motherhood Among Black Women*. Berkeley, CA: University of California Press.

Nash, Jennifer C. 2008. Strange Bedfellows. *Social Text* 26 (4(97)): 51–76.

Nash, Jennifer C. 2014. *The Black Body in Ecstasy: Reading Race, Reading Pornography*. Durham, NC: Duke University Press.

Nededog, Jethro. 2017. *VH1 Is in the Middle of a Ratings Resurgence and Beating Its Cable Competitors—Here's Why*. [Online article]. Business Insider. http://www.businessinsider.com/vh1-ratings-2017-3. Accessed July 19.

Plummer, Kenneth. 1995. *Telling Sexual Stories: Power, Change, and Social Worlds*. London: Routledge.

Rose, Tricia. 2008. *The Hip Hop Wars: What We Talk About When We Talk About Hip Hop—And Why It Matters*. New York: BasicCivitas.

Ross, Marlon B. 2005. Beyond the Closet as Raceless Paradigm. In *Black Queer Studies*, ed. E. Patrick Johnson and Mae G. Henderson, 161–189. Durham and London: Duke University Press.

Snorton, C. Riley. 2014. *Nobody Is Supposed to Know: Black Sexuality on the Down Low*. Minneapolis: University of Minnesota Press.

Spanos, Brittany. 2018. Janelle Monáe Frees Herself. *Rolling Stone*, April 26.

Stallings, LaMonda Horton. 2007. *Mutha' Is Half a Word: Intersections of Folklore, Vernacular, Myth, and Queerness in Black Female Culture, Black Performance and Cultural Criticism*. Columbus: Ohio State University Press.

Thompson, Lisa B. 2009. *Beyond the Black Lady: Sexuality and the New African American Middle Class, The New Black Studies Series*. Urbana: University of Illinois Press.

Walker, Alicia. 2014. "I'm Not a Lesbian; I'm Just a Freak": A Pilot Study of the Experiences of Women in Assumed-Monogamous Other-Sex Unions Seeking Secret Same-Sex Encounters Online, Their Negotiation of Sexual Desire, and Meaning-Making of Sexual Identity. *Sexuality & Culture* 18 (4): 911–935.

CHAPTER 6

"I Said What I Said": Final Notes on Ratchet/Boojie Politics

BAD AND BOOJIE

You know Young Rich Niggas
You know so we ain't really never had no old money
We got a whole lotta new money though

My bitch is bad and boujee (bad)
Cookin' up dope with a Uzi (blaow)
My niggas is savage, ruthless (savage)
We got 30's and 100 rounds too (grrah)
—Migos, "Bad and Boujee" (2017)

Hip-hop has a tremendous amount of influence within Black communities of practice. While not every Black person listens to hip-hop music regularly, or engages with its culture through fashion ("Skinny jeans or nah?"),[1]

---

[1] Trends in hip-hop fashion are constantly changing. As some younger rappers have taken up the "skinny jean," some continue to argue that this particular trend isn't "real" or authentic to hip-hop.

politics ("Who *really* killed Tupac?"),[2] or debates ("Who's your Top 5?"),[3] the language of hip-hop—what H. Samy Alim refers to as Hip-Hop Nation Language (HHNL) (Alim 2006)—often finds ways of exerting a great amount of influence over the daily lexical choices of many people living in and among African American speech communities. Further, there has been an increased mainstreaming and *pop*ularization of hip-hop personalities who bring HHNL to primetime with them. As hip-hop artists borrow from local Black discursive practices and terminology, taking them out of their original contexts, they make those words available within other local contexts. These terms then get laminated onto already rich and dense discursive fields where Black culture, practice, and ideologies bend and flex to accommodate the ideas contained in those terms: *shout out to my woes*.[4] It is no wonder then why *ratchet* has found its way into public and private discourses of Black Americans without much attention paid to the ways that it operates in and on the lives of those to whom it refers, those who fall outside of the notions of propriety, acceptability, and respectability.

When the rap trio Migos released their single "Bad and Boujee" in 2017, it became an anthem for young, Black and talented people who skirted the edges of respectability. The song seemed to capture the Black zeitgeist of the moment. Migos' "bitches" were bad *and* boojie (or boujee/boojee). Migos seemed to have flipped Geneva Smitherman's definition of "boojee":

> An elitist, uppity-acting African American. Generally, with a higher education and income level than the average Black, who identifies with European American culture and distances him/herself from other African Americans. Derives from 'bourgeois/bourgeoisie.' 2) Describes a person, event, style, or thing that is characteristic of elitist, uppity acting Blacks. 'It was one of them ol boojee thangs.' (Smitherman 1994, 66)

---

[2] Rapper Tupac Shakur was murdered in 1996 and his death remains unsolved. Ongoing questions and debates about who was responsible for his tragic murder remain topics of discussion.

[3] Refers to one's personal list under constant revision of the 5 greatest rappers of all of time. There is no definitive list.

[4] A "shout out" is a form of acknowledgment. "Woes" is an abbreviation of the New Orleans' African American English (AAE) term "Woadie" (pronounced WHOA-dee) referring to people who live in the same ward—think "Ward-ie" (Genius.com 2015). Canadian born, Grammy Award winning rapper Drake helped popularize "woes" in a song titled "Know Your Self."

For Migos, being boojie did not make one inauthentic. It didn't make someone *less* Black, or "uppity," a term often used to disparage Black people who *act* like they are better than others who might occupy a similar station. It also use as a racist epithet to refer to Black people who *act* above their station, and don't know their place at the bottom of the racial hierarchy. Situated squarely within what some consider to be a Black American cultural formation—hip-hop—it Migos' use of *boojie* distanced itself from the idea that *boujie* necessarily was about identifying with European American culture all while moving away from African American culture. Keith Bryant Alexander approaches boojie performativity as a set of restrictive dictates on one's behavior.

> For me a boojie performativity references those perceived repetitive actions performed by black people, plotted within grids of power relationships and social norms that are presumably relegated exclusively to white people; hence, by virtue of their enactment and in the presumed absence of black folk, these performances are critiqued as rejecting or abandoning some organic construction of black character and black people. (Alexander 2011, 311)

Alexander points out the underlying racist ideas that underpin the deployment of the use of *boojie* as an epithet. It rests on the idea that only white people are naturally capable of behaving properly, and that whatever white folks deem "proper," even if the guide post is constantly in flux, is the only way to behave properly. Presumably, acting "right" is simply not something that comes natural to Black people. When Black people demonstrate middle-class and upper-class proclivities, or if they are educated, speak American "Standard" English, or enjoy fine goods, they are accused of *pretending* to be white. Like Keith Bryant Alexander (2011, 311), Migos took issue with the idea that they (and "their bitches") could not be both "authentically" Black *and* boojie. They took issue with the idea that they didn't deserve to have money because they happened to be from "bad" neighborhoods, and continued to engage in bad behaviors while also enjoying fine luxury goods from European businesses. For them, being boojie and bad were not mutually exclusive. Being Black and being upper-class was not mutually exclusive.

During my research, I came upon middle-class and upwardly mobile Black people who went out of their ways to self-select into the category of ratchet. Not long after Migos' hit single "Bad and Boojie" dropped did the word *ratchet* start to make the leap from the "classless" to the classy. CNN political commentator, popular Black liberal pundit Angela Raye started a podcast in 2017 and described it as being for the "woke" and the "sophistiratchet." This blending of *ratchet* with the word *sophisticated* was a way to acknowledge the simultaneous existence of the "bad," or *ratchet*, and her enjoyment of middle-class notions of propriety. Interestingly enough, Raye names her middle-classness *sophisticated*, avoiding the epithet *boojie*. The point remains the same: you could now have the economic resources that place you outside the working-class, multiple advanced degrees, *and* like to "get ratchet." *Boojie*, for Migos and others, was a designation which made one attractive, and desirable. *Boojie* gets recuperated through a ratchet hip-hop song by a ratchet hip-hop group. They bend and twist the meaning of *boojie*, critiquing the view that to be boojie one had to reject ratchetness, Blackness, Black people, and Black cultural practices. As I have attempted to show throughout this book, it is precisely because the song is a ratchet hip-hop song, precisely because they put to work a ratchet performance that makes their anti-racist critique of *boojie* possible.

At the same time that we are witnessing an expansion in the realm of representation of Black queer people, we also are witnessing a cultural politic emerge around who is and what is ratchet/boojie. In Chap. 2, I described this as ratchet/boojie politics. Just as *ratchet* has derogatory, racist and a class racist connotation, so does *boojie*. However, as Migos demonstrates, both possess the potential to critique the politics of respectability *and* notions of authenticity as they relate to Black bodies and therefore engage in the work of (anti)respectability.

Pickens (2014) identifies the ratchet imaginary as being a space where racialized and gendered identity can be performed outside of the normative prescriptions. The ratchet imaginary calls into question the very tenants of the politics of respectability which assume that if a Black female subject *acts right*, then and only then, can she expect to be treated with respect, and thus be successful. I have argued that the work a Black woman's does to act upon her own self-determination *is* a matter of collective and political importance. Further, even if her quest for individuality and self-determination cause her and her sexuality to be read in terms of preexisting racist, sexist, and homophobic stereotypes regarding Black female sexuality, that does not mean that she cannot be engaged in politics of antiracist. Quite the contrary, part of the work that the ratchet imaginary does is call out the notion that one must *earn* basic decency and dignity (Cooper 2017). Instead, it says rather boldly, "you will respect me, because I am here." When that is questioned by naysayers, a ratchet imaginary responds: "I said what I said."

It is not a surprise that there are those who consider ratchet behaviors and people to be the antithesis to a collective, progressive racial politic. A notion of "progress" denotes that there is movement forward and *upward*, toward the mythical place of broad, mainstream (read: white) acceptance. This is not a coincidence. Throughout this book, I have argued that *ratchet* serves as a compelling site to think through the *work* that individuals do to perform a kind of *anti*-respectability that does not *insist* on acceptance from anyone, let alone a mainstream which would rather see them dying or dead anyway. We learn that ratchet people and things thought to be in a steady state—fixed. Ratchet things are and always have been ratchet. Ratchet becomes a tool for encoding certain persons, places, or things with particular ideas—classless, improper, inarticulate, "hyper" sexual, non-hetero/homonormative, hip-hop, and young—marking them for exclusion from "respectable" institutions. This implies, of course, that those persons deemed ratchet, wanted to be apart of these "respectable," mainstream institutions in the first place. If *ratchet* functions as a spaces of exclusion, outside the mainstream, what happens there is fascinating (see Chap. 4).

My research has found that there are at least three different ways that people engage with *ratchet*: (1) persons may begin to enact the very technologies of control used to exclude them by deploying *ratchet* as a means of distinguishing themselves from those who are undeserving of "a seat at the table"; (2) people learn to adapt, changing the way they behave based on context so that they can gain access to spaces and groups their working-class behaviors might be excluded from while maintaining access to working-class spaces where they can practice, at least somewhat privately, a "little bit ratchet"; and (3) one might completely dismiss calls for their behavior to be consistent with what makes others feel comfortable, opting to express their ratchetness in ways that purposefully exceed the limits of middle-class behavior whenever and wherever they want. The way this final engagement is embodied by those who already hold memberships to the Black middle-class—heterosexual, gender conforming, well-educated Black people—however, looks very different from the way it is embodied by lesbians whose Black middle-class membership is complicated by their sexuality.

"Am I Freak for Getting Down?"

In 2018, as I was finishing this manuscript, Black Jesus blessed us with Janelle Monáe's latest album, *Dirty Computer*. Black Jesus also saw fit that Monáe would confirm rumors of her non-heterosexuality (see Chap. 5). She disclosed in an interview published in the *Rolling Stone* magazine, describing herself as a "Black queer woman" and a "free ass motherfucker." The album and the accompanying visual album *Dirty Computer*, and what some will refer to as Monáe's "coming out," represented a culmination of the work she's done along the edges of hip-hop and pop. Janelle Monáe's song "Q.U.E.E.N." from her critically acclaimed third album,[5] *Electric Lady*, interrogates the boundaries often placed on Black women to perform in ways that are deemed acceptable. She addresses the Black church, a common "character" in the narrative of Black queer lives and in Black queer culture:

> Hey brother, can you save my soul from the devil?
> Say is it weird to like the way she wear her tights?
> And is it rude to wear my shades?
> Am I a freak because I love watching Mary? (Maybe)
>
> Hey sister, am I good enough for your heaven?
> Say will your God accept me in my black and white?
> Will he approve the way I'm made?
> Or should I reprogram the programming and get down

While most would never describe Janelle Monáe as ratchet, her stunning Black and white costumes and perfectly coiffed tresses, I would argue that both her aesthetics and the questions she poses in her music, often evoke ratchet/boojie politics. She simultaneously calls out the boundary work of Black respectability politics while evoking inappropriate, non-normative behaviors and ways of being. She wears suits, ties, oxfords, often in white and Black—clothing often associated with menswear. She wears a bold red lip and dances along the boundaries of gender non-conformity. In "Q.U.E.E.N.," she evokes the homoerotic, the gen-

---

[5] Received wide acclaim and also spent 34 weeks on Billboard's R&B Charts. See Billboard's listing for *The Electric Lady* https://www.billboard.com/music/janelle-monae-chart-history/r-and-b-albums/song/79618.

6 "I SAID WHAT I SAID": FINAL NOTES ON RATCHET/BOOJIE POLITICS

der non-conforming, and what she calls the "programming," or normative ideologies which work to the detriment of those who refuse to be "normal" when they find themselves in the places where conservative, Black middle-class rules of normativity are the principle organizing forces. This calls to mind E. Patrick Johnson's essay "Feeling the Spirit in the Dark" where he borrows from French theorist Michel de Certeau's formulation of the difference between "place" and "space," where "place" allows only for a set of prescriptive interpretations and possibilities for the performances of Black sexuality. Alternatively, in "space" there are a broader range of interpretations as it allows for multiple ways of performing and doing Black sexuality (Johnson 1998, 400). Places, such as the Black Church, are sites where one must play a particular role, talk a specific way, do what is expected. Monáe, similarly questions the performative possibilities in the Black Church. Considering that she might enjoy the "way she wear her tights" and that she "love[s] watching Mary," Monáe asks, "am I good enough for your Heaven?" Does a Black woman who experiences same-sex attraction fit in the prescriptive place of the Black Church? Would "*your* God accept me in my black and whites," she asks. And more broadly, does a woman who experiences same-sex attraction fit within the notion of morality? And, therefore, respectability? Monáe concludes by asking, incredulously, if she should "reprogram the programming." As I've argued here, BQW regularly create Black queer spaces in order to do just that—shake the foundations of what is deemed proper—engage in anti-respectability.

In contrast to "places," "spaces" are sites where one is able to "act up" and act out; spaces are sites where performances occur and are interpreted outside of normative constructions. Johnson (1998) offers analysis of an ethnographic instance where Black gay men remove Christian discourse from the "place" of the Black Church, shifting that discourse instead into the "space" of the night club. He describes the mood of the space shifting as the DJ plays gospel music and entreats the club goers to look next to them, because "somebody that was here last year ain't make it ... Somebody's lover has passed on" (Johnson 1998, 409). As the D.J. mixes gospel songs into the dance music, the club erupts into a mass of synergistic dancing, shouting, testifying, and a rapturous same-sex eroticism (Johnson 1998, 409). He writes,

> The echoes of my Southern Baptist minister's sermons consume my thoughts ... yield not to temptation ... I dance on ... something got a hold on me ... Kevin pins me against the wall ... it's just like fire! ... I consume his tongue ... "There was sin among them." ... I feel the tears well up in my eyes ... "It seemed that he could not breathe, that his body could not contain this passion" ... I dance on ... Somebody say yes (yes), say yes (yes), yes (yes) ... (Johnson 1998, 409, emphasis in original)

The nightclub in Johnson's analysis becomes a Black queer space for Black gay men where the DJ marks the lives and deaths of Black men important, over and against dominant discourses that would suggest those lives are insignificant (Johnson 1998, 409). The use of gospel music and Black Christian discursive practices, which might be thought of as out-of-place in a normative gay club, calls attention to the homophobia of the Black church and the racism often embedded within normative gay spaces, all while marking Black queer space as something other than purely secular and sexual. Within this Black queer space, we see Black cultural and discursive practices congeal with same-sex eroticism, marking it as a site where being African American, homosexual, and Christian is not only possible, but an acceptable interpretative framework for understanding one's place in the world (Johnson 1998, 409). The introduction of Black discursive practices into the gay nightclub opens up a unique opportunity for the expression of Black same-sex eroticism. In fact, same-sex eroticism and same-sex love are what inform the DJ's original call: "Somebody's lover has passed on," which thus transformed the nightclub into a space where the eroticism between two Black men was not only "appropriate," but sat comfortably among Black cultural values and discourse. Both the discourse of spirituality and the club had effectively been *reprogrammed* as Monáe might posit. When BQW enter the *spaces* of the hip-hop, they *reprogram* it. They do so to create spaces where they can get caught up in the rapturous nature of performing same-sex desire. They revel in the experience of being unlady like, and watching other women do the same.

In Chap. 3, I argued that it was in the space of the strip club and with the lyrics of a problematic, cisgender, heterosexual male rapper, Kanye West, that they staked a claim to their presence within the realm of hip-hop. Similarly, in my analysis of Shanovia McKenzie's *District Heat* in Chap. 4, I suggested that her insistence on screening Black lesbian sex brings to the melodrama genre that which is often left out of mainstream depictions of Black (lesbian) life—their sex, in all its complicated,

6 "I SAID WHAT I SAID": FINAL NOTES ON RATCHET/BOOJIE POLITICS

sometimes *seemingly* gender normative ways. It is in these spaces both real and imagined, however, that BQW are able to work out the terms of their inclusion within Black cultural life.

"We All Need to Get a Little Ratchet"

Throughout my research, what has consistently surprised me is the use of *ratchet* to describe mundane behaviors. For example, in a post by one Twitter user she includes a blurry photo of herself or a friend, crossing her eyes the 35-character caption reading: "We all need to get a little ratchet." This constitutes a gross misuse of the word and its attendant discourses, but more importantly it is just one of thousands of such examples. In her book, *The Everyday Language of White Racism*, Jane Hill (2008) remarks that white people frequently attempt to use non-white language styles that they feel will make them appear more "cool." In so doing, they often misuse the words and language practices. Talking about the specific case of white people's use of "Spanglish," the Anglocizing of the Spanish language, which serves only to bring into sharp relief the distinction between those using or pronouncing the words incorrectly—white people—and those who use the words natively. As an even more striking example, in my research, I found a website[6] dedicated to posting pictures and videos of fights between individuals whom the site referred to as "ratchets." They'd turned the word *ratchet*, which typically operates in AAE as an adjective or adverb, into a plural noun—one they reserved exclusively for Black people, primarily Black women who were filmed either with or without their knowledge engaging in physical violence against one another. Not only had the word been misused, but it was used—I would argue—to help justify racist ideas and the State-sanctioned violence against Black people that those racist ideas empower. The logic goes: "If they do it to themselves, then why can't we?" *Ratchet*, as I have argued, is a word steeped in racial, class, and sexual politics, and so when it is used by those who themselves never have to face the consequences of being ratchet such as white, cisgender, heterosexual, middle-class people, it brings to bear the wide gap between those who face daily, intermingled racist, sexist, classist, and homophobic violence both physical and symbolic against their bodies and

---

[6]While the creators of the site are impossible to determine, the site has the common markings of white supremacists, and therefore, I do not feel compelled to give the URL for this site for lack of an interest in adding to their clicks.

those who do not. It especially hides the fact that it is primarily Black women who are considered ratchet, and being considered ratchet may or may not benefit them. In Chap. 5, I discussed how Black women put ratchet to work for their benefit, but they do so under harsh criticism, often by those who are affected by negative stereotypes of Blackness.

Ratchet TV comes under fire constantly for its portrayals of Black women, as do the women who benefit from the representations of ratchetness. As Kristen J. Warner explains, much of the anxiety about Black women's representations on Ratchet TV is rooted in a fear that portrayals will damage the reputation of *all* Black women (Warner 2015). This sentiment is rooted in both the politics of respectability and in an unquestioned belief that these portrayals and situations are oppositional to progressive racial politics. It is important to distinguish between representations of ratchet, and ratchet as an actual embodied way of being. The way that one treats ratchet analytically is rooted in the distinction. Warner deals with representations of ratchet, therefore, works with a definition of ratchet as "over-the-top," and by effect, in excess of reality. But ratchet isn't simply "unrealistic," and "campy" portrayals of Blackness. I know some Black women who really *would* jump across a table and fight a bitch if she was talking crazy. I also know Black women who would never even let the "b-word" cross their lips, let alone fight some one, but frequently use the word *ratchet* to describe themselves. E. Patrick Johnson's reading of Marlon Riggs' 1995 documentary *Black Is… Black Ain't* in the essay "The Pot is Brewing" is instructive here. After demonstrating the ways Blackness is embedded within overlapping sociopolitical networks of class, sexual and gendered, Johnson (2003) argues that Riggs' metaphor of gumbo, which he uses to describe the diversity of people's experiences of Blackness, "draws our attention to the discursive constitution of the recipe for blackness and celebrates its improvisational aspects as well as the materiality of the pot" (Johnson 2003, 47). Part of the work that *ratchet* does is that it calls attention to the myriad ways that Blackness can be done. It also reveals the "pot," or the boundaries of Blackness placed by those who are Black and those who are not.

When anxieties are expressed about representations of ratchet, particularly in American popular culture, the fear is that there is some truth in them. It is ratchet to jump across a table in 5-inch heels, full make-up and weave to fight someone, but in truth, and here is where the anxiety lies, there are situations where if a bitch is being violent and disrespectful, you might need to fight. And every Black person beholden to middle-class notions of propriety knows that there are situations where they might be forced to defend themselves, talk loud, or perhaps they just want to wear sweatpants and hoodies or not worry about what they look like when they leave the house, and they know in those moments where their "mask" becomes askew, that they could be in danger of being mistaken for someone who is ratchet. The anxiety about white folks knowing that some Black people are ratchet—that some Black people really don't care what white people or other Black people think—or that any Black person could at any point become ratchet, fuels the politics of respectability. The politics of respectability is meant to compel us to invest so much of our daily existence to the management of what other people think that we would deny simply *being* ourselves, especially if being ourselves evokes what others have deemed irresponsible, hypersexual, or inappropriate. It also denies the truth: some of us do behave in ratchet ways, enjoy ratchet places and things. It also produces the idea that if and when Black people do get an opportunity to be seen in public, they should represent the race according to the terms of middle-class behavior. Within this frame of thought, only those of us who aren't ratchet should be seen, or should benefit from being seen. Somehow, the logic goes, this will lead to white people seeing Black people as capable of being "normal," just like them. According to assimilationist ideas, that is the goal—for white people to think we're "okay." These discursive frameworks point to a commitment to "uplift suasion" (Kendi 2016).

"Uplift suasion," as defined by Ibram X. Kendi, refers to the belief that "White people could be persuaded away from their racist ideas if they saw Black people improving their behavior, uplifting themselves from their low station in American society" (Kendi 2016, 124). The problem of course with this idea is that it places the burden of fixing racism and its attendant racist ideas onto Black people. What's so fascinating about Ratchet TV and the Black women who star in them is that they are, first and foremost, *individuals*; yet, in the racist imagination an individual Black person can be the representative for all other Black people, and uplift suasion buys into this racist idea. It goes a step further by placing the blame on Black people and their "behaviors" for the problem of racism. But this logic simply doesn't add up, because even when Black people do "lift ourselves up," even to the highest station in American society—think Barack Obama—neither racism nor racist ideas go away. As Ibram X. Kendi has pointed out, even W. E. B. Du Bois, a stalwart for assimilationist ideas for most of his career as a Black intellectual, came to understand by the end of his career that changing racist ideas should not be the goal of a true anti-racist struggle (Kendi 2016). It can't be the goal, because in the racist imagination anything Black people do that "confirms" stereotypes works in favor of their already racist ideas, and anything we do that doesn't confirm those stereotypes simply points out an individual Black person's, *exceptional* behavior. No number of good, wholesome Black families, characters, or documentary series on television about real Black people, can convince someone who doesn't want to see Black people's humanity, to abandon their racist ideas.

> Everyone who has witnessed the historic presidency of Barack Obama—and the historic opposition to him—should now know full well that the more Black people uplift themselves, the more they will find themselves on the receiving end of a racist backlash. Uplift suasion, as a strategy for racial progress, has failed. Black individuals must dispose of it as a strategy and stop worrying about what other people may think about the way they act, the way they speak, the way they look, the way they dress, the way they are portrayed in the media, and the way they think and love and laugh. Individual Blacks are not race representatives. They are not responsible for those Americans who hold racist ideas. Black people need to be their imperfect selves around White people, around each other, around all people. Black is beautiful *and* ugly, intelligent *and* unintelligent, law-abiding *and* law-breaking, industrious *and* lazy—and it is those imperfections that make Black people human, make Black people equal to all other imperfectly human groups. (Kendi 2016, 505)

Kendi implores us to abandon our belief that Black people need to be perfect all the times in public in order to be able to claim that we are deserving of basic human rights collectively or individually. We don't all have to be Barack Obama and Michelle Obama, cisgender, heterosexual, beautiful, middle aged, highly educated, and wealthy, in order to be treated with dignity.

Lingering Questions

Class

While I have been more interested in the class *politics* that undergird the language practices of my informants, rather than their actual socioeconomic positions, this book would have greatly benefited from a more in-depth analysis of socioeconomic conditions of Black LGBTQ folks. What I have found in the sociological data about BQW is severely lacking, however. Further, the "go-to" statistics often cited to "prove" the loose values of Black people, their "broken" families, and the general immorality of Black women such as the number of "single-mothers" and out-of-wedlock" births, might tell us something about BQW as they may erroneously (or not) included in those numbers. Statistics have a way of reinforcing heteronormative scripts about Black sexuality because those using them sometimes assume that women not in heterosexual marriages are indeed "single-mothers," and that a "female headed household" doesn't have multiple women raising children together. This is especially true in situations where same-sex couples could not get legally married and before the Census Bureau collected information on same-sex couples. There remain few sources to draw from which address the specific ways that non-heterosexuality structures Black women's access to social, economic, cultural, and symbolic capitals. Further, there is little information about the way that flows structures their experiences, their talk, or their relationships to social space. The dearth of information pertaining to Black lesbians and class, what Evelynn Hammonds calls one of the many (w)holes that exists where it pertains to Black women's sexuality (Hammonds 1994) lead me to ask the kinds of questions that this book has, but there are many more outstanding questions about this link that I employ researchers to undertake.

The South

Washington, DC is a city that is at once considered "Southern," and by those from the South, "Northern." Before the Civil War, there was slavery in the city. On April 16,[7] 1862, President Abraham Lincoln signed the Compensated Emancipation Act of 1862 into law that would purchase the freedom of the remaining roughly 3,000 enslaved men, women, and children in DC. As the city grew, developed suburbs, attracted "transplants" for work in politics, and the African American population swelled, a *distinctive* character came to characterize the city. Treva Lindsey describes the city at the turn of the twentieth century as a "corridor city—a city through which distinctly Northern and Southern roots converged" (Lindsey 2017, 137). This remains true. At present, DC has a larger

---

[7] This day is presently celebrated as "Emancipation Day" in the District.

population of those who have moved to the city from various parts of the country for work as opposed to being both born and raised in the city.

While over half of my informants were from the South or from DC with parents who migrated to DC during the 60s and 70s, it is important to note that I have not placed DC's social life nor the use of the word *ratchet* in a distinct set of Black Southern politics. And yet, *ratchet* is a Southern word that gets transported on the backs of Southern hip-hoppers to the internet and to the mouths of people all over the country. The people who are most often described as *ratchet* are Southern, a geographic area often equated with racist ideas and practices, antimodern and backward ways of being, and whose people are slow talking, "nice," but unintelligent. Meanwhile, the North gets to maintain the fiction that racist ideas are only located in the South. As such it is a geographic region ripe for exploration on how this word emerges and travels. As I have described it, *ratchet* can be understood as a politic of being, or a desire to perform what could be understood as "stereotypical" (working-class, Southern) Blackness without pretense. Southern working-class Blackness is both perpetually linked to notions of "authentic" Blackness, and carries the full weight of the negative stigma for Blackness inside and outside of Black cultural life. There are still so many questions outstanding about how the word traffics within the class and cultural politics of the South and how ratchet/boojie politics animate the experiences of Southern Black queer men and women.

Final Remarks

Ratchet *and the* "*Nigga*"

When asked to define *ratchet*, often my informants answered by describing ratchet aesthetics. That is, instead of defining *ratchet*, they told me what *ratchet* looked, sounded, and acted like. Indeed, people spend considerable amounts of time talking about who or what is ratchet. They sometimes framed ratchet in terms of references from Black popular culture. For example, Tamar Braxton, reality television star and R&B singer, catapulted to fame because of her behavior on the reality television show *Braxton Family Values*.[8] Tamar's frequent outbursts and general bad

---

[8] The show centered on the lives of Toni Braxton, the Grammy Award winning singer, her sisters, and their mother.

behavior, would earn her fans and followers. People seemed to enjoy seeing Tamar, the youngest sister, behave like a "spoiled brat" with a tendency to be messy.[9] Tamar's messy behavior quickly earned her the label: ratchet. As a result of her work on *Braxton Family Values*, Tamar would go on to be a co-host of the daytime talk show *The Real*. In 2016, Tamar Braxton was fired from the show. Reporting on the story, celebrity gossip blogger B. Scott reported that a source suggested that following market tests, Tamar didn't "play well" among "middle-class" and "educated" women. In other words, Tamar's Southern, high-femme, loud personality and temperament had been positioned as low-class, ghetto, and ratchet to the point where middle-class and educated women found her unlikable.[10] What had initially made Tamar a breakout star in Ratchet TV, her over-the-top, diva-antics, her made-up catch phrases, her Black drag queen inspired looks and attitude, made her unbearable for a "middle-class, educated" viewership of the daytime talk show. Tamar's frequent use of phrases such as "bomb dot com" and "get ya life," that would later become popular among Black women and gay men, positioned her as outside of the markers of palatable Black womanhood. Further, her "excessive" femininity positioned her outside the boundaries of Black middle-class respectability even though she's rich and her behavior was exactly what makes many Black women reality television stars so valuable (Chap. 5). Black women in popular media are frequently rewarded for their confirmation of stereotypes of "bad" Black female behavior (Pickens 2014). However, as I have already argued about the nature of *ratchet*, it is both a technology of control and a resource from which one can draw from for a variety of reasons including to get paid in a society which reminds us daily that it hates Black women, regardless of how we behave.

Within a boojie imaginary, calling something or someone *ratchet* is a way of categorizing their behavior as unfit for public consumption. In *Race Rebels*, Robin D.G. Kelley (1994) argues that Black working-class acts of resistance are often subtle, incomplete, and are often framed by the Black middle-class as "setting the race back." Similar discourses have

---

[9] Being "messy" refers to actions or behaviors that bring conflict to otherwise uncomplicated situations. Simply put, it is when an individual (who can also be referred to as "messy") causes a "mess." They make drama where it would otherwise not exist. For example, see Season 3, Episode 3 of Braxton Family Values—a family dinner that turns into a shouting match due to something Tamar says.

[10] *The Real* is a daytime talk show. As a daytime talk show, it is surprising that middle-class, educated women would be the target demographic.

played out throughout the history of Black people within American Popular Culture. When Black popular culture has been consumed by whites, there has always been the fear that those representations of Blackness will "confirm" stereotypes about Black behavior. Thus, some take it upon themselves never to represent such stereotypes—as a strategy of "racial uplift." Here the notion of "racial uplift" is positioned as another technology of coercing working-class Black people to "act right."

> The ideal, desired product, then, of this supplemental string—coloniality, subordinativity, necropolitics, and the duppy state—is the convenient and necessary other of the citizen: the exploitable, expendable, and disposable (and blackened) body (aka "the nigger"). (Iton 2008, 135)

"The nigger" is one of America's most popular tropes. Speaking specifically of Chris Rock's infamous "black-versus-niggas" joke, Iton argues that part of what made this joke, and subsequently Chris Rock, so famous was America's "widespread appetite for disparaging tales of the nigger" (Iton 2008, 177). Chris Rock's joke begins with "Black people aren't afraid of welfare going away. Niggas are." Others have discussed Rock's joke in terms of its class politics, and Iton, in terms of its racial politics, however, I want to emphasize also the gendered and sexual politics that also operate within the joke.

Black women have historically been disproportionately affected by welfare policy. As Iton (2008) argues, Ronald Reagan's deployment of the specter of the undeserving "Welfare Queen" taking unearned tax payer money to fund a "lavish" lifestyle is what sets the stage for the Bill Clinton's promise to "end welfare as we know it." It was when welfare gets a Black female face—a blackened and improperly heterosexual (some might say "queer") face—that the dissolution the social safety net becomes necessary (Cohen 2005; Collins 2008). As I've attempted to demonstrate, there is a strong link between to work that "the nigger" does, and the deployment of *ratchet* as a disciplinary technique. I would go so far as to say that *ratchet* might be another way of calling Black people "niggers". In the conservative Black middle-class imagination it is one's lack of skills, knowledge, moral fortitude, and ability to manage their behavior to avoid being seen as "the nigger" which marks one as ratchet. Therefore, anyone can be read as ratchet if they animate the anxiety of "setting the race back," a metaphor of progress of an entire group of people, impeded by the bad behavior of one or a few.

> Let me be clear: as long as there is a regime of representation that consistently recirculates Black images as part of long-standing tropes and types, the politics of respectability can hardly compete, never mind win, in this battle of images. I am not advocating that respectability politics, with its tendency to shame black bodies, *should* win. Yet the idea that it *could* win persists because respectability is easily digestible and presents a problem that, in theory, can be solved. (Warner 2015, 138)

Warner makes an extremely important point here about the losing strategy of respectability politics. The belief that *more* Black images of upstanding Black citizens can and will sway racists into believing in the humanity of Black people has been proven time and time again to be unfounded (Kendi 2016). Black folks have consistently tried to "earn" the respect of white folks, and in so doing, have drawn boundaries around what Blackness can be in response to racist ideas. But Black women have also *demanded* being treated with dignity, because they were born worthy of it. As Brittany Cooper explains in her book *Beyond Respectability: The Intellectual Thought of Race Women*, "demands for respectability assume that unassailable social propriety will prove one's dignity. Dignity, unlike respectability, is not socially continent. It is intrinsic and therefore, not up for debate" (Cooper 2017, 5). As homonormativity prepares to slice up Black queer communities into the "haves" and "have nots," *ratchet* still sits within the borderlands creating spaces and opportunities for the release from the pressures of having to perform proper middle-classness in order for white people and straight people to see us as deserving of basic human rights and dignity. This quare work that *ratchet* does calls out the white-washing, conservative, classist, racist, and assimilationist impulses within Black queer communities and attends to the needs of the *flesh* of bodies, while pointing out their individual erotic sovereignty. This quare work of *ratchet* is vital to our sustenance within the oppressive conditions which shape our everyday lives. So, in the words of Hurricane Chris, "Let's get ratchet. Let's get ratchet."

References

Alexander, Bryant Keith. 2011. 'Boojie!': A Question of Authenticity. In *From Bourgeois to Boojie: Black Middle-Class Performances*, ed. Vershawn Ashanti Young and Bridget Harris Tsemo, 309–330. Detroit: Wayne State University Press.

Alim, H. Samy. 2006. *Roc the Mic Right: The Language of Hip Hop Culture*. London and New York: Routledge.

Cohen, Cathy J. 2005. Punks, Bulldaggers, and Welfare Queens: The Radical Potential of Queer Politics. In *Black Queer Studies: A Critical Anthology*, ed. E. Patrick Johnson and Mae Henderson, 21–51. Durham: Duke University Press.

Collins, Patricia Hill. 2008. *Black Feminist Thought: Knowledge, Consciousness, and the Politics of Empowerment*. New York and London: Routledge.

Cooper, Brittney C. 2017. *Beyond Respectability: The Intellectual Thought of Race Women*. Champaign: University of Illinois Press.

Hammonds, Evelynn. 1994. Black (W)holes and the Geometry of Black Female Sexuality. *Differences: A Journal of Feminist Cultural Studies* 6 (2/3): 126–145.

Hill, Jane H. 2008. *The Everyday Language of White Racism, Wiley Blackwell Studies in Discourse and Culture*. West Sussex: Wiley-Blackwell.

Iton, Richard. 2008. *In Search of the Black Fantastic: Politics and Popular Culture in the Post-Civil Rights Era*. New York: Oxford University Press.

Johnson, E. Patrick. 1998. Feeling the Spirit in the Dark: Expanding Notions of the Sacred in the African-American Gay Community. *Callaloo* 21 (2): 399–416.

———. 2003. The Pot Is Brewing: Marlon Riggs' Black Is… Black Ain't. In *Appropriating Blackness: Performance and the Politics of Authenticity*. Durham and London: Duke University Press.

Kelley, Robin D.G. 1994. *Race Rebels: Culture, Politics, and the Black Working Class*. New York: Free Press.

Kendi, Ibram X. 2016. *Stamped from the Beginning: The Definitive History of Racist Ideas in America*. New York: Nation Books.

Lindsey, Treva B. 2017. *Colored No More: Reinventing Black Womanhood in Washington*. University of Illinois Press.

Pickens, Therí A. 2014. Shoving Aside the Politics of Respectability: Black Women, Reality TV, and the Ratchet Performance. *Women & Performance: A Journal of Feminist Theory* 25 (1): 1–18.

Riggs, Marlon T. 1995. *Black Is… Black Ain't*. San Fransisco: California Newsreel.

Smitherman, Geneva. 1994. *Black Talk: Words and Phrases from the Hood to the Amen Corner*. Boston: Houghton Mifflin.

Warner, Kristen J. 2015. They Gon' Think You Loud Regardless: Ratchetness, Reality Television, and Black Womanhood. *Camera Obscura: Feminism, Culture, and Media Studies* 30 (1(88)): 129–153.

Index[1]

A
Authenticity, 11, 29, 30, 37, 85n11, 87, 92, 114, 120, 131n14, 150

B
Being ratchet, 4, 7, 31, 44, 54, 60, 67–89, 108, 143, 155
Bisexual, 6, 11, 15, 23, 25, 30, 31, 61, 77, 85n11, 92, 93, 118, 120, 126, 128, 131n14, 133, 136–138, 141
Black
 middle-class, 3–5, 8, 9, 14–25, 27–28, 30, 31, 41–44, 49, 53, 60, 61, 64, 69, 70, 72, 112, 117, 130, 135, 139, 140, 142, 151, 153, 161, 162
 queer, 1–31, 35–64, 67–89, 92–95, 113, 114, 116, 138, 140, 150, 152–154, 163
 women, 5, 7, 12–15, 18, 19, 21, 22, 25–31, 40, 45, 50, 53, 58, 62, 69, 70, 78, 92, 94, 95, 98, 102, 108, 109, 111–144, 152, 155–157, 159, 161–163
Blackness, 3, 4, 10, 15, 16, 37, 38, 40, 60, 63, 95, 102, 108, 121, 133, 150, 156, 160, 162, 163
Blues, 13, 128
Bodies, 9, 10, 14, 21, 28–31, 40, 43, 53, 60, 69, 70, 98, 108, 109, 111, 114, 116, 127, 129, 136, 140, 143, 144, 150, 154, 155, 162, 163
Boojie/*boojie*, 17, 35–64, 70, 71, 74, 75, 80, 87, 91, 92, 95–98, 107n10, 112, 117, 135, 140, 147–163
BQW, 1, 2, 6, 9, 10, 12–15, 19, 23, 25, 28–31, 41–46, 48, 49, 51, 53–56, 58, 60, 62, 69–72, 74,

[1] Note: Page numbers followed by 'n' refer to notes.

75, 77, 78, 80–82, 85–87, 91–94, 98, 102, 113, 114, 116–136, 140, 141, 143, 144, 153–155, 159
Braxton, Tamar, 26, 160, 161

C
Class, 2, 6, 7, 11, 12, 14, 16, 19, 25, 28–30, 38, 39, 42–44, 50, 52–55, 52n7, 59–61, 70, 72, 91, 107, 109, 136, 140, 150, 155, 158–159
Class politics, 5, 6, 10, 71, 107, 158, 162
Coming out, 30, 81, 111–144, 152
Culture, 16, 28, 49, 50, 61, 62, 81, 91, 93, 96, 103, 107, 108, 116, 121, 124, 140, 143, 144, 148, 149, 152, 156, 160, 162

D
Desire, 19, 21, 22, 26, 27, 43, 49, 53, 63, 69, 81–83, 85, 91, 97, 104, 113, 114, 117, 121, 124, 126–128, 139, 140, 142, 154, 160
District Heat, 30, 92, 98–105, 107–109, 154

F
Femininity, 25, 62, 107, 109, 161
Femme, 50, 56, 85, 95–98, 101, 103–107, 109

G
Gender, 6, 7, 11, 12, 14, 19, 22, 28–31, 40, 42, 43, 50, 60, 69, 70, 83, 92, 95–98, 103, 106, 107, 109, 121, 125, 128, 131, 132, 138, 143, 151–153, 155
Get ratchet, 36, 150
Ghetto/*ghetto*, 9, 9n12, 16, 44, 52, 127, 161
Gucci Mane, 82, 83

H
Hernandez, Joseline, 75, 113, 116, 117, 143
Heteronormativity, 12, 14, 15, 23, 30, 42, 135, 140
Heterosexual, 9, 12, 13, 23, 25, 27, 43, 58, 69, 75, 83, 86, 103, 104, 113, 116, 118, 122, 123, 129, 131n14, 132, 137, 144, 151, 154, 158, 159, 162
Hip-hop, 2, 3, 5, 6, 8, 9, 26, 50, 61, 62, 70, 75–78, 81–83, 85, 86, 91, 92, 107, 108, 111, 113–118, 120–122, 124–128, 131n14, 143, 144, 148, 149, 152, 154
Homonormative, 23, 28, 61, 73, 74, 109, 114, 140, 142

I
Identity, 17, 23, 26, 44, 61, 97, 104, 113, 114, 116–118, 121, 122, 124, 126, 132, 136–138, 150

L
Language, 1–31, 40, 44, 101n2, 127, 129, 138, 155, 158
Lesbian, 6, 11, 13–15, 23–25, 30, 31, 43–46, 50, 54, 55, 61, 69, 71, 73, 77, 85, 86, 91–110, 118, 123, 125, 128, 131–133, 131n14, 135, 137–141, 151, 154, 159

Love & Hip-Hop: Atlanta (LHHAtl), 111, 113–136

M

Masculine, 23, 47, 50, 78, 81, 92, 94, 95, 97, 99, 101, 101n2, 103, 104, 107, 130
Masculinity, 13, 50, 95, 102–107, 109, 120, 125
Middle-class, 2, 8, 9n13, 12, 15–17, 19, 23, 25, 28–30, 42–45, 48, 50, 51, 53, 54, 57, 59–61, 64, 69, 71–75, 80, 91, 96, 98, 106–109, 113, 127, 128, 140, 142, 149–151, 156, 157, 161, 161n10
Migos, 148–150
Monáe, Janelle, 30, 136–138, 152–154
Morality, 18, 19, 69, 70, 114, 131n14, 133, 135, 153

N

Narrative, 26, 30, 69, 101, 104, 113, 114, 116, 122, 136–138, 141, 144, 152
Normative/normativity, 5, 10, 13, 19, 25, 42, 43, 60–63, 81, 82, 87, 100, 109, 113, 128, 135, 140, 142, 150, 153–155

P

Party, 1, 30, 45–48, 46n4, 51, 52, 54–59, 71, 73–75, 78–80, 107, 115, 130, 131
Performance, 1, 2, 15, 26, 27, 37, 40, 43, 46, 47, 49, 52, 53, 69, 74, 77–80, 95–97, 103, 104n6, 106, 107, 117, 118, 120, 123–126, 128, 139–141, 143, 149, 150, 153
Performativity/performative, 15, 123, 149, 153
Place, 4n7, 6–9, 13, 18, 25, 28–30, 36, 41, 42, 44–46, 49, 53, 56, 58, 60, 63, 64, 70, 71, 73, 76n7, 78, 80, 99, 100, 102, 104, 109, 110, 116, 118, 128, 129, 135, 144, 149, 151, 153, 154, 157
Popular, 6, 14, 30, 50, 62, 77, 81, 91–93, 100, 113, 115, 116, 120, 140, 149, 156, 160–162
Professional, 1, 30, 39, 42, 45–50, 53, 57, 58, 61, 62, 73, 75, 100, 103, 107, 109, 117, 140

Q

Quare, 10, 11, 35, 36, 108–109, 114, 163
Queer, 1, 10–13, 23, 25, 30, 31, 36, 51, 61, 69, 70, 77, 85, 85n11, 86, 93, 94, 113, 114, 121, 128, 136–138, 140, 144, 162
Queer space, 13, 35–64, 67–89, 153, 154

R

Racial, 4, 8, 12, 17–20, 22, 26, 37, 40, 44, 73, 121, 135, 142, 143, 151, 155, 156, 158, 162
Racialized, 5, 6, 12, 26, 42, 48, 55, 73, 83, 109, 114, 120, 142, 143, 150
Ratchet, 1–31, 35–64, 67–89, 91–144, 147–163
Ratchet politics, 39, 40
Ratchet TV, 30, 112–118, 122, 125, 126, 135, 144, 156, 157, 161

Relationships, 12, 14, 23, 24, 26, 41, 59, 63, 70, 75, 78, 92, 93, 97, 103, 104, 104n6, 106, 109, 115–118, 121, 123, 126, 130, 131n14, 132, 134, 136, 149, 159
Represent, 13, 23, 29, 62, 63, 69, 91, 93, 105, 108, 116, 139, 140, 142–144, 152, 157, 162
Representation, 7, 10, 14n14, 16, 19, 21, 26, 27, 29, 30, 81, 87, 91–93, 95, 98, 102, 104, 108, 110, 116, 117, 126, 128, 140–142, 150, 156, 162, 163
Respectability, 3, 5–8, 10, 12, 14–22, 25–29, 39, 43, 50, 67–89, 92, 102, 108, 114, 137–139, 141, 143–144, 148, 150, 152, 153, 156, 157, 161, 163
Rihanna, 67, 127, 128

S

Sexuality, 2, 5–7, 11, 12, 14, 22–25, 28–31, 42–44, 48, 50, 52, 55, 60, 69, 70, 78, 87, 91–93, 95, 98, 104, 108, 109, 113, 114, 116, 117, 120–122, 125–128, 132, 133, 135, 137–142, 150, 151, 153, 159
Space, 1, 2, 13, 14, 23, 26, 28, 31, 42–45, 47–49, 53–55, 58–62, 71, 73–75, 77–81, 87, 91, 94, 103, 107, 108, 118, 135–137, 140, 142–144, 150, 151, 153–155, 159, 163
Stripping, 3, 46, 46n4, 75, 77, 87
Stud, 49, 54, 77, 94–96, 101, 101n2, 103–106, 106n9, 109

T

Twerk/*twerk*, 5, 126

W

West, Kanye, 2, 81, 86, 87, 154
Whiteness, 10, 17, 38, 44
Womanhood, 9, 12, 15, 25, 69, 108, 113, 117, 125, 126, 128, 161
Women, 1, 39, 69, 92, 113, 154
Working-class, 8, 9n13, 10, 16, 23, 24, 38, 41, 44, 52, 53, 55, 58–60, 63, 69, 71–73, 93, 96, 101, 106, 107, 109, 140, 151, 160–162

Y

Young, 4, 18, 23, 25, 44, 45, 47, 49, 54, 55, 59–61, 93, 94, 117, 126, 127, 129, 138, 140, 148

Printed in the United States
By Bookmasters